Miller & Levine

Biology

Laboratory Manual B

PEARSON

Boston, Massachusetts Chandler, Arizona Glenview, Illinois Upper Saddle River, New Jersey

ISBN-13: 978-0-13-368714-9

ISBN-10: 0-13-368714-7

1 2 3 4 5 6 7 8 9 10 V016 13 12 11 10 09

Contents

Unit 6 From Microorganisms to Plants

Unit 7 Animals

Unit 8 The Human Body

Data Analysis Activities

Additional Hands-On Activities

Safety in the Biology Laboratory

Working in the biology laboratory can be exciting, but it can also be dangerous if you do not follow the proper safety guidelines. You are responsible for helping to maintain a safe environment in the laboratory. Unsafe practices endanger not only you but also the people who work near you.

Safety Rules

To prepare yourself for a safe year in the laboratory, review the following safety rules. Make sure you understand each rule. Ask your teacher to explain any rules you do not understand.

Dress Code

- To protect your eyes, wear safety goggles when you see the safety goggles symbol. This symbol will appear when you work with chemicals that are corrosive, such as acids or bases. The symbol will also appear when a chemical has irritating vapors.

  Avoid wearing contact lenses when you work with chemicals. If you need to wear contact lenses in the lab to see clearly, talk with your teacher about your need.
- Wear a laboratory apron or coat when you are working with chemicals that are corrosive or can stain your clothing. Also wear an apron when you are heating materials.
- Tie back long hair to avoid contact with chemicals, flames, or biological cultures.
- Remove, tie back, of avoid wearing any clothing or jewelry that can hang down and touch chemicals, flames, or cultures.
- Do not wear sandals or open-toed shoes in the laboratory. Never walk around barefoot or in stocking feet in the laboratory.

General Safety Rules

- Read the procedure for a lab in advance. Follow the steps of the procedure exactly as they are written unless your teacher tells you otherwise. If you do not understand a step, ask your teacher for help.
- Never do an experiment that your teacher has not approved. Do not use any lab equipment without permission or without the supervision of your teacher.
- Never eat or drink anything while you are in the laboratory. Do not bring food into the lab that you intend to eat later. Do not chew gum. Do not apply cosmetics.
- If you spill a chemical, check with your teacher right away about the proper cleanup procedure.
- Do not pour chemicals or other materials into the sink or place items in a trash container unless specifically instructed to do so by your teacher.

Emergencies and First Aid

- Know the location and proper use of safety equipment such as the fire extinguisher, fire blanket, eye-wash station, and first-aid kit.
- Learn what to do in response to specific emergencies, such as cuts, burns, or contact with chemicals.
- Immediately report all accidents, no matter how minor, to your teacher.
- Your teacher will help you determine the proper response to an accident. He or she may administer first aid, send you to the school nurse, or call a physician.
- Report any fires to your teacher at once. Know the location of the fire alarm and know where and how to report a fire or other emergency requiring outside assistance.

Heating and Fire Safety

- Always wear safety goggles when you use a candle or gas burner as a heat source.
- Make sure you know how to safely light a gas burner. Your teacher will demonstrate the proper procedure for lighting a burner. Also refer to the section in Appendix D on gas burners.
- If the flame leaps out of a burner toward you, turn the gas off immediately. Do not touch the burner, which may be hot.
- Never leave a lighted burner unattended.
- Never reach across a flame.
- Never heat a chemical that you are not told to heat. A chemical that is harmless when cool can be dangerous when heated.
- Make sure that there are no open containers of flammable liquids in the laboratory when flames are being used.
- When you heat a test tube with a flame, point the opening of the tube away from yourself and others. Chemicals can splash or boil out of a heated test tube.
- Never heat a closed container. Expanding gases inside the container may cause the container to blow apart, causing injury to you or others working nearby.
- Never pick up a container that has been heated without first holding the back of your hand near it. If you can feel the heat on the back of your hand, the container may be too hot to handle. Use a clamp or tongs when handling hot containers, or, if appropriate, wear heat-resistant gloves.
- Maintain a clean work area and keep materials other than the ones you are heating away from flames or hot plates.

Using Chemicals Safely

- Never mix chemicals for the "fun of it." You might produce a dangerous, possibly explosive, substance.
- Chemicals used in labs may be poisonous. Never touch, taste, or smell a chemical that you do not know for a fact is harmless. If you are instructed to smell the fumes in an experiment, gently wave your hand over the opening of a container and direct the fumes toward your nose. Do not inhale the fumes directly from the container.
- Use only those chemicals needed in the investigation. Keep all lids closed when a chemical is not being used. Notify your teacher whenever chemicals are spilled.
- Dispose of all chemicals as instructed by your teacher. To avoid contamination, never return chemicals to their original containers.
- Be extra careful when working with acids or bases. Pour such chemicals from one container to another over the sink, not over your work area.
- When diluting an acid, pour the acid into water. Never pour water into the acid.
- Notify your teacher immediately if you spill an acid or a base.
- Use a continuous stream of water from the tap to rinse acid or bases off your skin or clothing.
- If an acid or base splashes in your eyes, go to the eye-wash station immediately to flush the liquid from your eyes.

Using Glassware Safely

- Before you heat a beaker or other glass container, make sure the outside of the container is dry.
- If you use a gas burner as a heat source, use a wire screen to protect glassware from the flame.
- Keep in mind that hot glassware will not appear hot. Never pick up a heated glass object without first checking to see if it is hot. If you can feel the heat on the back of your hand, use a clamp or tongs to handle the container or wear heat-resistant gloves if appropriate.
- Never use broken or chipped glassware.
- If a glass object breaks, notify your teacher. Then use a brush and dustpan to collect and dispose of the broken glass in the proper trash container. Never pick up broken glass with your hands.
- Never eat or drink from laboratory glassware. Thoroughly clean glassware before putting it away.
- If you need to insert a glass tube into a rubber stopper or rubber tubing, use a lubricant and a gentle turning motion to reduce the risk of breaking the glass.

Using Sharp Instruments

- Handle scalpels, scissors, and knives with extreme care. Always cut away from yourself.
- Always use sharp instruments only as instructed.
- Notify your teacher immediately if you cut yourself while working in the laboratory.

Working With Live Organisms

- No experiments that will cause pain, discomfort, or harm to animals should be done in the classroom or at home.
- Treat all living organisms with care and respect. Limit your interaction with organisms to only what is required to complete an experiment.
- Pay close attention to the instructions in the procedure and any additional instructions from your teacher.
- Use sterile procedures, as instructed by your teacher, when working with microbes.
- Wash your hands thoroughly after you handle any organisms or their containers.

End-of-Experiment Rules

- Before you leave the laboratory, clean up your work area and return all equipment to its proper place.
- Make sure you turn off and disconnect burners from the gas supply. Also turn off and unplug hot plates.
- Wash your hands thoroughly with soap and warm water before you leave the lab.

Safety Alerts

All the labs in this manual have been designed with safety in mind. When appropriate, you will find a paragraph about safety after the list of materials. Some of the safety symbols shown on the next page will also be included to alert you to possible dangers and to remind you to work carefully.

Watch for statements within a procedure that are labeled "CAUTION." These statements focus on possible risks related to specific steps in the procedure. The possible risk may be to yourself, to an organism, or to equipment.

Safety Symbols

Safety Goggles Always wear safety goggles to protect your eyes during any activity involving chemicals, flames or heating, or the possibility of flying objects, particles, or substances.

Lab Apron Wear a laboratory apron to protect your skin and clothing from injury.

Plastic Gloves Wear disposable plastic gloves to protect yourself from contact with chemicals or organisms that could be harmful. Keep your hands away from your face, and dispose of the gloves according to your teacher's instructions at the end of the activity.

Breakage Handle breakable materials such as thermometers and glassware with care. Do not touch broken glass.

Heat-Resistant Gloves Use an oven mitt or other hand protection when handling hot materials. Heating plates, hot water, and glassware can cause burns. Never touch hot objects with your bare hands.

Heating Use a clamp or tongs to hold hot objects. Do not touch hot objects with your bare hands.

Sharp Object Scissors, scalpels, pins, and knives are sharp. They can cut or puncture your skin. Always direct sharp edges and points away from yourself and others. Use sharp instruments only as directed.

Electric Shock Avoid the possibility of electric shock. Never use electrical equipment around water or when the equipment or your hands are wet. Be sure cords are untangled and cannot trip anyone. Disconnect equipment when it is not in use.

Flames Tie back loose hair and clothing, and put on safety goggles before working with fire. Follow instructions from your teacher about lighting and extinguishing flames.

No Flames Flammable materials may be present. Make sure there are no flames, sparks, or exposed sources of heat present.

Corrosive Chemical This symbol indicates the presence of an acid or other corrosive chemical. Avoid getting the chemical on your skin or clothing, or in your eyes. Do not inhale the vapors. Wash your hands when you are finished with the activity.

Poison Do not let any poisonous chemical get on your skin, and do not inhale its vapor. Wash your hands when you are finished with the activity.

Fumes Poisonous or unpleasant vapors may be produced. Work in a ventilated area or, if available, in a fume hood. Avoid inhaling a vapor directly. Test an odor only when directed to do so by your teacher, using a wafting motion to direct the vapor toward your nose.

Physical Safety This activity involves physical movement. Use caution to avoid injuring yourself or others. Follow instructions from your teacher. Alert your teacher if there is any reason that you should not participate in the activity.

Animal Safety Treat live animals with care to avoid injuring the animals or yourself. Working with animal parts or preserved animals may also require caution. Wash your hands when you are finished with the activity.

Plant Safety Handle plants only as your teacher directs. If you are allergic to any plants used in an activity, tell your teacher before the activity begins. Avoid touching poisonous plants and plants with thorns.

Disposal Chemicals and other materials used in the activity must be disposed of safely. Follow the instructions from your teacher.

Hand Washing Wash your hands thoroughly when finished with the activity. Use soap and warm water. Lather both sides of your hands and between your fingers. Rinse well.

General Safety Awareness You may see this symbol when none of the symbols described earlier applies. In this case, follow the specific instructions provided.

Safety Contract

Once you have read the information on pages vi–ix and are sure you understand all the rules, fill out the safety contract below. Signing this contract tells your teacher that you are aware of the safety rules and agree to follow them. Return your signed contract to your teacher. You will not be allowed to work in the laboratory until you have signed the contract.

Safety Contract

I, ____,

- agree to be responsible for my own safety and behavior in the lab and to do everything I can to ensure the safety of others.
- agree to read all labs in advance and come to class fully prepared and dressed appropriately.
- agree to follow all written instructions in the manual and any additional instructions given to me by my teacher.
- agree to use great caution when handling items that are potentially dangerous including glassware, sharp instruments, heat sources, and chemicals.
- agree to treat all living organisms with care and respect.
- agree that I know the locations and use of all safety equipment.

Signature ____________________________________ Date ____________

Lab Skills 1 Lab Equipment and Safety

Problem

What can you do to ensure that you work safely and efficiently in the science laboratory?

Introduction

Lab activities give you an opportunity to practice the process of science. They allow you to do what scientists all over the world do in research labs and in the field. Like all scientists, you must follow procedures that ensure your safety. These procedures also ensure that the data you collect is reliable. Unlike most scientists, you will need to fit your experiments into a set block of time. Thus, your ability to work efficiently will be important to your success.

In this lab, you will draw a map of the room in which you will do labs. You will note the locations of safety equipment and other supplies. Finally, you will identify some pieces of equipment that may be unfamiliar and infer the purpose of these items.

Skills Focus

Observe, Infer, Compare and Contrast

Materials

- graph paper
- colored pencils

Build Vocabulary

Term	Definition
ensure	To make certain, or make *sure,* that something will happen
efficient	Producing the result you want with the least possible effort, cost, or waste
procedure	A list of steps that describe how to carry on, or *proceed,* with a task
infer	To offer a reasoned opinion, or *inference,* based on observations and experience

Pre-Lab Questions

1. **Infer** Why is it important to know the location of equipment, such as a fire extinguisher, before you begin working in the lab?

2. **Relate Cause and Effect** How could reading a lab in advance contribute to both safety and efficiency?

3. **Use Analogies** Give an example of an activity that takes place outside of school in which people are expected to review safety cautions before taking part in the activity.

Procedure

Part A: Mapping the Lab

Use a sheet of graph paper to make a map of your science lab. Use abbreviations instead of full names to record the locations of items. Use the space at the top of page 3 to make a key with abbreviations, such as FB for fire blanket.

1. Start by marking the locations of doors, windows, lab benches, and any desks.
2. Next, walk around the room and locate the following safety equipment: safety goggles, fire extinguisher, fire blanket, safety shower, eyewash station, fume hood, plastic gloves, first-aid kit, and broken glass disposal box. Use a red pencil to record the locations of these items on the map.
3. Then, find the locations where common lab equipment such as beakers, graduated cylinders, microscopes, and thermometers are stored. Use a green pencil to mark these locations on your map. Add the abbreviations you choose to your key.
4. After each lab period, your lab station should be cleaned and organized. To help reach this goal, use a blue pencil to mark the locations for items such as the following on your map: sink, paper towels, test-tube brush, hand soap, and dishwashing liquid. Add the abbreviations for these items to your key.

Name ______________________ Class ________ Date ________

Key to Map Abbreviations

Part B: Identifying Lab Equipment

5. Your teacher will place ten pieces of lab equipment labeled A–J on your lab bench or table. Choose a name for each item from the list of items that your teacher will give you.
6. Choose a possible use for each item from the list of uses that your teacher will give you.
7. In the column titled Safety Issues, note which items might require one or more of the following safety warnings: safety goggles, breakage, electric shock, sharp object, and disposal.

Data Table

Item	Name	Possible Use	Safety Issues
A			
B			
C			
D			
E			
F			
G			
H			
I			
J			

Analyze and Conclude

1. **Infer** Why is there a general safety rule to never bring food or drinks into the lab?

2. **Sequence** Describe what you would do if a glass beaker drops and breaks. List the correct steps in order.

3. **Design an Experiment** Graduated cylinders, beakers, and pipettes are all used to measure liquids. What are two factors that could help you decide which of these items to use for a given task?

4. **Compare and Contrast** When the method used to do a task changes, often the safety warnings change, too. Compare the warnings for heating water with a burner to the warnings for a hot plate.

Build Science Skills

Biologists develop detailed safety plans to protect themselves and the organisms they are studying. Each of the fields described on pages 17–18 of your textbook has different safety issues. Work in small groups to research the safety rules for one of these fields. Consult with your teacher about possible topics.

Guided Inquiry • Skills Lab

Lab Skills 2 Applying Scientific Methods

Problem

How will light affect the sprouting of eyes on a potato?

Introduction

Doing experiments is a central part of science. For a controlled experiment, you need both an experimental setup and a control setup. The setups must be exactly the same except for the independent variable. With this approach, you will know that your results are due to that variable.

In this lab, you will use a potato to do a controlled experiment. Figure 1 shows where the potatoes are located in a growing potato plant. Along the surface of a potato are buds, or "eyes," which look like small dimples in the potato skin. The eyes can sprout and grow into new potato plants. In your experiment, you will determine whether more eyes sprout in the dark or in the light.

Figure 1 Potato plant

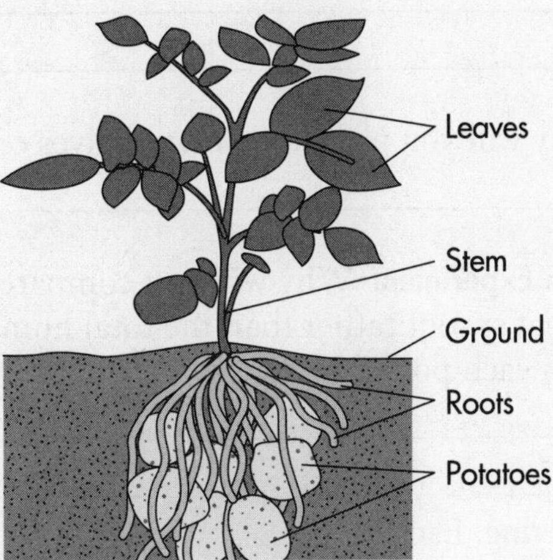

Build Vocabulary

Term	Definition
variable	Something that is able to change, or *vary*
control	The setup used to test the results of a managed, or *controlled,* experiment
determine	To find out or come to a decision by investigation, thinking, or calculation

Skills Focus

Form a Hypothesis, Control Variables, Organize Data

Materials

- medium-sized potato
- scrub brush
- knife
- dissection tray
- 2 paper towels
- 2 plastic bags with twist ties
- permanent marker

Safety

When using the knife to cut the potato, keep your fingers out of the path of the blade. Wash your hands thoroughly with soap and warm water after handling the potatoes.

Pre-Lab Questions

1. **Control Variables** How does cutting one potato in half help control the variables in this experiment?

____

____

____

2. **Infer** Why will you place the potato halves on wet paper towels?

____

3. **Design an Experiment** Why will you compare the percentage of eyes that sprout rather than the total number of eyes that sprout on each potato half?

____

____

Procedure

1. As a group, discuss how the presence or absence of light will affect the sprouting of a potato. Record your hypothesis.

   Hypothesis: ____

   ____

   ____

2. Put on your safety goggles and lab apron. Scrub the potato with a firm brush to remove any wax coating from the potato.

3. Using a dissection tray, carefully cut the potato from end to end into equal halves. Choose one half to put in the dark and one half to keep in the light. Count the number of eyes on each potato half and record this information in the data table below.
4. Fold each paper towel until you have rectangles about equal in size to your potato halves. Moisten the towels with water. Place a folded paper towel in each plastic bag. **CAUTION:** The paper towels should be slightly damp, but not soaked.
5. Place a potato half in each plastic bag with the cut surface on the paper towel as shown in Figure 2. Tie each bag with a twist tie. Use the marker to label one bag Light and the other Dark.

Figure 2 Potato half in plastic bag

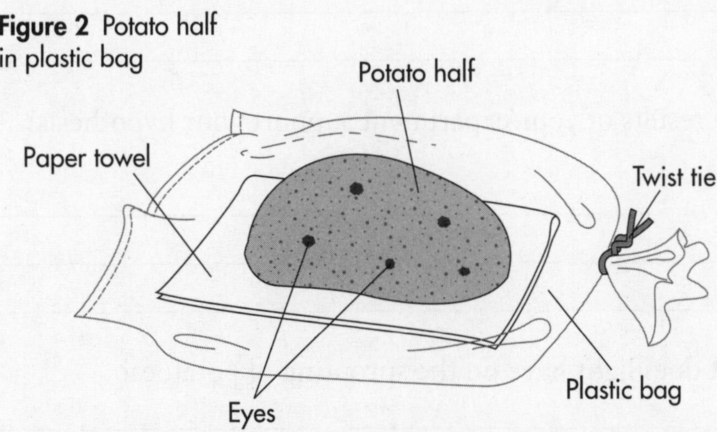

6. Your teacher will provide a cool, dark place and a cool, well-lit place where you will keep the bags. Place the bags in the correct locations. Make sure that the potato halves are resting on top of the paper towels after you place the bags.
7. After one week, open the bags and count the number of sprouts on each potato. Record these numbers in the data table.
8. To calculate the percentage of eyes that sprouted, divide the number of sprouts by the number of eyes. Then, multiply the result by 100. Record your answers in the data table.

$$\text{Percentage of eyes sprouted} = \frac{\text{Number of sprouts}}{\text{Number of eyes}} \times 100\%$$

9. When the experiment is over, follow your teacher's instructions for cleanup and disposal of materials.

Data Table

Location of Potato	Number of Eyes	Number of Sprouts	Percentage of Eyes Sprouted
Dark			
Light			

Analyze and Conclude

1. **Design an Experiment** What was the independent variable in this experiment? What was the dependent variable?

2. **Design an Experiment** Which was the experimental setup in this investigation? Which was the control? Explain.

3. **Evaluate** Did the results of your experiment support your hypothesis? Explain.

4. **Infer** What effect does light have on the sprouting of potatoes?

5. **Control Variables** Why was it important to keep both the control setup and the experimental setup at the same temperature throughout the experiment?

Build Science Skills

Design an experiment to investigate whether temperature or amount of water affects the percentage of sprouts. Before you begin, have your teacher approve your plan.

Lab Skills 3 Using a Compound Microscope

Problem

What is the proper way to use a compound microscope and prepare a wet-mount slide?

Introduction

A microscope is a device that magnifies objects that are too small to be seen by the eye alone. A compound microscope has three main parts that work together to bring a magnified image to your eye. A light source illuminates, or lights up, the object being observed. A lens on the nosepiece magnifies the image of the object. A lens in the eyepiece further enlarges the image and projects the image into your eye.

Thin glass plates, or slides, are used to observe biological samples under a microscope. The slides are made in one of two ways. A prepared slide is made by enclosing a sample in glass. This permanent slide can be stored and viewed many times. A wet-mount slide is made by placing a drop of liquid containing the sample between the slide and a thin glass coverslip. This temporary slide is made to last only a short time—usually one lab period.

Build Vocabulary

Term	Definition
magnify	To cause an object to appear larger than it is
magnification	The amount by which an image is made larger, or *magnified*
objective lens	The lens nearest to the *object* being viewed with a microscope
focus	To alter the location or shape of a lens so that an image seen with the lens is clear and sharp
adjustment	A change that is made to make something work better
fine	Very tiny, as in the small distance a lens moves when the fine adjustment knob is turned

The microscope you will use will be similar to the one shown in Figure 1. A microscope is an instrument that requires careful handling. In this lab, you will learn how to use a compound microscope. You will also learn how to prepare a wet-mount slide.

Figure 1 Parts of a microscope

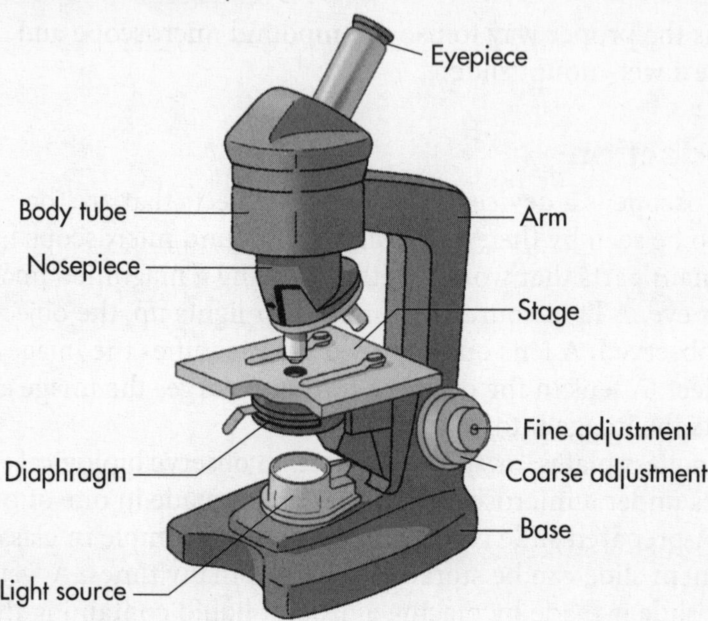

Skills Focus

Observe, Calculate, Compare and Contrast

Materials

- compound microscope
- lens paper
- prepared slide
- scissors
- newspaper
- microscope slide
- dropper pipette
- coverslip
- dissecting probe

Safety

To avoid damaging a microscope, follow the rules that are stated in this lab. Handle slides gently to avoid breaking them and cutting yourself. Alert your teacher if you break a glass object. To avoid electrical shocks, make sure that cords, plugs, and your hands are dry when using the light source. Use the scissors only as instructed. Do not direct the points of the scissors toward yourself or others.

Name ______________________ Class ________ Date ________

Pre-Lab Questions

1. **Infer** Why is it important to keep a microscope away from the edge of the table?

____

____

____

2. **Predict** How will the image of the letter *e* change when you switch from low power to high power?

____

____

____

Procedure

Part A: Prepare the Microscope

1. Collect a microscope and bring it to your workstation. Grasp the arm of the microscope with one hand, and place your other hand under the base. Place the microscope at least 10 cm from the edge of your table or desk with the arm facing you.

   RULE 1: Always carry a microscope with both hands.

2. You can find the magnification for a lens on the side of the objective. In Figure 2, the lens has a 10× magnification. This value means that the lens will produce an image that is ten times the actual size of the object being viewed.

Figure 2 Nosepiece with objective lens

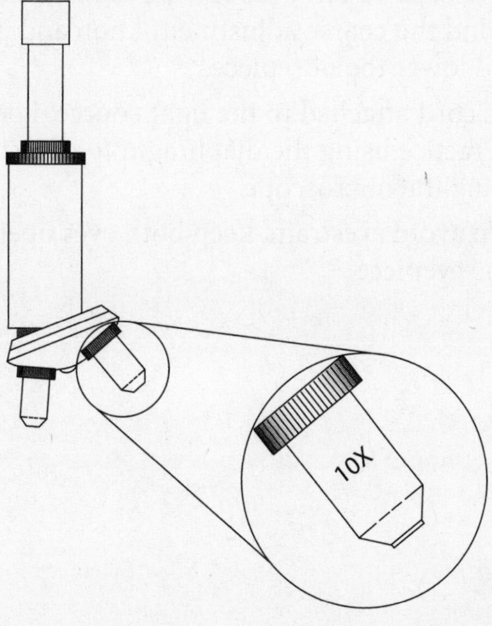

3. Find the magnification for each objective lens and record this data in the table. Then find and record the magnification for the eyepiece. To find the total magnification under each power, multiply the objective magnification by the eyepiece magnification. Record the results in the table.

Total magnification = Objective magnification × Eyepiece magnification

Data Table

Objective	Objective Magnification	Eyepiece Magnification	Total Magnification
Low power			
Medium power			
High power			

4. Before you use a microscope, you should clean the objective lenses and the lens in the eyepiece.

   RULE 2: To avoid scratching the lenses, always use lens paper to clean the lenses. Never touch a lens with your finger.
5. Look at the microscope from the side. The low-power objective should be about 3 cm from the stage. Rotate the nosepiece until you hear the high-power objective click into position. Note that the high-power objective is longer than the low-power objective.

   RULE 3: Always view the microscope from the side when you move an objective to avoid damaging the lens or a slide.
6. Rotate the nosepiece until the low-power objective clicks into position. Find the coarse adjustment knob and practice using it to raise and lower the nosepiece.
7. Plug in the cord attached to the light source. Look through the eyepiece. Practice using the diaphragm to adjust the amount of light entering the microscope.

   RULE 4: To avoid eyestrain, keep both eyes open while looking through the eyepiece.

Part B: View a Prepared Slide

8. Center the prepared slide over the opening in the stage. Hold the slide by its edges to avoid leaving fingerprints that could blur the image. Use the stage clips to hold the slide in place.
9. Make sure the low-power objective is still in position. While you look from the side, use the coarse adjustment to move the objective as close to the stage as possible without touching the stage.
10. Use both eyes to look through the eyepiece. Turn the coarse adjustment to move the low-power objective *away* from the stage until the object comes into focus.

    RULE 5: To avoid hitting a slide, never move an objective toward the stage while looking through the eyepiece.
11. Use the fine adjustment to bring the object into sharp focus. You may need to adjust the diaphragm to see the object clearly. Draw what you can see under low power in Figure 3.
12. While you view the lenses from the side, rotate the high-power objective into position. Look through the eyepiece and use the fine adjustment to bring the object into focus. Draw what you can see under high power in Figure 3.

    RULE 6: Never use the coarse adjustment when you are using a high-power objective.
13. Move the low-power objective back into position. Remove the slide from the stage.

Figure 3 Prepared slide under low power and high power

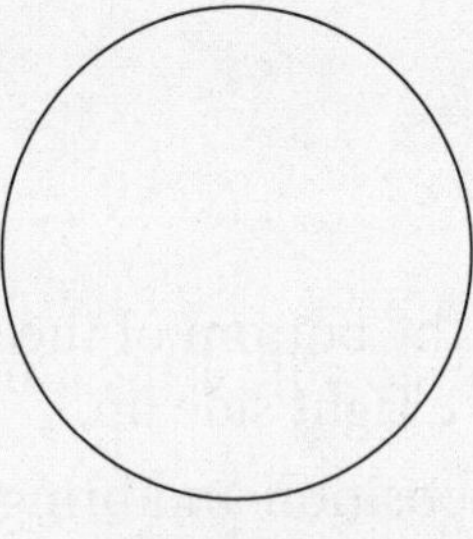

Low Power

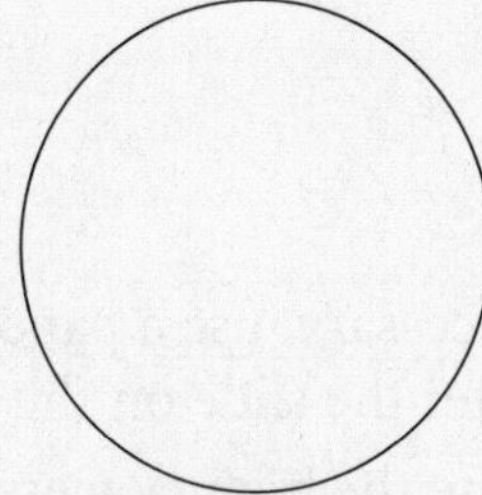

High Power

Part C: Prepare a Wet-Mount Slide

14. Look for the smallest lowercase letter *e* you can find in a newspaper. Cut out the letter and place it on the center of a slide.

15. Use a dropper pipette to place one drop of water on the letter, as shown in Figure 4.

Get Ready! When you place a coverslip on a slide, you need to lower it slowly to keep air bubbles from being trapped between the slide and the coverslip.

16. Place a coverslip so that one edge touches the side of the drop at a 45° angle, as shown in Figure 4. Use a dissecting probe to slowly lower the coverslip onto the paper.

Figure 4 How to prepare a wet-mount slide

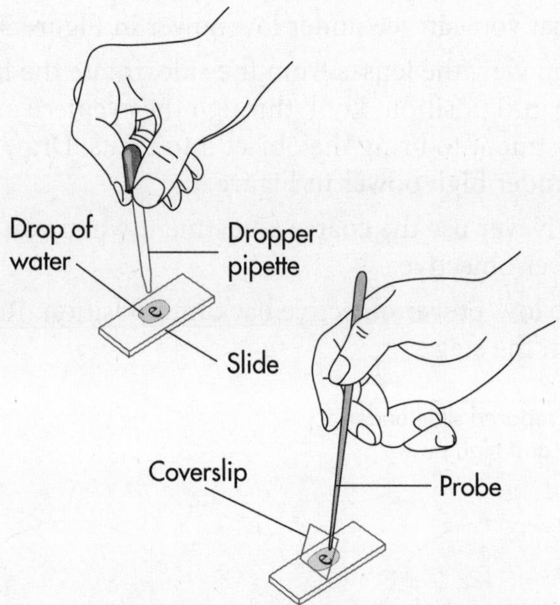

17. If necessary, use a paper towel to dry the bottom of the slide. Center the slide on the stage with the e right side up.

18. Rotate the high-power objective into position and bring the *e* into focus. Draw what you can see under high power in Figure 5.

19. As you look through the eyepiece, move the slide to the left. Notice the way the image of the letter moves. Now move the slide to the right and notice the way the image moves. Move the slide toward the arm and away from the arm and observe how the image of the letter moves.

20. Rotate the high-power objective into position and focus the *e*. Draw what you can see under high power in Figure 5.

 •

Figure 5 Wet-mount slide under low power and high power

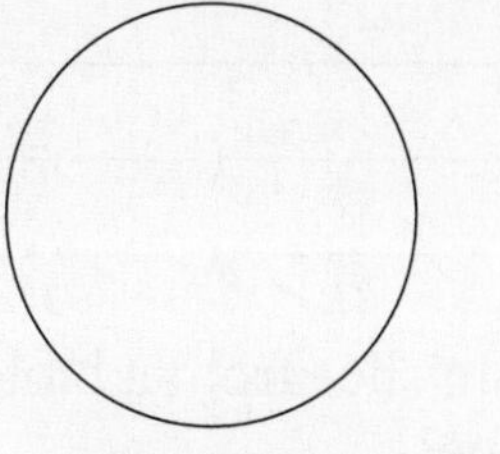

Low Power **High Power**

21. Take apart the wet mount. Discard the newspaper. Clean the slide and coverslip with soap and water. Carefully dry the slide and coverslip with paper towels and return them to their boxes.
22. Rotate the low-power objective into position and use the coarse adjustment to place it as close to the stage as possible without touching the stage.
23. Carefully pick up the microscope and return it to its storage area.

Analyze and Conclude

1. **Apply Concepts** The adjective *compound* means "made by the combination of two or more parts." In a compound microscope, which are the parts that are being combined? Why are they being combined?

____

____

____

2. **Compare and Contrast** How is the image of an object seen through a high-power objective different from the image seen through a low-power objective?

____

____

____

3. **Observe** How did the position of the *e* appear to change when it was viewed through the microscope?

____

____

____

4. **Draw Conclusions** You observe an ant through the eyepiece of a microscope. The ant moves toward the bottom of the slide and then it moves to the right. In which direction is the ant actually moving?

5. **Form a Hypothesis** Why must scientists cut a thin slice from a biological sample before they can view it with a microscope?

Build Science Skills

Use the microscope to view a small piece of a color photograph from a magazine or newspaper. Draw or describe the details you are able to see when the photograph is magnified.

Chapter 1 Lab Using a Microscope to Estimate Size

Problem

How can you use a microscope to estimate the size of an object?

Introduction

When you view objects with a microscope, the objects appear to be much larger than they really are. When an object is magnified, you can get a false sense of its actual size.

You can estimate the size of magnified objects if you know the size of the field of view. The field of view is the brightly lit circle you see as you look through the eyepiece of a microscope. The size of the field depends on which objective lens you are using. When you switch from a low-power to a high-power lens, you zoom in on an object. The field of view decreases as you zoom in.

In this lab, you will determine the diameter of the field of view for each objective lens. Then you will use your results to compare the sizes of a plant cell and a bacterial cell.

Skills Focus

Observe, Measure, Calculate, Predict

Materials

- compound microscope
- transparent 15-cm plastic ruler
- prepared slide of a plant root or stem
- prepared slide of bacteria

Build Vocabulary

Term	Definition
field of view	The area in which an image is able to be observed, or *viewed*
diameter	The length of a straight line passing through the center of a circle from one side to the other
determine	To find out or come to a decision by investigation, thinking, or calculation

Safety

Handle slides gently to avoid breaking them and cutting yourself. Alert your teacher if you break a glass object. Review the rules for handling a microscope. To avoid electrical shocks, make sure that cords, plugs, and your hands are dry when using the light source.

Pre-Lab Questions

1. **Review** Which lens provides more magnification—a low-power lens or a high-power lens?

2. **Infer** Which lens will provide the larger field of view—a low-power lens or a high-power lens?

3. **Calculate** Eight cells fit across a field of view of 160 μm. What is the width of each cell?

4. **Predict** Which cell do you think will be larger, the plant cell or the bacterial cell? Give a reason for your answer.

Procedure

Part A: Determine a Field of View for Each Objective Lens

1. Make sure the low-power lens is in place. Place the ruler on the microscope stage so that the millimeter marks are lined up on the diameter of the lit circle as shown in the drawing.

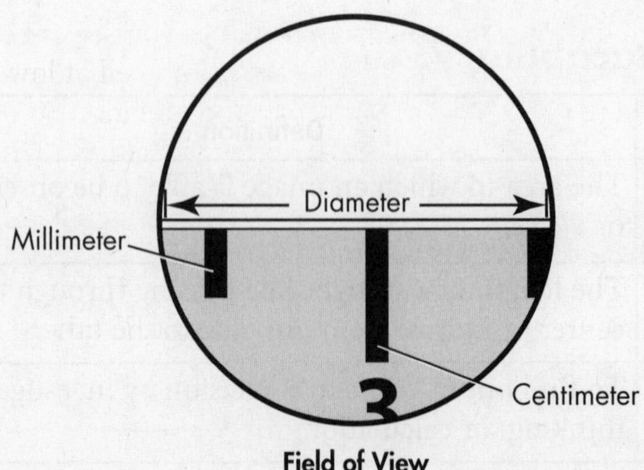

Field of View

2. Look through the eyepiece of the microscope. Look at the millimeter marks. Slowly move the ruler until a millimeter mark is lined up with the left edge of the circle.
3. Count the number of whole millimeters you see. If a millimeter mark does not line up with the right edge of the circle, estimate what fraction of the partial millimeter is visible. Record the diameter in millimeters in the data table below.
4. To convert the diameter from millimeters to micrometers, multiply the diameter by 1000.

   1000 micrometers = 1 millimeter

Get Ready! You will use the data for the low-power objective to calculate the field of view under medium power and high power.

5. Record the power of the low-power, medium-power, and high-power objective lenses in the data table.
6. Divide the power of the low-power lens by the power of the medium-power lens. Multiply the result by the diameter of the low-power field of view to calculate the diameter of the medium-power field of view.
7. Repeat Step 6 for the high-power lens.

Data Table: Field of View

Objective	Power	Diameter (mm)	Diameter (µm)
Low power			
Medium power			
High power			

Part B: Compare the Size of a Plant Cell and a Bacterial Cell

8. Examine a prepared slide of a plant stem or root at low power and at high power. The small round shapes you see are cells. Decide whether to estimate the size of a plant cell at low power or at high power. Using the diameter of the field of view you choose, estimate and record the size of a typical plant cell.

   ______

   ______

9. Repeat Step 8 with a prepared slide of bacteria. Estimate and record the size of a typical bacterial cell.

   ______

   ______

Analyze and Conclude

1. **Infer** Why didn't you use the ruler to measure the field of view of the medium-power and high-power lenses?

2. **Classify** Are bacteria unicellular organisms or multicellular organisms? Provide evidence for your answer.

3. **Control Variables** How did you decide which lens to use to estimate the size of the plant cell?

4. **Control Variables** How did you decide which lens to use to estimate the size of the bacterial cell?

5. **Predict** Some plant diseases are caused by bacteria. Could bacteria injure plant cells by surrounding and eating them? Could bacteria injure plant cells by entering them? Explain your thinking.

Build Science Skills

With your teacher's permission, use the microscope to observe a hair from your head. Use the data you collect to estimate the width of the hair. You and your classmates might want to pool your data to establish a range of widths for human scalp hair.

Chapter 2 Lab Temperature and Enzymes

Problem

How does temperature affect the rate of an enzyme-catalyzed reaction?

Introduction

Some cells in your body can produce hydrogen peroxide to help fight infections. Hydrogen peroxide (H_2O_2) is one of many chemicals that can help cells at low levels and harm them at high levels. Therefore, the level of hydrogen peroxide in a cell must be controlled.

Hydrogen peroxide can break down into water (H_2O) and oxygen gas (O_2). An enzyme called catalase helps speed up this reaction. In this lab, you will observe this enzyme-catalyzed reaction. Then you will design an experiment to determine the effect of temperature on the reaction.

Skills Focus

Form a Hypothesis, Design an Experiment, Measure, Interpret Graphs

Materials

- raw liver
- forceps
- petri dish
- dropper pipette
- 1% hydrogen peroxide solution
- 25-mL graduated cylinder
- 50-mL beakers
- pureed liver
- filter-paper disks
- paper towels
- timer or clock with second hand
- water baths
- thermometers
- beaker tongs
- graph paper

Build Vocabulary

Term	Definition
rate	The speed at which an event, such as a reaction, takes place
enzyme-catalyzed	Describes a reaction in which an enzyme is used as a *catalyst* to increase the rate of the reaction
trial	One of a series of tests done under controlled conditions

Safety

Hydrogen peroxide solution can be irritating. If the solution gets in your eye, tell your teacher and immediately use the eye wash fountain. Rinse off any solution that spills on your skin or clothing. Alert your teacher if you break a glass object. To avoid electrical shock, make sure that cords, plugs, and your hands are dry when using a hot plate. Wash your hands thoroughly with soap and warm water before leaving the lab.

Pre-Lab Questions

1. **Relate Cause and Effect** How will you know that a chemical reaction is taking place in Part A? How will you know in Part B?

____

____

____

2. **Control Variables** In Part B of the lab, which variable will you manipulate? Which variable is the dependent variable?

____

____

3. **Relate Cause and Effect** How is the time required for the filter-paper disk to float related to the activity of the enzyme?

____

____

____

____

Procedure

Part A: Observe the Catalase Reaction

1. Put on your apron, gloves, and safety goggles.
2. Liver cells contain catalase. Use forceps to place a small piece of raw liver in an open petri dish. Use a pipette to put a drop of hydrogen peroxide solution on the liver. Observe what happens. CAUTION: Rinse off any solution that spills on your skin or clothing or splashes in your eye.

   Get Ready! Steps 3–6 describe how to use a filter-paper disk to measure the rate of reaction. If you will be using an oxygen probe to measure the rate, see your teacher for instructions.
3. Use a graduated cylinder to place 25 mL of hydrogen peroxide solution in a 50-mL beaker.

4. Use forceps to dip a filter-paper disk in liver puree. Place the disk on a paper towel for 4 seconds to remove any extra liquid.
5. Use the forceps to place the filter-paper disk at the bottom of the 50-mL beaker. Observe the disk, and record the number of seconds it takes to float to the top of the liquid.

   Number of seconds: ______________________________

Part B: Design an Experiment

6. **Form a Hypothesis** How will changing the temperature affect the rate of the hydrogen peroxide reaction? You may find it useful to set up your hypothesis as an if…then statement.

   Hypothesis: ______________________________

   ____

7. **Describe Your Plan** Describe the procedure you will use to test your hypothesis. You will use some steps from Part A. Other steps in your procedure will be new. Focus on the new steps in your description.

   Experimental Plan: ______________________________

   ____

   ____

   ____

   ____

   ____

8. **Organize Data** Make a three-column data table in the space below to record your measurements and your observations. Include a row for each trial you plan to do.
9. **Disposal** When you are done with your trials, follow your teacher's instructions for cleanup and disposal of materials. Wash your hands thoroughly with soap and warm water.

Analyze and Conclude

1. **Graph** Use the data you collected to make a graph of your results. Plot the independent variable on the *x*-axis and the dependent variable on the *y*-axis.

2. **Interpret Graphs** How did increasing the temperature affect the reaction time?

3. **Draw Conclusions** How did increasing the temperature affect the activity of the enzyme?

4. **Analyze Data** At what temperature was the enzyme most active? Why is this temperature significant?

5. **Infer** Why was raw liver used in this experiment rather than cooked liver?

6. **Apply Concepts** Why is it important for your body to maintain a stable internal temperature?

Build Science Skills

How can pH affect catalase activity? Design an experiment to test your hypothesis. Ask your teacher for comments on your design. With your teacher's permission and supervision, carry out your experiment.

Guided Inquiry • Real-World Lab

Chapter 3 Lab The Effect of Fertilizer on Algae

Problem

How do excess nutrients affect the growth of algae?

Introduction

As primary producers, algae form the base of the food web in the upper layers of the ocean and in freshwater lakes and ponds. The term algae is used to describe a range of organisms from the large brown kelp found attached to rocks at the seashore to the tiny green algae found in fish tanks. Like other plants, green algae need nitrogen, phosphorus, and potassium in order to grow. All three nutrients must be available for the algae to grow and reproduce.

Have you ever seen a pond with a thick, green layer of algae on its surface? This layer is a sign that the pond ecosystem has been disturbed by the presence of too much nitrogen or phosphorus in the water. Fertilizers contain these nutrients, which can end up in bodies of water when rainfall flows downhill from farms.

In this lab, you will work with *Chlorella,* a type of algae that is commonly found in ponds and aquariums. You will compare the growth of *Chlorella* when nutrients are limited and when nutrients are plentiful.

Skills Focus

Predict, Compare and Contrast, Infer

Build Vocabulary

Term	Definition
nutrient	A chemical substance that an organism needs in order to stay alive
excess	An amount of something, such as a nutrient, that goes beyond, or *exceeds,* the amount that is needed
control	The setup used to test the results of a managed, or *controlled,* experiment.
summarize	To state briefly or *sum* up; to prepare a brief statement or *summary*

Materials

- 2 test tubes
- glass-marking pencil
- test-tube rack
- 2 dropper pipettes
- algae culture
- 25-mL graduated cylinder
- spring water
- fertilizer
- 2 cotton balls
- grow light

Safety

Wear safety goggles and plastic gloves when handling cultures. If you have glass test tubes or cylinders, check for cracks or chips. Alert your teacher if you break a glass object. Wash your hands thoroughly with soap and warm water before leaving the lab.

Pre-Lab Questions

1. **Design an Experiment** What is the independent variable in this experiment?

   ______

2. **Predict** After four days, how will you be able to tell which test tube has more algae?

   ______

3. **Control Variables** Why will you grow *Chlorella* in spring water instead of pond water?

   ______

Procedure

1. Use a glass-marking pencil to label one test tube Control and the other Fertilizer. Place the test tubes in a test-tube rack.
2. Put on your safety goggles and plastic gloves.
3. Use a dropper pipette to add 20 drops of algae culture to each test tube.
4. Add 19 mL of spring water to each test tube.
5. Use a second dropper pipette to add 4 drops of fertilizer solution to the test tube labeled Fertilizer.

6. Loosely plug each test tube with a cotton ball to slow the evaporation of the water.
7. Place the test-tube rack under a grow light. Turn on the light. Adjust the position of the rack so that each test tube will receive an equal amount of light.
8. Observe the test tubes each day for the next four days. Record your observations in the data table.

Data Table: Observations		
Day	**Control**	**Fertilizer**
1		
2		
3		
4		

Analyze and Conclude

1. **Compare and Contrast** Summarize your observations of the two test tubes over four days.

2. **Draw Conclusions** How did the addition of fertilizer affect the growth of the algae?

3. **Infer** In Step 6, why did you use cotton balls instead of rubber stoppers to plug your test tubes? *Hint:* Review the diagram of the carbon cycle on page 83 of your textbook.

4. Apply Concepts How could a thick layer of algae on the surface of a pond affect producers that live on or near the bottom of the pond?

Build Science Skills

Design an experiment to see whether the percentage of nitrogen in a fertilizer affects the growth of *Chlorella*. Compare the fertilizer you used in this lab, which has a high percentage of nitrogen, with a low-nitrogen fertilizer. Ask your teacher for instructions on preparing a solution of fertilizer.

Open-Ended Inquiry • Real-World Lab

Chapter 4 Lab **Abiotic Factors and Plant Selection**

Problem

How can you decide which plants will thrive in a garden?

Introduction

The first humans arrived in New Zealand about 1000 years ago. They crossed the Pacific Ocean from Polynesia in large canoes. The climate in Polynesia is tropical, with abundant rainfall and warm temperatures. New Zealand has a more temperate climate. The days and nights tend to be cooler, and there is less rainfall.

The immigrants brought crops with them, such as yams, taro, and gourds, that they wanted to grow in their new home. They looked for regions in New Zealand where the soil type and other abiotic factors were similar to those in their former home. Sometimes the farmers had to adjust the soil to make it easier for the plants to thrive.

Modern gardeners deal with some of the same issues. They need to find a location where the conditions are right for the plants they want to grow, or they need to select plants that will grow successfully in the existing conditions.

In this lab, you will collect data about abiotic factors in your region. Then, you will plan a small garden and select plants that can grow successfully in that garden.

Build Vocabulary

Term	Definition
thrive	To grow strong and healthy
conditions	Factors that affect whether an event or a process, such as the growth of a plant, can take place
hardiness	The quality of being able to survive rough, or *hard,* conditions; a quality that plants must have to live outdoors in winter
scale	A ratio that relates the size of a model, such as a drawing, to the size of the object it represents
indirect	Not following a straight, or *direct,* path from one place to another

Skills Focus

Classify, Analyze Data, Use Models

Materials

- plant hardiness zone map
- plant catalogs
- graph paper
- tape measure or metersticks

Pre-Lab Questions

1. **Predict** How will knowing the plant hardiness zone for your area help you plan a garden?

2. **Relate Cause and Effect** What is the relationship between the last frost and the length of the growing season?

3. **Infer** A plant species grows well in one location in a small garden but does not grow as well in another location. Suggest one possible reason for this difference.

Procedure

Part A: Investigate Your Area

Before you can decide which plants could thrive in your garden, you need to research several abiotic factors for your area. Record the data you collect in the data table on the next page.

1. Use a plant hardiness zone map to identify your area's plant hardiness zone. In the lower 48 states of the United States, there are 8 hardiness zones, numbered 3 through 10. Some parts of Alaska are in Zones 1 and 2. Most of Hawaii is in Zone 11.

2. Find your region's average lowest temperature. This data will be presented as a temperature range. From this information, you can infer whether the soil in your region is likely to freeze in winter and how quickly frozen soil will thaw in the spring.
3. Identify the time of year when your area will typically have its last frost. From this information, you can tell when it is safe to plant seeds or seedlings and you can estimate the length of your growing season.
4. Use an almanac or an online resource to find the average annual, or yearly, rainfall for your area.

Data Table 1: Local Abiotic Factors	
Plant Hardiness Zone	
Lowest Average Temperature	
Last Frost	
Average Annual Rainfall	

Part B: Investigate Your Garden Site

When you select plants for a garden, you have to consider local conditions as well as regional factors. Your teacher may select a site that you can use to plan a garden. Or your teacher may ask you to suggest some possible sites.

5. Once you have agreed on a site, members of your group need to visit the site. Ideally, you should visit the site at different times of day to make observations. Use the data table to summarize your observations. Two factors have been entered to get you started.

Data Table 2: Summary of Observations	
Factor	**Observations**
Amount of Light	
Exposure to Wind	

6. As a group, use a sheet of graph paper to make a scale drawing of your site. Note the location of large objects, such as trees or fences. Record where north is in relation to your site.

   Get Ready! You will be adding information to the drawing in Part C. If you will be working as individuals on Part C, make a copy of the drawing for each team member.

Part C: Plan Your Garden

For Part C, your teacher may ask you to work as a team or as individuals.

7. Decide what type of garden you want to plan—a vegetable garden or a flower garden. Then browse through plant catalogs, looking for plants that can thrive at your site.
8. List the plants you choose below. Include useful information about each plant, such as whether it needs direct sunlight, indirect sunlight, or shade. For vegetables, include the number of days from when seeds or seedlings are planted until the vegetable can be picked.

   ____

   ____

   ____

   ____

   ____

   ____

   ____

   ____

   ____

   ____

   ____

   ____

   ____

   ____

   ____

9. Update your scale drawing of the garden site to show where each species would be planted. Use different colors or symbols to represent each species and include a key.

Analyze and Conclude

1. **Infer** What abiotic factor was used to classify regions into plant hardiness zones? Why do you think this factor was chosen?

2. **Relate Cause and Effect** In general, what is the relationship between the distance of a region from the equator and its plant hardiness zone?

3. **Evaluate** Which of the local factors that you identified in Part B had the greatest effect on which plants you chose, and why?

4. **Control Variables** How do people who live in dry regions grow plants that typically thrive in wetter regions?

5. **Control Variables** How do people who live in temperate regions grow plants that typically thrive in tropical regions?

6. **Infer** Why would someone living in Zone 3 or Zone 4 decide to plant seedlings rather than seeds?

Build Science Skills

Some people make their living growing crops. Besides abiotic factors, what factors must a farmer consider when he or she chooses to plant a crop?

Guided Inquiry • Skills Lab

Chapter 5 Lab The Growth Cycle of Yeast

Problem

What type of population growth occurs in a yeast culture?

Introduction

Yeast have two traits that make them a good choice for studies of population growth. Large numbers of these tiny organisms can live in a small space, and yeast are able to reproduce quickly.

Your teacher has prepared five yeast populations, or cultures, by adding yeast to diluted white grape juice. The cultures were grown under similar conditions. The youngest culture is three days old; the oldest culture is seven days old. Your team will be assigned one culture. You will use the microscope to count yeast cells in your culture, and then share your data with the rest of the class. As part of your analysis, you will graph the class results.

Skills Focus

Measure, Calculate, Interpret Graphs

Materials

- yeast culture
- stirring rod
- 3 dropper pipettes
- 3 microscope slides
- 3 coverslips
- microscope
- 10-mL graduated cylinder
- 2 test tubes
- test-tube rack
- graph paper

Build Vocabulary

Term	Definition
culture	A population of cells or organisms grown under conditions that allow the cells or organisms to be used for scientific study
dilute	To lower the concentration of a mixture by adding a liquid, such as water, to produce a weaker mixture, or *dilution*

Safety

Handle slides and coverslips carefully to avoid breaking them and cutting yourself. Alert your teacher if you break a glass object. Review the rules for use of a microscope. To avoid electrical shocks, make sure the cords, plugs, and your hands are dry when using the light source. Wash your hands thoroughly with soap and warm water before leaving the lab.

Pre-Lab Questions

1. **Infer** Why was grape juice used to prepare the yeast cultures instead of plain water?

   ____

   ____

   ____

2. **Calculate** Suppose you have to do one dilution of your culture before you are able to count the yeast cells. If you count 21 yeast cells in the diluted sample, how many yeast cells were in the same area of the undiluted sample?

   ____

3. **Predict** What do you think will happen to the yeast populations between Day 3 and Day 7? Give a reason for your answer.

   ____

   ____

   ____

Procedure

Part A: Count the Yeast Cells

1. Stir the yeast culture well with a stirring rod. Then use a dropper pipette to place a small drop of the culture on a slide. Add a coverslip and place the slide on the microscope stage.

   Get Ready! When you observe the yeast cells, you may see both single oval-shaped cells and colonies in which several cells are attached together.

2. First view the drop under low power. Once you locate some yeast cells, switch to high power and focus with the fine adjustment. **CAUTION:** When you move an objective lens, always observe the movement from the side of the microscope.

3. If you can count the yeast cells in your field of view, move on to Step 4. If there are too many yeast cells to count, follow the instructions in Part B for diluting the culture.

4. Find an area that is representative of the sample as a whole. Count and record the number of yeast cells. Include both single cells and cells in colonies. Record the count in the correct row of the data table. **NOTE:** If you had to dilute the culture, also record the dilution factor. If you did not have to dilute the culture, record 1 as the dilution factor.
5. To determine the number of yeast cells present, multiply the observed count by the dilution factor.
6. To complete the data table, collect data from the other teams.

Part B: Diluting the Culture

7. Stir the culture. Use a clean dropper pipette to transfer 1 mL of culture into a 10-mL graduated cylinder.
8. Add 9 mL of tap water to the graduated cylinder. Empty the graduated cylinder into a test tube. This procedure dilutes the culture by a factor of 10.
9. View the diluted sample under the microscope as in Step 2. If there are still too many yeast cells to count, repeat Steps 7 and 8. Repeating Steps 7 and 8 will dilute the original culture by a factor of 100.
10. You can repeat Steps 7 and 8 as often as necessary as long as you multiply the dilution factor by 10 each time. Stop diluting the sample when you are able to count the yeast cells. Once you are able to count the yeast cells, go back and complete Steps 4–6.

Data Table

Age of Culture	Yeast Cells Observed	Dilution Factor	Yeast Cells Present
3 days			
4 days			
5 days			
6 days			
7 days			

Analyze and Conclude

1. **Graph** Determine which variable is the independent variable and which is the dependent variable. Then make a graph of the class results. Plot the independent variable on the *x*-axis and the dependent variable on the *y*-axis.

   Independent Variable: ______________________

   Dependent Variable: ______________________

2. **Interpret Graphs** Compare your graph to the graph of logistic growth on page 110 of your textbook.

   ____

   ____

   ____

3. **Apply Concepts** What density-dependent limiting factor might cause a yeast population to decline rather than level off?

   ____

   ____

   ____

4. **Design an Experiment** Describe how you could modify the procedure to ensure that the results were not affected by any variables other than age.

   ____

   ____

5. **Perform Error Analysis** You do not notice a yeast cell near the edge of your field of view. What effect would the dilution factor have on the size of the error?

   ____

   ____

   ____

Build Science Skills

For the cultures you observed in this lab, your teacher used a culture medium that was 25 percent grape juice by volume. How would changing the concentration of the grape juice affect the rate of growth? Form a hypothesis and design an experiment to test your hypothesis. Ask your teacher to approve your design and provide instructions for preparing the cultures.

____

____

____

Chapter 6 Lab Acid Rain and Seeds

Problem

How does acid rain affect seed germination?

Introduction

Every seed contains a tiny living plant and a food supply to nourish that plant when it first begins to develop. The plant and the food supply are enclosed in a protective coat, which keeps the contents of the seed from drying out. The tiny plant can survive for weeks, months, or even years. Factors such as temperature and moisture determine when the plant within the seed will start to grow again. This resumption of growth is called germination.

Before seeds can germinate, they must absorb water, which causes the food-storing tissues to swell and crack the seed coat. The root is the first part of the plant to emerge from the seed.

All rain is mildly acidic because carbon dioxide forms a weak acid when it dissolves in water vapor. If the pH of rain falls below 5.0, the rain is usually classified as acid rain. In this lab, you will design an experiment to determine whether the pH of the water that a seed absorbs can affect germination.

Skills Focus

Design an Experiment, Organize Data, Measure, Graph

Build Vocabulary

Term	Definition
resumption	The act of continuing with, or *resuming,* a process that has been stopped for a while
absorb	To soak up a liquid; to take in nutrients or other chemicals gradually
emerge	To come into view or appear
variable	Something that is able to change, or *vary*
construct	To build something by putting together separate parts to form a planned *structure*

Materials

- 5 large test tubes
- test-tube rack
- glass-marking pencil
- 25-mL graduated cylinder
- 5 solutions of vinegar and water
- pH paper
- 120 dried beans
- paper towels
- zip-close plastic bags
- stick-on labels
- hand lens
- graph paper

Safety

Wear goggles and a lab apron when you handle the solutions. Rinse off any solution that spills on your skin or clothing. If you use glass test tubes or graduated cylinders, check for cracks or chips. Alert your teacher if you break a glass object. Wash your hands thoroughly with soap and warm water before leaving the lab.

Pre-Lab Questions

1. **Compare and Contrast** How are the solutions you will use in this experiment similar? How are they different?

____

____

____

2. **Use Models** What do the solutions represent?

____

____

____

3. **Infer** How will you know that a seed has germinated?

____

____

Procedure

Your teacher has prepared 5 solutions of vinegar and water, which are labeled A–E. Each solution in the series is 8 times as dilute as the previous solution. Solution A is the most concentrated. Solution B is 8 times as dilute as Solution A, Solution C is 8 times as dilute as solution B, and so on.

Part A: Measure the pH of the Solutions

1. Put on your safety goggles and apron.
2. Place 5 large test tubes in a rack. Label the test tubes A, B, C, D, and E.
3. Use the graduated cylinder to place 15 mL of Solution A in the test tube labeled "A." Rinse out the cylinder.
4. Repeat Step 3 for each of the other solutions. Be sure to place each solution in the correct test tube.
5. With your teacher's guidance, select the proper equipment to measure the pH of each solution—either pH paper or a pH probe. If you will be using a probe, see your teacher for instructions. Record the results in Data Table 1.

Data Table 1: pH of Solutions

Solution	Dilution Compared to Solution A	pH
A	none	
B	8×	
C	64×	
D	512×	
E	4096×	

Part B: Design an Experiment

6. **Form a Hypothesis** How will changing the pH of a water-based solution affect the percentage of seeds that germinate? Record your hypothesis as an if…then statement. If the pH of the solution…then the percentage of seeds that germinate…

   Hypothesis: ______________________________

   ____

7. **Control Variables** What will your independent variable be? What will your dependent variable be?

   Independent Variable ______________________________

   Dependent Variable: ______________________________

8. **Describe Your Plan** Record the details of your plan. You will have 120 dried beans and 5 solutions to work with. Which variables will you need to control? Before you begin, have your teacher review your plan.

   Experimental Plan: ______________________________

9. **Organize Data** Construct a data table in the space below. You will need columns for the pH values of the solutions being tested and for the number of seeds that germinate. You might want to include a third column for other observations.

10. **Disposal** After you gather your data, follow your teacher's instructions for cleanup and disposal of materials. Then wash your hands thoroughly with soap and hot water.

Analyze and Conclude

1. **Calculate** Use your data to calculate the percentage of seeds that germinated at each pH. Record the results in Data Table 3.

Data Table 3	
pH of Solution	Percentage of Seeds Germinated

2. **Graph** Use the results from Data Table 3 to make a graph. Plot pH on the *x*-axis and the percentage of seeds germinated on the *y*-axis.

3. **Interpreting Graphs** Does the graph support the hypothesis you made in Part B of the procedure? Why or why not?

______

______

______

______

4. **Infer** At the time that bean plants and other seed plants evolved, what do you think the pH of rainfall was, and why?

______

______

______

5. **Evaluate** Identify at least one way that this lab was not a perfect model for the effect of acid rain on the germination of seeds.

______

______

______

6. **Relate Cause and Effect** Explain why acid rain could harm animals as well as plants. Which types of animals do you think would be most at risk from acid rain?

Build Science Skills

Is the average pH of rain the same in all parts of the United States? Look at a recent map of pH data collected from field stations across the lower 48 states. Identify any pattern in the data and try to explain this pattern.

Chapter 7 Lab **Detecting Diffusion**

Problem

How can you determine whether solutes are diffusing across a membrane?

Introduction

A cell membrane is a selectively permeable barrier. In other words, some particles can pass through the cell membrane while other particles are held back. Solutes that can move across the membrane generally do so by diffusion. When solutes diffuse, they move from an area of high concentration to an area of lower concentration.

In this lab, you will use a small plastic bag to represent the cell membrane. The bag has small openings, or pores, that allow the passage of relatively small molecules. You will use an indicator to determine which molecules diffuse through the pores.

Skills Focus

Use Models, Analyze Data, Infer

Materials

- 400-mL beaker
- 25-mL graduated cylinder
- 1% starch solution
- plastic sandwich bag
- twist tie
- iodine solution
- forceps

Build Vocabulary

Term	Definition
permeable	Letting liquids or gases pass through, or *permeate,* a barrier such as a membrane
selective	Able to choose, or *select,* some options and reject others
solute	A substance that dissolves in another substance, such as water, to form a solution
indicator	Something that is used to show, or *indicate,* the presence of a solute in a solution

Safety

Iodine solution can irritate the eyes and skin and can stain clothing. Wear safety goggles, gloves, and a laboratory apron while handling any solution that contains iodine. Rinse off any solution that spills on your skin or clothing. Wash your hands thoroughly with soap and warm water before leaving the lab.

Pre-Lab Questions

1. **Draw Conclusions** How will you know whether starch has diffused across the membrane?

   ____

   ____

   ____

2. **Draw Conclusions** How will you know whether iodine has diffused across the membrane?

   ____

   ____

   ____

3. **Use Analogies** How is a window screen similar to a cell membrane?

   ____

   ____

   ____

   ____

Procedure

You will use iodine as an indicator to determine whether the plastic bag is permeable to starch. Iodine will turn blue-black when it comes into contact with starch.

1. Put on your goggles, apron, and gloves.
2. Add about 200 mL of water to a 400-mL beaker.
3. Pour 25 mL of starch solution into the plastic sandwich bag.
4. Use a twist tie to tightly seal the bag.
5. Use tap water to thoroughly rinse the outside of the bag in case any starch solution spilled onto the outside of the bag. Be sure to rinse the twist tie as well.

6. Place the plastic bag in the beaker so that the bag is completely covered with water.
7. Add 8 drops of iodine solution to the water in the beaker. Record your initial observations in the data table. Wait 10 minutes, and then record your final observations.
8. Use a forceps to remove and dispose of the plastic bag as instructed by your teacher.

Data Table						
	Inside Bag			Outside Bag		
	Color	Is starch present?	Is iodine present?	Color	Is starch present?	Is iodine present?
Initial						
Final						

Analyze and Conclude

1. **Infer** After you placed the plastic bag in the beaker, what happened to the iodine? What happened to the starch?

2. **Apply Concepts** Use what you know about the structure of starch molecules to explain your results.

3. **Infer** Did water move into the bag or out of the bag? Why?

4. **Perform Error Analysis** When Alyssa did the experiment, she observed the solution outside the plastic bag turn black. What might have happened?

5. **Use Models** Describe two functions of a cell membrane that cannot be modeled with a plastic bag.

6. **Predict** Red blood cells are placed in water that has been distilled so that there are no dissolved substances in the water. Are the red blood cells likely to swell up or shrink? Why?

Build Science Skills

Is a sandwich bag permeable to glucose? Describe how you could modify the procedure in this experiment to answer this question. What could you use to test for the presence of glucose?

Guided Inquiry • Skills Lab

Chapter 8 Lab Plant Pigments and Photosynthesis

Problem

Do red leaves have the same pigments as green leaves?

Introduction

Through the process of photosynthesis, plants convert energy from the sun into energy that is stored in food. The molecules in plants that absorb light are called pigments. Chlorophyll is the primary pigment in most plants. Light energy is converted to chemical energy within chlorophyll molecules. Chlorophyll also gives green plants their color. What about plants that do not have green leaves? What pigments are found in these plants?

Scientists can use paper chromatography to determine which pigments are found in a plant. A mixture of pigments is deposited on a piece of paper. A solvent, such as alcohol, is used to carry the pigments along the paper. Because each pigment moves at a different rate, the pigments become separated. The paper with the separated bands of pigments is called a chromatogram. The prefix *chroma-* comes from a Greek word meaning "color."

In this lab, you will use chromatography to find out whether a red-leafed plant has the same pigments as a green-leafed plant.

Skills Focus

Predict, Analyze Data, Draw Conclusions

Build Vocabulary

Term	Definition
convert	To change from one form to another
primary	The main or most important item in a group of similar items
solvent	A substance that can dissolve other substances and form a solution
control	The setup used to test the results of a managed, or *controlled,* experiment.

Materials

- 2 paper clips
- 2 one-hole rubber stoppers
- 2 chromatography paper strips
- sheet of clean paper
- green and red leaves
- metric ruler
- quarter
- 2 large test tubes
- test-tube rack
- glass-marking pencil
- 10-mL graduated cylinder
- isopropyl alcohol
- colored pencils

Safety

Because alcohol evaporates easily, you should work in a well-ventilated area. If you use glass test tubes or cylinders, check for cracks or chips. Alert your teacher immediately if you break a glass object. Do not pick up broken glass. Wash your hands thoroughly with soap and warm water when you have completed the lab.

Pre-Lab Questions

1. **Design an Experiment** What is the purpose of this lab?

____

____

2. **Control Variables** What is the control in this lab?

____

____

3. **Design an Experiment** Why must the pigment line be at least 2 cm from the bottom of the paper?

____

____

____

4. **Predict** Will red leaves contain the same amount of chlorophyll as green leaves? Why or why not?

____

____

____

Procedure

1. Straighten both paper clips. Bend each into a hook shape.
2. Push the straight end of each bent clip through the hole in a rubber stopper.

   Get Ready! When you transfer pigments from a leaf to a paper strip, the line you produce must be straight.
3. Lay one strip of chromatography paper flat on a sheet of clean paper. Place the green leaf at one end of the strip, as shown in Figure 1. Rock the edge of a quarter back and forth over the leaf at a location about 2 cm from the end of the strip. This motion will transfer leaf pigments to the paper.

Figure 1 How to transfer pigment

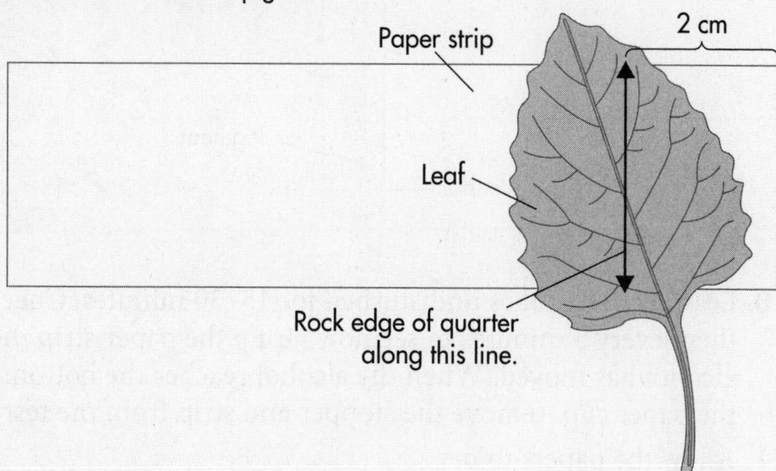

4. Punch the hook end of a paper clip through the strip near the end without the pigments.
5. Repeat Steps 3 and 4 with the red leaf and the second strip of chromatography paper.

   Get Ready! As you do Steps 6–9, try not to let the paper strip touch the inside of the tube.
6. Place two test tubes in the test-tube rack. Insert the stopper and strip with the pigments from the green leaf into one test tube. Make a mark on the test tube about 1 cm below the pigment line. Use the glass-marking pencil to label the test tube Green.
7. Repeat Step 6 with the second test tube. Use the stopper and strip that has pigments from the red leaf. Label the test tube Red.

8. Remove each stopper and strip from its test tube. Add alcohol to each tube until the surface of the alcohol reaches the mark you made on the tube.
9. Reinsert each stopper and strip into its test tube. The alcohol should cover the bottom of the paper but not touch the pigment, as shown in Figure 2.

Figure 2 Completed setup

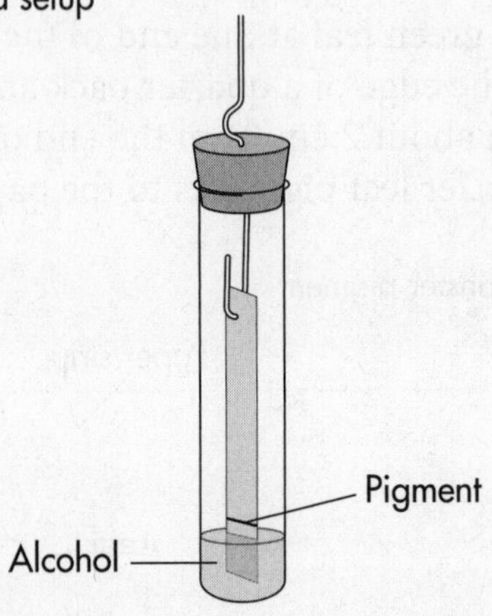

10. Leave the test tubes undisturbed for 15–30 minutes. Check them every 5 minutes to see how far up the paper strip the alcohol has moved. When the alcohol reaches the bottom of the paper clip, remove the stopper and strip from the test tube.
11. Allow the papers to dry.
12. Use colored pencils to draw what you observe on each strip in the space below. Label the drawings Green Leaf and Red Leaf.

Analyze and Conclude

1. **Compare and Contrast** How are the two chromatograms similar? How are they different?

2. **Analyze Data** Your teacher will provide a chart that matches the color bands to pigments. Use the chart to identify the pigments that are visible on your chromatograms.

3. **Apply Concepts** Based on your results, does photosynthesis take place in a red-leafed plant? Explain your answer.

4. **Predict** During the fall, the chlorophyll in the leaves of many plants starts to break down. The colors of other pigments present in the leaf are revealed. How do you think a chromatogram of a leaf that just turns red in the fall would compare with your chromatogram of a leaf that is red all year?

5. **Apply Concepts** What advantage could there be for a leaf to have pigments other than chlorophyll? *Hint:* Do all pigments absorb the same wavelengths of light?

Build Science Skills

If possible, repeat the experiment using a leaf that turns red only in the fall. Compare the chromatogram from that leaf with the chromatogram from the leaf that is red all year. Record your results.

Guided Inquiry • Real-World Lab

Chapter 9 Lab Comparing Fermentation Rates of Sugars

Problem

How does the type of sugar affect the rate of fermentation?

Introduction

Fermentation is the process that releases energy from food in the absence of oxygen. Fermentation can be used to make foods, such as cheese and bread. Early in the bread-making process, yeast is added to the bread dough. Yeast are unicellular organisms that can break down carbohydrates in dough to produce carbon dioxide and ethanol. The bubbles of carbon dioxide gas that collect in the dough give bread its volume and texture. The alcohol evaporates as the dough rises and the bread is baked.

Sugars ferment at different rates. In this lab, you will measure and compare rates of fermentation for five different sugars.

Skills Focus

Predict, Measure, Analyze Data, Infer

Build Vocabulary

Term	Definition
rate	The speed at which an event, such as a reaction, takes place
gas pressure	The force applied by a gas as it pushes, or *presses,* against the walls of its container
disaccharide	A sugar whose molecules form when two simple sugars join together
interface	A connection between two devices, such as a probe and a computer
suspension	A mixture that contains materials, such as yeast, that do not dissolve
monitor	To keep close watch over something, such as the temperature of a water bath

Materials

- probe interface
- gas pressure probe
- hot plate
- 400-mL beaker
- thermometer
- ring stand
- test-tube clamp
- medium test tube
- test-tube rack
- sugar solution
- yeast suspension
- 2 pipettes
- vegetable oil
- 1-hole rubber stopper
- plastic tubing with lock fitting

Safety

Always wear goggles and an apron when using a water bath. If you have glass beakers or test tubes, check for cracks or chips. Alert your teacher if you break a glass object. Avoid contact with the surface of the hot plate. To avoid electric shocks, make sure cords, connections, and your hands are dry. Wash your hands thoroughly with soap and warm water at the end of the lab.

Pre-Lab Questions

1. **Infer** What is the purpose of adding a layer of vegetable oil above the sugar and yeast mixture?

   ____

   ____

   ____

   ____

2. **Relate Cause and Effect** How will the rate of fermentation affect the gas pressure in a test tube?

   ____

   ____

   ____

   ____

3. **Predict** Which of the sugars do you think will have the highest rate of fermentation, and why?

   ____

   ____

   ____

Procedure

As a class you will test glucose and fructose, which are simple sugars. You will also test sucrose, lactose, and maltose, which are disaccharides. Each group will test one sugar and share its data with the rest of the class.

Part A: Set Up the Water Bath and Probe Interface

1. Put on goggles and an apron.
2. Plug in your hot plate and use a setting that will produce a temperature between 37°C and 40°C.

   Get Ready! You will need a water bath to control the temperature of the yeast throughout the experiment.
3. Pour about 300 mL of water into a 400-mL beaker and place the beaker on the hot plate. Heat the water until it reaches a temperature between 37°C and 40°C. **CAUTION:** Make sure the water bath is placed away from the edge of the lab bench or table.
4. While the water is heating, follow your teacher's instructions for setting up your probe interface. Set the pressure scale on the vertical axis for 90 to 130 kPa. Set the time scale on the horizontal axis for 0 to 15 minutes. Set the data collection rate to 6 samples per minute.

Part B: Prepare the Reactants

5. Use a test-tube clamp to attach the test tube to a ring stand, as shown in Figure 1.

Figure 1 Overall setup

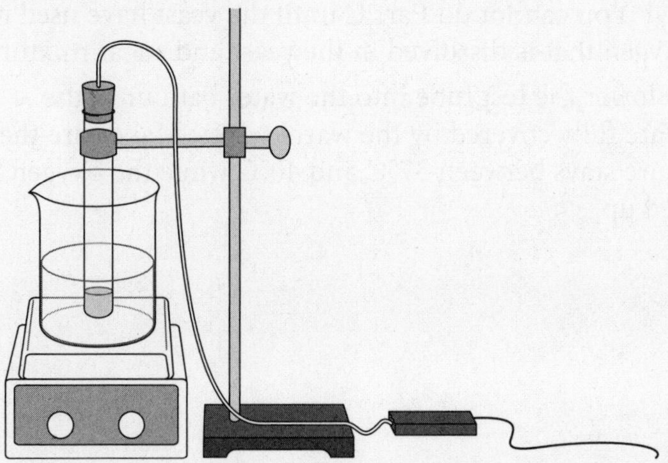

Get Ready! Choose someone with a steady hand to do Steps 6–8.

6. Use a pipette to add 1 mL of the sugar solution to the test tube. **CAUTION:** Do not allow the solution or the pipette to touch the sides of the test tube.
7. Use a second pipette to gently stir the yeast suspension. Then use the pipette to add 1 mL of the suspension to the test tube. **CAUTION:** Do not allow the solution or the pipette to touch the sides of the test tube.
8. Use a dropper to carefully construct a layer of vegetable oil above the yeast and sugar mixture, as shown in Figure 2. Add enough oil to make a layer that is about 0.5 cm deep.

Figure 2 Test tube with liquids

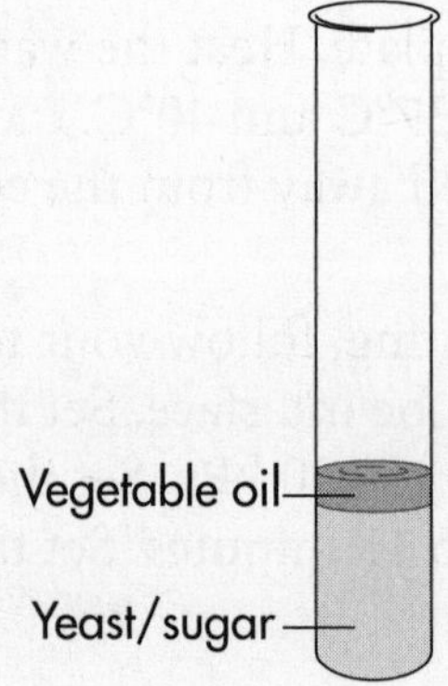

9. Insert the rubber stopper with the post for connecting the tubing to the stopper. **CAUTION:** Don't connect the tubing to the stopper at this time. You don't want pressure to build up in the test tube before you are ready to measure the pressure.

Get Ready! You cannot do Part C until the yeast have used up all the oxygen that is dissolved in the yeast and sugar mixture.

10. Carefully lower the test tube into the water bath until the contents are fully covered by the warm water. Make sure the temperature stays between 37°C and 40°C while the oxygen is being used up.

Part C: Collect Data

11. After 10 minutes, connect the plastic tubing to the rubber stopper. Collect data for 15 minutes. Keep monitoring the temperature during this time. **CAUTION:** If the pressure exceeds 115 kilopascals, the stopper will pop off. Disconnect the tubing if the pressure reaches 113 kilopascals.
12. After 15 minutes, find the value of the slope, *m*, for the change in pressure in the test tube. This is the rate of fermentation.
13. Record the slope in the appropriate row of the data table. Post your data on the board and record data from other groups in your table.
14. Turn off the hot plate. Follow your teacher's instructions for breaking down the setup and for cleanup. Wash your hands thoroughly with soap and warm water before leaving the lab.

Data Table	
Sugar	**Rate of Fermentation (kPa/min)**
Glucose	
Fructose	
Sucrose (glucose + fructose)	
Lactose (galactose + glucose)	
Maltose (glucose + glucose)	

Analyze and Conclude

1. **Interpret Tables** Which sugar had the highest rate of fermentation? Which sugar had the lowest rate?

___

___

2. **Draw Conclusions** Use what you know about the structures of the sugars to explain the results for glucose, fructose, sucrose, and maltose.

___

___

___

___

___

3. **Infer** Why do you think little or no fermentation occurred with lactose? *Hint:* Recall the role that enzymes play in reactions that take place in cells.

4. **Predict** The solutions used in this lab contained only 5 percent of sugar. Would an increase in the concentration of sugar change the rate of fermentation? Explain.

5. **Apply Concepts** Why did all of the oxygen in the mixture have to be used up before fermentation could begin?

Build Science Skills

Find a recipe for bread and make one or more loaves. Record your observations at each stage in the process. Use as many of your senses as possible.

Open-Ended Inquiry • Design Your Own Lab

Chapter 10 Lab **Regeneration in Planaria**

Problem

How potent are the stem cells in planaria?

Introduction

Planarians are flatworms that live in fresh water. They are able to replace, or regenerate, body parts. Figure 1 is a diagram of a planarian. When a planarian is cut, stem cells collect at the site of the injury. Stem cells have the ability to differentiate into other types of cells. Stem cells that can form any tissue in an organism's body are *totipotent.* Stem cells that can differentiate into some, but not all, cell types are *multipotent.*

In this lab, you will design an experiment to determine how potent planarian stem cells are. Then you will share your results with the rest of the class. From these combined results, you should be able to infer where stem cells are found in a planarian's body.

Figure 1 External anatomy of planarian

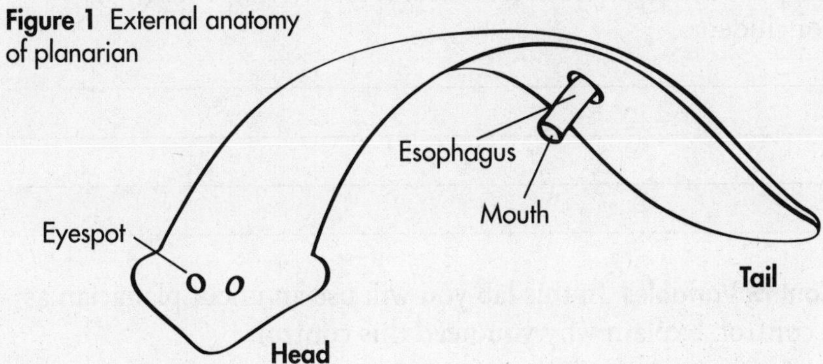

Skills Focus

Form a Hypothesis, Design an Experiment, Draw Conclusions

Build Vocabulary

Term	Definition
differentiate	To change an object so that it is not the same as, or *different* from, the original
infer	To offer a reasoned opinion, or *inference*, based on observations and experience
partial	Having an effect on only some, or *part*, of an object

Materials

- fresh water or spring water
- planarians
- petri dishes
- glass-marking pencil
- forceps
- scalpel
- dissecting microscope
- glass microscope slide
- lens paper
- pipette
- small paintbrush
- clear ruler

Safety

A scalpel is an extremely sharp instrument. Never hold a flatworm with your fingers while making a cut. If you are using glass petri dishes or pipettes, check for cracks or chips. Alert your teacher if you break a glass object. Wash your hands thoroughly with soap and warm water before leaving the lab.

Pre-Lab Questions

1. **Draw Conclusions** Suppose a cut planarian regenerates completely. What would you conclude about its stem cells? Suppose the regeneration is incomplete. What would you conclude?

____
____
____
____

2. **Control Variables** In this lab you will use an uncut planarian as a control. Explain why you need this control.

____
____
____
____

3. **Infer** Two planarians are cut at different locations. Regeneration occurs in one planarian, but not in the other. Based on these results, what might you infer about stem cells in planarians?

____
____
____

Name ____________________ Class ________ Date ________

Procedure

Part A: Care and Handling of Planarians

Your teacher may ask you to care for the planarians as you observe them for one or two weeks. If so, follow your teacher's instructions.

1. **Water** Planarians need to be kept in fresh water or spring water in a dark area at room temperature. **CAUTION:** Never add tap water or distilled water to the petri dish.
2. **Food** The planarians need to be fed once a week.
3. **Moving Planarians** When you need to move a planarian from one dish to another, use a pipette. **CAUTION:** If a planarian attaches itself to a petri dish, do not use a hard object to scrape it off the dish. Use a small paintbrush instead.
4. **Making Cuts** Figure 2 shows a vertical cut and a horizontal cut. It also shows the difference between a partial cut and a complete cut.

Figure 2 Examples of cuts

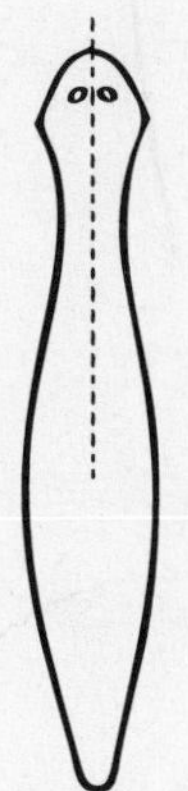

Partial Vertical Cut

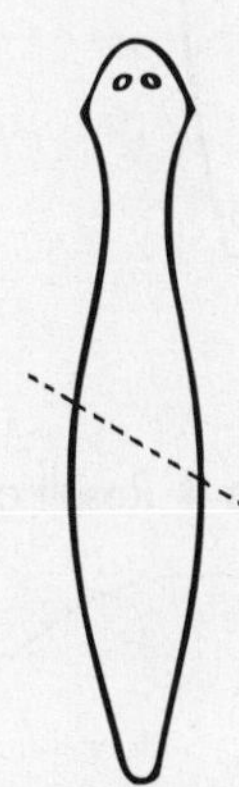

Complete Horizontal Cut

Part B: Design an Experiment

Assume you will have three planarians to work with.

5. **Form a Hypothesis** Are stem cells in planaria multipotent or totipotent? Record your hypothesis as an if…then statement: If the cut planarians…then stem cells in planaria are…

   Hypothesis: ____

   ____

   ____

   ____

6. **Control Variables** Decide which independent variable you will investigate—the type of cut (complete or partial) or the location of the cut. Record your independent variable.

   Independent Variable: ______________________

   Dependent Variable: amount of regeneration

7. **Describe Your Plan** Use Figure 3 to record the cuts you intend to make. Use Figure 4 to draw what your planarians will look like right after the cuts. Depending on the cuts you make, you may have as many as five planarians to observe.

Figure 3 Planned cuts

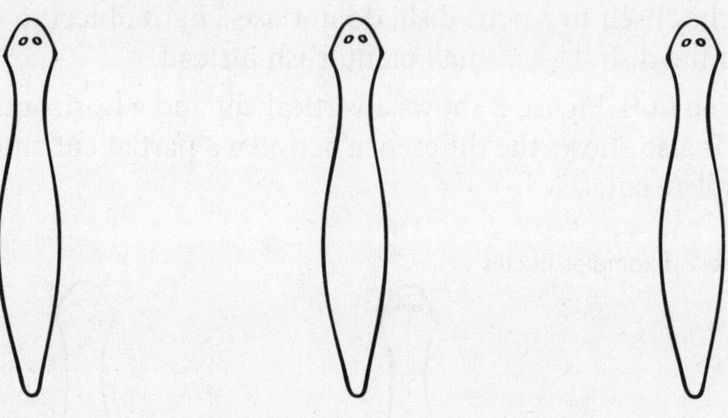

Figure 4 Result of cuts

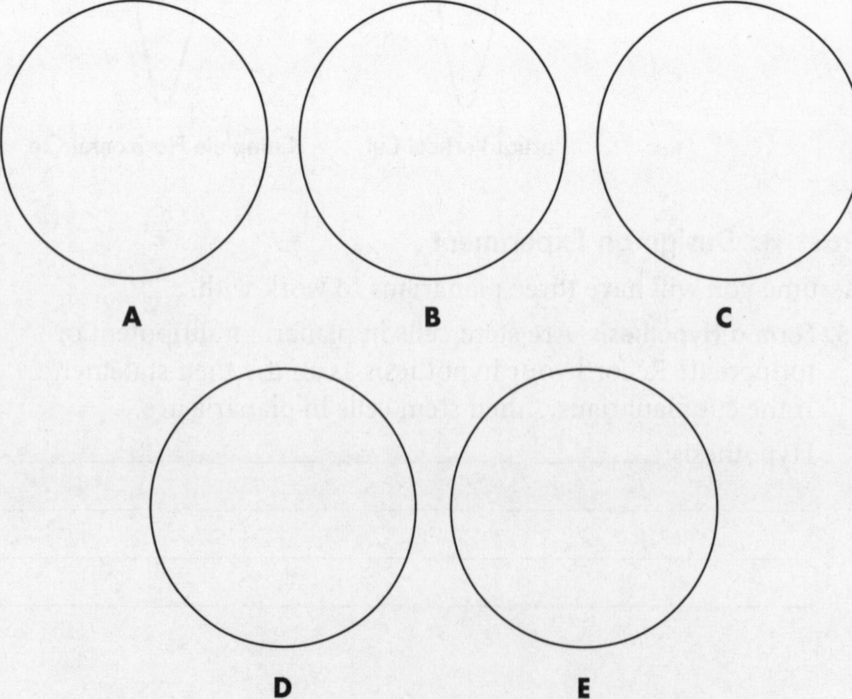

8. **Making Observations** Decide how you will track changes in the dependent variable. Will you use drawings, measurements, or written observations?
9. **Organize Data** Use the data table to record your observations.
10. **Disposal** After handling the planarians, wash your hands thoroughly with soap and warm water. When the experiment is over, follow your teacher's instructions for cleanup and disposal of materials.

Data Table: Observations

Day	Planarian A	Planarian B	Planarian C	Planarian D	Planarian E
3					
5					
7					
9					
12					
14					

Name ______________________ Class ________ Date ________

Analyze and Conclude

1. **Infer** What evidence do you have that planarians have more than one type of tissue in their bodies?

2. **Apply Concepts** What must happen to the stem cells before the different kinds of tissues can be regenerated?

3. **Evaluate** How complete was the regeneration of your cut planarians? Use Figure 1 to help you evaluate the results.

4. **Draw Conclusions** Was your hypothesis supported or not supported? Use your results to explain your answer.

5. **Analyze Data** As a class, look at the results from all the groups. What can you conclude about the location of stem cells in a planarian's body?

6. **Apply Concepts** Why can the human body heal a cut on a finger but not regenerate a finger that is cut off?

Build Science Skills

Planarians naturally swim away from bright light. How could you demonstrate that regenerated eyespots are functional?

Guided Inquiry • Skills Lab

Chapter 11 Lab Modeling Meiosis

Problem

How does meiosis increase genetic variation?

Introduction

Most cells in organisms that reproduce sexually are diploid. They have two sets of chromosomes and two complete sets of genes. Gametes are the exception. Gametes are the cells that combine during sexual reproduction. In animals, these cells are called sperm and eggs. Gametes are haploid cells, which means that they have only one set of chromosomes. Meiosis is the process in which haploid cells form from diploid cells.

In this lab, you will model the steps in meiosis. You will make drawings of your models. You will also identify points in the process that can lead to greater genetic variation.

Skills Focus

Use Models, Sequence, Draw Conclusions

Materials

- pop-it beads
- magnetic centromeres
- large sheet of paper
- colored pencils
- scissors

Safety

Do not direct the points of the scissors toward yourself or others. Use the scissors only as instructed.

Build Vocabulary

Term	Definition
model	A structure that helps you form a picture of an object or process you cannot see directly
variation	The degree, or extent, to which a set of similar items differ, or *vary*
independent	Is not affected by, or does not *depend* on, another person or thing

Pre-Lab Questions

1. **Control Variables** Why must you use the same number of beads when you construct the second chromosome in Step 1?

2. **Infer** Why is the longer chromosome pair used to model crossing-over?

3. **Calculate** A diploid cell has two pairs of homologous chromosomes. How many different combinations of chromosomes could there be in the gametes?

Procedure

The diploid cell in your model will have two pairs of homologous chromosomes. In order to keep track of the pairs, you will make one pair longer than the other. The beads will represent genes. Use the large sheet of paper to represent the cell.

Part A: Interphase

Just before meiosis begins, the chromosomes are copied, or replicated.

1. Use ten beads and a centromere of one color to build the long chromosome. Use ten beads and a centromere of a second color to build the second chromosome in the long pair. Refer to the drawing below.
2. For the shorter pair of chromosomes, use only five beads.

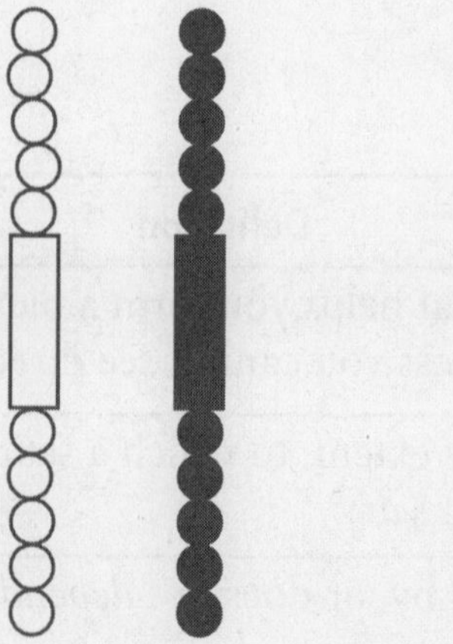

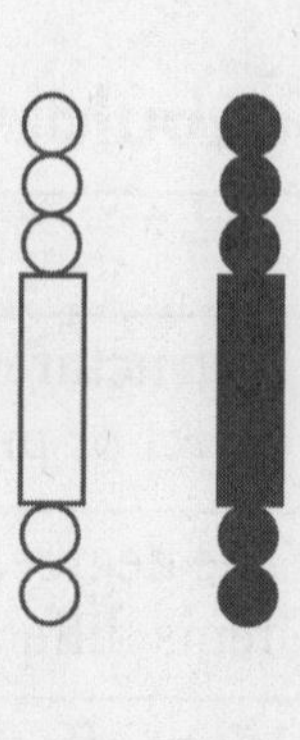

3. Now model the replication of the chromosomes. Use the magnetic centromeres to attach each copy to its original.
4. Make a drawing of your model in the space below.

Part B: Meiosis I

During meiosis I, the cell divides into two diploid daughter cells.

5. Pair up each replicated chromosome with its homologous chromosome to form a tetrad. When you are done you will have two tetrads.
6. Use the longer tetrad to model crossing-over.
7. Make a drawing of the tetrads in the space below.

8. Line up the tetrads across the center of your "cell." Separate the chromosomes in each tetrad.
9. Move one chromosome from each pair of chromosomes to the left side of the cell and the second chromosome to the right side.
10. Divide the cell into two daughter cells.
11. Use the space below to make a drawing of the result.

Part C: Meiosis II

During meiosis II, the daughter cells divide again.

12. Line up the chromosomes at the center of the first cell, one above the other. Separate the chromatids in each chromosome and move them to opposite sides of the cell.
13. Repeat Step 12 for the second cell.
14. Divide each cell into two daughter cells.
15. Use the space below to make a drawing of the four haploid cells.

Name ______________________ Class ________ Date ________

Guided Inquiry • Skills Lab

Chapter 11 Lab **Modeling Meiosis**

Problem

How does meiosis increase genetic variation?

Introduction

Most cells in organisms that reproduce sexually are diploid. They have two sets of chromosomes and two complete sets of genes. Gametes are the exception. Gametes are the cells that combine during sexual reproduction. In animals, these cells are called sperm and eggs. Gametes are haploid cells, which means that they have only one set of chromosomes. Meiosis is the process in which haploid cells form from diploid cells.

In this lab, you will model the steps in meiosis. You will make drawings of your models. You will also identify points in the process that can lead to greater genetic variation.

Skills Focus

Use Models, Sequence, Draw Conclusions

Materials

- pop-it beads
- magnetic centromeres
- large sheet of paper
- colored pencils
- scissors

Safety

Do not direct the points of the scissors toward yourself or others. Use the scissors only as instructed.

Build Vocabulary

Term	Definition
model	A structure that helps you form a picture of an object or process you cannot see directly
variation	The degree, or extent, to which a set of similar items differ, or *vary*
independent	Is not affected by, or does not *depend* on, another person or thing

Pre-Lab Questions

1. **Control Variables** Why must you use the same number of beads when you construct the second chromosome in Step 1?

____

____

2. **Infer** Why is the longer chromosome pair used to model crossing-over?

____

____

3. **Calculate** A diploid cell has two pairs of homologous chromosomes. How many different combinations of chromosomes could there be in the gametes?

____

____

Procedure

The diploid cell in your model will have two pairs of homologous chromosomes. In order to keep track of the pairs, you will make one pair longer than the other. The beads will represent genes. Use the large sheet of paper to represent the cell.

Part A: Interphase

Just before meiosis begins, the chromosomes are copied, or replicated.

1. Use ten beads and a centromere of one color to build the long chromosome. Use ten beads and a centromere of a second color to build the second chromosome in the long pair. Refer to the drawing below.
2. For the shorter pair of chromosomes, use only five beads.

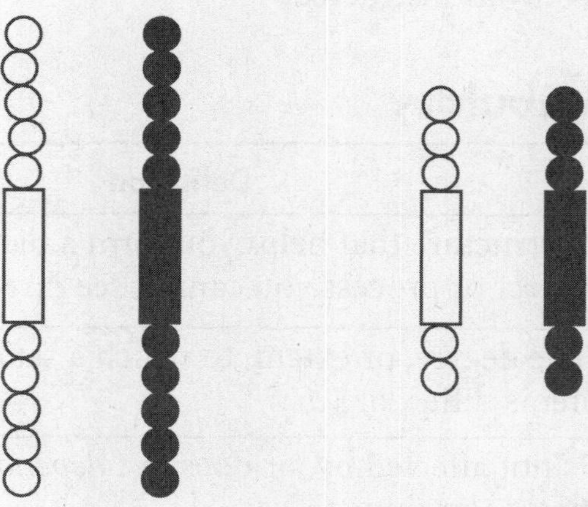

Name ________________ Class ________ Date ________

Analyze and Conclude

1. **Relate Cause and Effect** How does crossing-over increase variation in genes?

2. **Use Models** Suppose no crossing-over takes place. Use Step 9 to explain why meiosis will still increase genetic variation.

3. **Compare and Contrast** Compare your models of the four haploid cells with those of other groups. Describe and explain any variation that you observe.

4. **Calculate** What would happen to the possible variation in gametes if the number of chromosome pairs increased from two to three? What if the number increased again from three to four?

5. **Apply Concepts** How can independent assortment help explain genetic diversity in humans? *Hint:* How many pairs of chromosomes are in a human diploid cell?

6. Perform Error Analysis Suggest a way you could improve the models to better represent the process of meiosis.

7. Draw Conclusions In terms of adaptation, what advantage does sexual reproduction provide for a species?

Build Science Skills

Join with another group to model how genetic variation will increase during fertilization. Make a drawing of your model in the space below.

Guided Inquiry • Skills Lab

Chapter 12 Lab Extracting DNA

Problem

What properties of DNA can you observe when you extract DNA from cells?

Introduction

A strawberry is an excellent choice for a DNA extraction. Because each strawberry cell has eight copies of its chromosomes, you will be able to collect a large amount of DNA. Ripe strawberries also contain enzymes that help break down cell walls.

In this lab, you will extract the DNA from a strawberry. You must crush the strawberry to break apart its cells, and then add a detergent to dissolve the cell membranes. You will use a filter to remove the solids from the mixture. The solution that you collect will contain DNA, proteins, sugars, and other dissolved molecules. You will use ethanol to isolate the DNA from the other dissolved molecules in the solution.

Skills Focus

Predict, Observe, Draw Conclusions

Materials

- self-sealing plastic freezer bag
- ripe strawberry
- detergent solution
- 25-mL graduated cylinder
- cheesecloth
- funnel
- test tube, medium-sized
- test-tube rack
- chilled 95% ethanol
- stirring rod

Build Vocabulary

Term	Definition
extract	To remove a substance from a mixture, often by dissolving it
solution	A mixture in which all the substances are spread out evenly throughout the mixture
isolate	To separate out a substance in order to identify and study it
dispose of	To throw away or get rid of

Safety 

The ethanol used in this lab could be toxic if absorbed through the skin. So rinse off any solution that spills on your skin immediately. Wash your hands thoroughly with soap and hot water at the end of the lab. Do not handle broken glassware.

Pre-Lab Questions

1. **Apply Concepts** Why do strawberry cells need DNA?

2. **Infer** If you observe a cell nucleus under a compound microscope, you will not see a molecule of DNA. Why will you be able to see the DNA you extract?

3. **Predict** Use what you know about DNA to predict some of the physical properties of DNA.

Procedure

1. Place your strawberry in the freezer bag. Press the bag to remove as much air as possible and then seal the bag. Crush the strawberry by mashing it with your fist for about 2 minutes.
2. Open the bag and add 10 mL of detergent solution. Carefully press out the air and reseal the bag.
3. Squeeze or mash the strawberry and detergent mixture for about 1 minute.
4. Prepare the setup shown in Figure 1. If you have a test-tube rack, place the test tube in the rack. Make sure the cheesecloth hangs over the funnel at all points.
5. Pour the liquid from the freezer bag into the funnel. When the test tube is about one-eighth full of liquid, remove the funnel.
6. Discard the cheesecloth and any leftover strawberry pulp.

Figure 1 Filtration setup

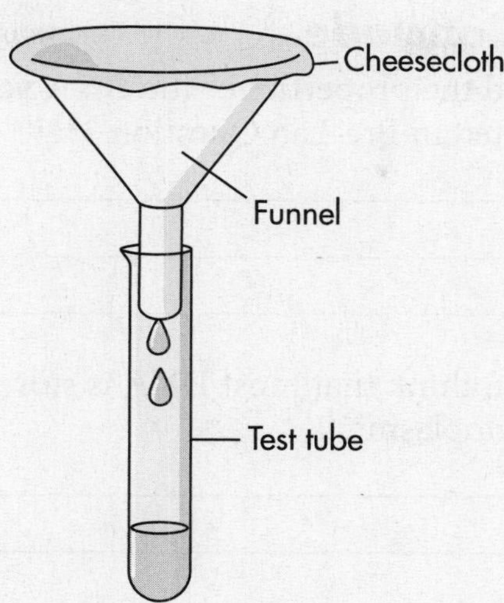

Get Ready! You are going to use a dropper to slowly add ethanol to the test tube. You will need to hold the dropper so that the drops run down the side of the test tube.

7. Slowly add drops until the test tube is half full. The ethanol should form a separate layer above the filtered solution. Record what you observe.

____

____

8. Place the tip of the stirring rod at the point where the two layers meet, as shown in Figure 2. As you gently twirl the rod, bend down so you can observe what is happening at eye level. Record what you observe.

____

____

9. Dispose of the materials as instructed by your teacher. Wash your hands thoroughly with soap and warm water.

Figure 2 Placement of stirring rod

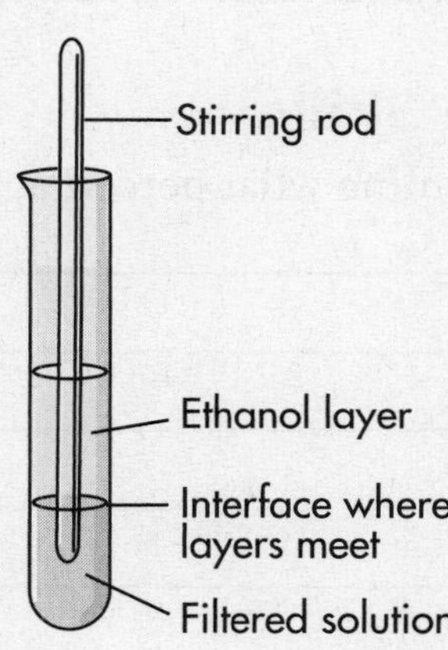

Analyze and Conclude

1. **Evaluate** How did the properties of the DNA you observed compare to those you predicted in Pre-Lab Question 3?

2. **Infer** Why do you think that most DNA is stored in the nucleus of a cell and not in the cytoplasm?

3. **Use Analogies** Sewing thread is very thin and difficult to see once a length of thread is removed from its spool. How is the thread and spool an analogy for what happened to the DNA in Step 7.

4. **Draw Conclusions** Water is the main ingredient in the detergent solution. Ethanol is a type of alcohol. What can you conclude about how easily DNA dissolves in water and in alcohol?

5. **Predict** Do you think it would be easier or harder to extract DNA from animal cells than from plant cells? Explain your answer?

Build Science Skills

How could you determine what percentage of a strawberry's mass is DNA?

 •

Guided Inquiry • Skills Lab

Chapter 13 Lab **From DNA to Protein Synthesis**

Problem

What are the steps involved in making a protein?

Introduction

Before a protein can be built, the instructions must be packaged and transferred out of the DNA "library." First, the specific sequence of DNA that codes for the protein is transcribed into a complementary strand of mRNA. In eukaryotic cells, the mRNA then leaves the nucleus and enters the cytoplasm. In all cells, the mRNA molecule attaches to a ribosome. This is the location where tRNA anticodons translate the mRNA into amino acids. The completed amino acid chain, or polypeptide, then folds into its final shape as a protein.

In this lab, you will model transcription of DNA and translation of mRNA while you decode secret messages.

Skills Focus

Use Models, Sequence

Build Vocabulary

Term	Definition
synthesis	The process of joining, or combining, two or more objects into a new object
transcribe	To use a segment of DNA as a guide, or pattern, to build a complementary strand of messenger RNA (mRNA)
complementary	Used to describe either of two parts that *complete* each other; containing the information needed to build the other part
translate	To decode the instructions stored in mRNA for building a protein from amino acids
correspond	To have a clearly defined relationship; for example, the match between an mRNA codon and an amino acid

Pre-Lab Questions

1. **Sequence** Describe briefly the process you will use to decode the messages.

2. **Compare and Contrast** What role do stop codons play in protein synthesis? What are they used for in the coded messages?

3. **Predict** Which six letters will not appear in the coded messages? Give a reason for your answer.

Procedure

Part A: How to Decode Messages

1. Write the complementary mRNA strand for the DNA sequence given below by finding the mRNA codon that matches each DNA triplet, base for base. The mRNA strand has been started for you. Finish the transcription.

   DNA: TAC CGT TTT CTT ATT TAC ATA ACT CTG
   CGA ATG

   mRNA: AUG GCA AAA GAA UAA

2. Use Figure 1 on the next page to match each mRNA codon from Step 1 with its corresponding amino acid. When the codon is a "stop" codon, include "stop" in the sequence. The amino acid sequence has been started for you. Finish the translation.

   methionine, alanine, lysine, glutamic acid, stop,

Name ________________ Class ________ Date ________

Figure 1 Map of mRNA codons to amino acids

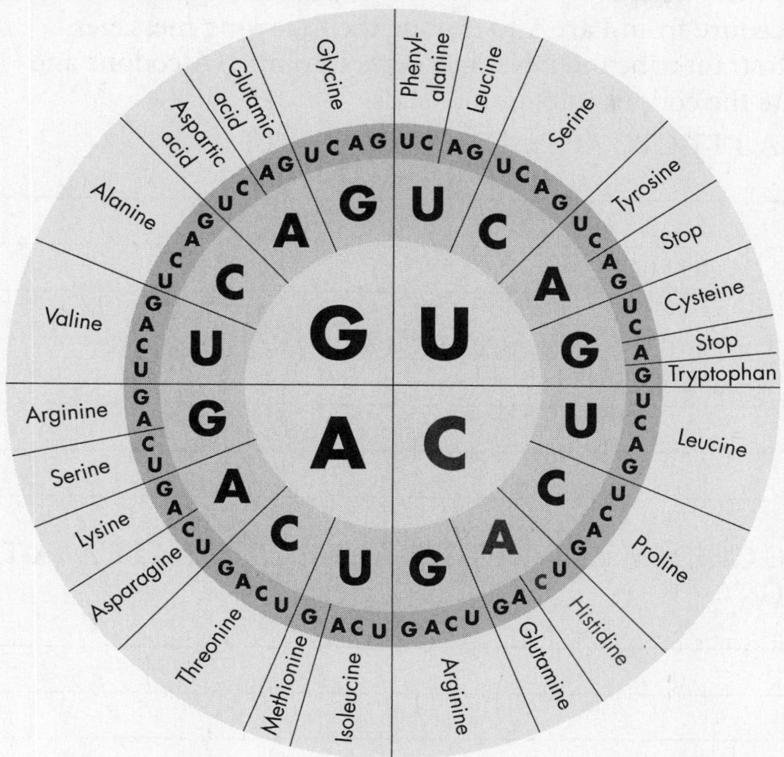

3. Use the table to find the single-letter symbol for each amino acid in the sequence from Step 2. The symbols will spell out a sentence or a familiar saying. The first word is already done.
MAKE ______________________________

Single-Letter Symbols for Amino Acids			
Amino Acid	**Symbol**	**Amino Acid**	**Symbol**
Alanine	A	Leucine	L
Arginine	R	Lysine	K
Asparagine	N	Methionine	M
Aspartic Acid	D	Phenylalanine	F
Cysteine	C	Proline	P
Glutamic Acid	E	Serine	S
Glutamine	Q	Threonine	T
Glycine	G	Tryptophan	W
Histadine	H	Tyrosine	Y
Isoleucine	I	Valine	V

Part B: Decoding Messages

4. Use the procedure from Part A to decode the following messages. Remember to transcribe the DNA messages into mRNA codons and then translate the codons into amino acids.

   a. TGA CGA TTT CTC ACT ACA CGC GCG CTT

   b. GTA CTT ATT TAA AGC ATC CGT ATT AGT GGC ATA

   c. TAC CTC CTT TGA ATT TAC CTT ACT CGT TGT ATT AAA TAT CAG CTC

   d. TGT GTA CTT ACT GGG GAT CGC TTG ATT GTA CGG AGC ATC ACG GTG CGA TTG CCC CTT CTG

   e. TGT GTG CTC ACT AGA GTA TAG GGA ATT AGG CGG TAT GAC AGC ATC CGA TGC ACT CTG CGC ACC TTA

Analyze and Conclude

1. **Apply Concepts** How did you know which bases to use when you transcribed the DNA sequence to mRNA codons?

2. **Predict** Suppose the DNA sequence for the first message in Part B began with TGT CGA instead of TGA CGA. Would the message change? Why or why not?

3. **Use Analogies** Suppose some codons mapped to two different amino acids? What would the effect be on your translation of coded messages? What would the effect be on the production of proteins?

4. **Sequence** During the actual production of proteins in a cell, what might happen to a strand of RNA before it leaves the nucleus?

5. **Evaluate and Revise** What step could you add after you transcribe the DNA to make a more complete model of protein synthesis?

Name ______________________ Class __________ Date __________

Build Science Skills

Write your own secret message using DNA triplets. Exchange messages with classmates and try to solve the messages you receive. Remember that there is no triplet for the letters B, J, O, U, X, and Z. You will need to be creative to come up with messages that don't use those letters.

Guided Inquiry • Forensics Lab

Chapter 14 Lab Using DNA to Identify Human Remains

Problem

How can pedigrees help scientists identify human remains?

Introduction

For 300 years the Romanov family ruled Russia. The last Romanov ruler was Tsar Nicholas II. His wife, Tsarina Alexandra, was descended from Queen Victoria of England, as shown in Figure 1.

In 1917, revolution swept through Russia. The royal family was killed on July 16, 1918. The official report said that all the bodies were buried in a single grave. However, some witnesses said that one or two of the children were not buried with the others. The new government kept the location of the burial site secret. In 1991, after the breakup of the Soviet Union, scientists were at last allowed to examine the burial site and remove the bones.

Figure 1 Simplified pedigree for Tsarina Alexandra

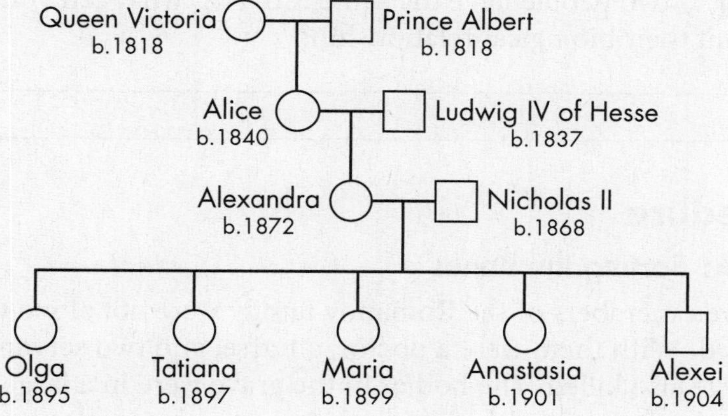

Build Vocabulary

Term	Definition
pedigree	A chart that shows the relationships within families; can be used to trace an inherited trait through generations; a family tree
descendants	A group of individuals related to, or *descended* from, a single common ancestor

In this lab, you will investigate how the scientists classified the skeletons that they found. You will also figure out how pedigrees helped the scientists find living relatives whose DNA could be compared with DNA extracted from the bones.

Skills Focus

Analyze Data, Draw Conclusions

Pre-Lab Questions

1. **Infer** The tsar and tsarina had five children. Did all seven family members have the same mitochondrial DNA (mtDNA)? Give a reason for your answer.

______

2. **Predict** To confirm that bones belonged to the Romanov children, which living relative would be more useful—a relative of the tsar or a relative of the tsarina? Why?

______

3. **Infer** If two people have the same mtDNA, what can you infer about their biological relationship?

______

Procedure

Part A: Sorting the Bones

The seven members of the Romanov family were not alone when they died. With them were a doctor, a nurse, and two servants, who were also killed. The bodies in the grave were in a large pile. When scientists sorted the bones, they were able to reconstruct only nine skeletons. To figure out who was missing, the scientists first needed to classify the skeletons by age and sex.

1. **Relative Age** Scientists can use wisdom teeth to determine the relative age of skeletons. The wisdom teeth are the last teeth to emerge from the gums. This event usually occurs between the ages of 17 and 21. Use the data in Table 1 to classify each skeleton by age. Classify skeletons with wisdom teeth as age 22 or older. Classify skeletons without wisdom teeth as younger than age 22.

2. Sex Scientists can use the shape of the pelvis to determine the sex of a skeleton. The pelvis is a ringlike structure of bones located at the base of the spine. The pelvis of a female is wider and has a wider opening than the pelvis of a male. Use the data in Table 1 to determine each skeleton's sex.

Table 1

Skeleton	Teeth	Pelvis	Age	Sex
1	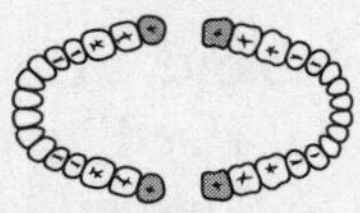	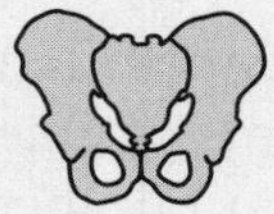		
2	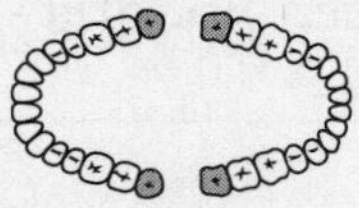	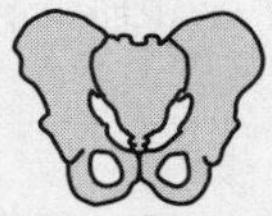		
3	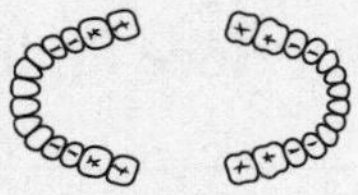			
4	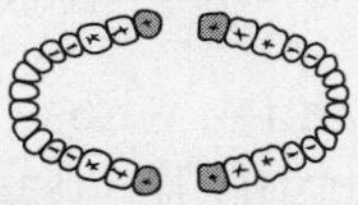			
5	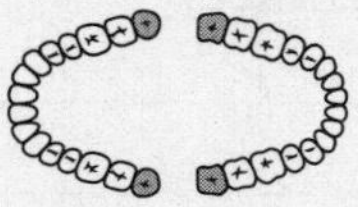	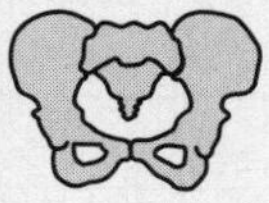		
6	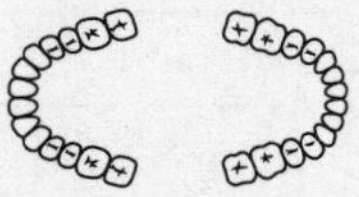			
7	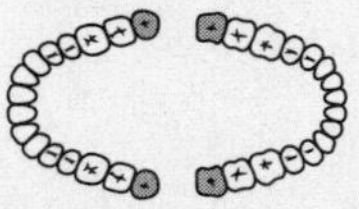			
8	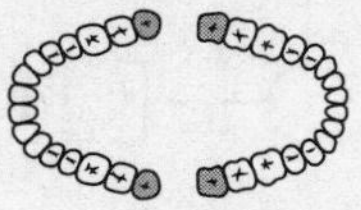			
9	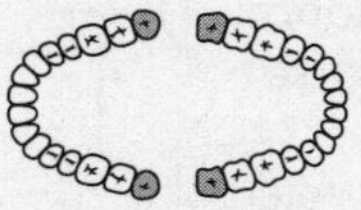			

Part B: Finding Living Relatives of the Tsarina and Tsar

After examining the skeletons, the scientists knew which skeletons were adult males and which were adult females. However, they did not know which of the adults were the tsarina and the tsar. For this task the scientists needed to use DNA.

The bodies had been burned before they were buried. They were repeatedly frozen and thawed for decades. Yet the scientists were still able to extract mitochondrial DNA (mtDNA) from the bones. Now they needed DNA from living relatives for a comparison.

3. Both Queen Elizabeth II and her husband, Prince Philip, are living descendants of Queen Victoria. Use Figure 2 to trace the descent of Queen Elizabeth II. List the descendants below. The first descendant will be one of Queen Victoria's children.

______

______

4. Use Figure 2 to trace the descent of Prince Philip.

______

______

5. Based on your findings in Steps 3 and 4, whose mitochondrial DNA did scientists use to try to identify the tsarina's bones—Elizabeth or Philip? Explain your choice.

______

______

______

______

Figure 2 Simplified pedigree for Queen Elizabeth and Prince Philip

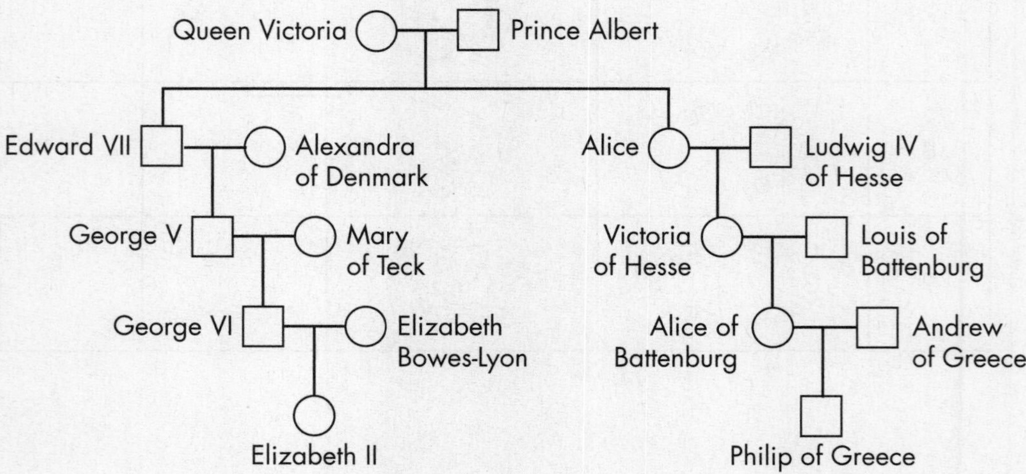

6. Tsar Nicholas II was descended from Louise of Hess-Cassel. Use Figure 3 to trace the tsar's descent.

____

____

7. Scientists identified two living descendants of Louise of Hess-Cassel who might be candidates for a DNA comparison—James Carnegie and Countess Xenia. Use Figure 3 to trace the descent of James Carnegie from Louise of Hess-Cassel.

____

____

8. Use Figure 3 to trace the descent of Countess Xenia from Louise of Hess-Cassel.

____

____

____

9. Based on your findings in Steps 6–8, what is the relationship between James Carnegie and Tsar Nicholas II? What is the relationship between Countess Xenia and Tsar Nicholas II?

____

____

____

Figure 3 Some descendants of Louise of Hess-Cassel

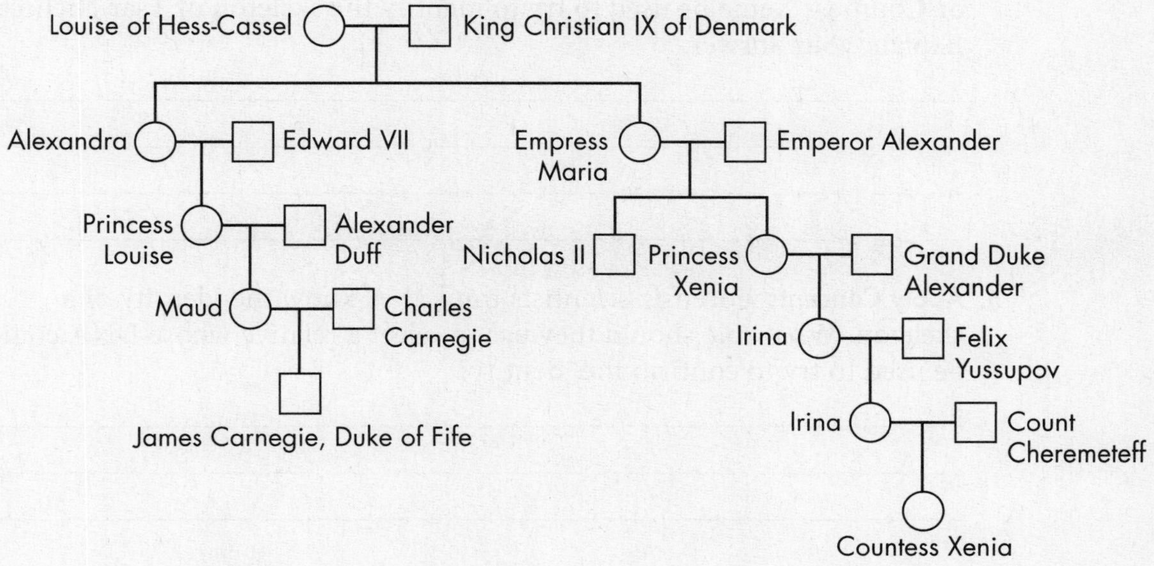

Analyze and Conclude

1. **Analyze Data** Table 2 lists the age and sex of each Romanov family member and their servants at the time of their deaths. The exact ages of the servants are not known. Compare the data in Table 2 with the data in Table 1. Who are the possible candidates for the two missing skeletons, and why?

Table 2

Female	Age	Male	Age
Tsarina	46	Tsar	50
Olga	22	Alexei	14
Tatiana	21	Doctor	Adult
Maria	19	Servant	Adult
Anastasia	17	Servant	Adult
Nurse	Adult		

2. **Draw Conclusions** Could the mitochondrial DNA of either James Carnegie or Countess Xenia be used to try to identify the skeleton of Tsar Nicholas? Explain your answer.

3. **Apply Concepts** Forensic scientists think they know the identity of a skeleton. What rule should they use to select a relative whose DNA could be used to try to confirm the identity?

4. **Infer** When mitochondrial DNA from living relatives was compared with mitochondrial DNA from the skeletons, scientists determined that skeletons 3, 4, 5, 6, and 7 were members of the Romanov family. Which of these skeletons can be identified by name based on the evidence you have? Explain your answer.

5. **Predict** Queen Elizabeth and Prince Philip have four children. Would these children have been a useful source of DNA for identifying the Romanov skeletons? Why or why not?

Build Science Skills

In 1920, before the discovery of DNA, a factory worker named Anna Anderson claimed to be Anastasia Romanov. Do research to find out what evidence Anna Anderson used to back up her claim. After Anna's death, how did scientists investigate her claim?

Guided Inquiry • Forensics Lab

Chapter 15 Lab Using DNA to Solve Crimes

Problem

How can DNA samples be used to connect a suspect to a crime scene?

Introduction

When biological evidence, such as blood, is found at a crime scene, a crime scene investigator can collect a sample and send it to a crime lab. At the lab, a forensic scientist extracts and purifies the DNA. The next step takes advantage of DNA's ability to replicate itself. Selected regions in the DNA are copied. The result is a mixture of DNA fragments with varied lengths.

Gel electrophoresis is one method used to sort DNA fragments by size. An electric field pulls the fragments through a thick gel. Shorter fragments travel farther than longer fragments in a given period of time. As a result, the fragments become grouped into a pattern of bands, which forensic scientists call a profile. In this lab, you will make and analyze four DNA profiles.

Skills Focus

Measure, Compare and Contrast, Draw Conclusions

Build Vocabulary

Term	Definition
profile	An analysis or summary of the specific features of a person or object; may be a graph or table
fragment	One of the parts that remains when an object is broken or cut into smaller pieces; a *fragile* object is easily broken
track	To follow the path, or trail, made by a person or object
electrode	A wire, plate, or rod through which *electric* current enters or leaves a device that is powered by *electricity*
terminal	The positive (+) or negative (–) end on a battery

Materials

- gel block
- electrophoresis chamber
- dilute buffer solution
- 250-mL beaker
- metric ruler
- 4 DNA samples
- 4 micropipettes
- five 9-volt batteries
- electric cords
- staining tray
- DNA stain
- 100-mL graduated cylinder
- clock or timer

Safety

Wear goggles, gloves, and a lab apron to avoid staining your skin or clothing. Wipe up spills immediately. To avoid electrical shocks, do not touch exposed metal in circuits. Alert your teacher if you break a glass object. Wash your hands thoroughly with soap and warm water before leaving the lab.

Pre-Lab Questions

1. **Control Variables** Why must you use a new pipette to load each DNA sample?

______

______

2. **Relate Cause and Effect** Why will the DNA samples separate into bands as they move through the gel?

______

______

______

3. **Infer** Why is purple tracking dye added to the DNA samples?

______

______

______

Procedure

Part A: Loading DNA Samples

Your teacher prepared gel blocks with depressions, or wells, to hold the DNA samples. A purple tracking dye was added to each DNA sample. You will use a buffer solution to keep the pH neutral, which is necessary for the DNA fragments to remain charged. Refer to Figure 1 as you do Part A of the procedure.

1. Put on your goggles, lab apron, and gloves.
2. Obtain a plastic tray with a gel block. **CAUTION:** Hold the tray parallel to the floor so that the gel block does not slip off the tray.
3. Locate the wells near one end of the block. Place the tray in the center of the electrophoresis chamber so that the wells are closest to the black (negative) electrode.
4. Add 200 mL of buffer solution to the chamber. Make sure the surface of the solution is 2–3 mm above the top of the gel block.
5. Obtain the DNA sample labeled Crime Scene.

   Get Ready! Before you open the tube, make sure the sample is at the bottom of the tube.
6. Push the plunger all the way to the bottom of the micropipette. Insert the end of the pipette into the tube, and gently pull the plunger to draw 10 μL (microliters) of liquid into the pipette.
7. Insert the end of the pipette into the first well in the gel block. **CAUTION:** Do not puncture the bottom of the well. Hold the pipette steady and gently press the plunger forward.
8. When the pipette is empty, discard it in the trash.
9. Repeat Steps 6–8 for the Suspect 1, Suspect 2, and Suspect 3 samples. Be sure to use a new pipette for each sample and to place each sample in a separate well.
10. Make sure the chamber cover is dry, and then place the cover on the electrophoresis chamber.

Figure 1 Placing the gel in the chamber

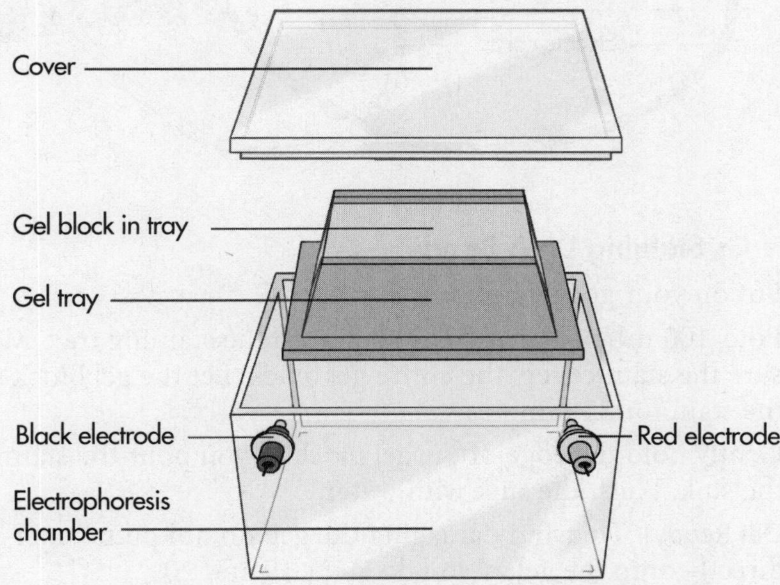

Part B: Separating DNA Fragments

11. Connect five 9-volt batteries as shown in Figure 2. Snap the positive terminal of one battery to the negative terminal of another battery. When you are done, you should have one open negative terminal and one open positive terminal.
12. Use the red cord to connect the open positive battery terminal and the red electrode on the chamber. Use the black cord to connect the open negative terminal and the black electrode.
13. If you do not see bubbles form along the wires at the bottom of the chamber, recheck all the connections.
14. You will see the purple dye from each DNA sample slowly move through the gel. **CAUTION:** When the dye reaches the end of the gel block, disconnect the batteries from the chamber.

    Get Ready! The gel block is fragile and could break when you transfer it from the chamber to the staining tray.
15. Remove the gel tray from the chamber and use your gloved fingers to gently push the gel block off the casting tray into a staining tray.

Figure 2 Connecting the batteries

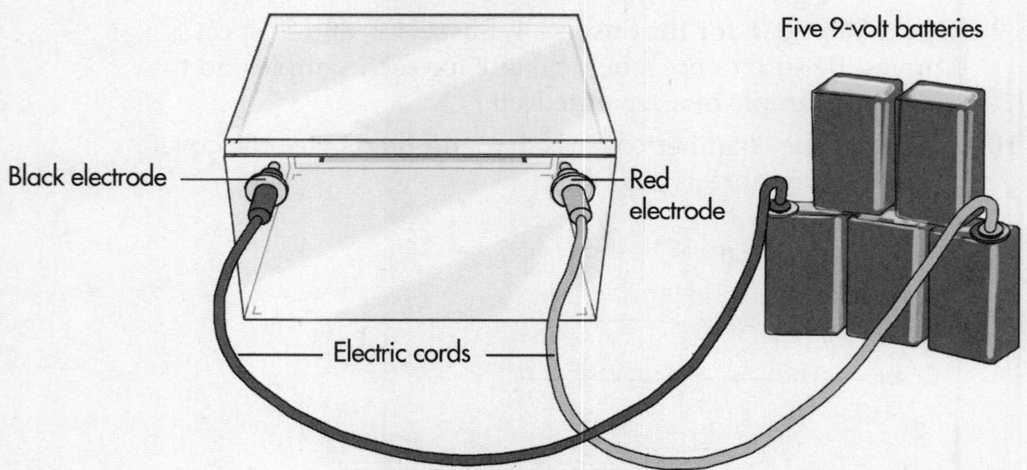

Part C: Staining DNA Bands

16. Put on your goggles, gloves, and apron.
17. Pour 100 mL of warm DNA stain into the staining tray. Make sure the stain covers the entire gel block. Let the gel block sit in the stain for 35 minutes.
18. Gently hold the edge of the gel block as you pour the stain into the sink. Flush the sink with water.

    Get Ready! To avoid damaging the gel, do not pour water directly onto the gel as you do Steps 19 and 20.

19. Slowly pour tap water into the staining tray until the water completely covers the gel block.

20. Gently rock the tray back and forth. After 5 minutes, hold the edge of the gel block as you pour the water into the sink.

21. Repeat Steps 19 and 20 four more times. When you are done, the gel should have a light blue tint and the DNA bands should be clearly visible as dark blue lines.

Part D: Sketching and Measuring DNA Bands

22. With the gel block still in the tray, place the tray on a light-colored surface. Sketch the DNA bands in Data Table 1.

Data Table 1

DNA From Crime Scene	DNA From Suspect 1	DNA From Suspect 2	DNA From Suspect 3

23. For each DNA sample, measure the distance from the edge of its well to the center of each DNA band. Record the measurements in Data Table 2.

Data Table 2

Band	Crime Scene	Suspect 1	Suspect 2	Suspect 3
1				
2				
3				
4				
5				
6				
7				

Analyze and Conclude

1. **Apply Concepts** Where are the shortest fragments of DNA located? Where are the longest fragments located?

2. **Analyze Data** Based on Data Table 1, which suspect's profile most closely matches the profile of the crime scene DNA? Explain.

3. **Analyze Data** Based on Data Table 2, which suspect's profile most closely matches the profile of the crime scene DNA? Explain.

4. **Compare and Contrast** How are Data Table 1 and Data Table 2 similar? How are they different?

5. **Draw Conclusions** Based on your results, what can you conclude about the person whose profile matched the crime scene profile? What can't you conclude based on this evidence?

Build Science Skills

Research possible errors that could occur when biological evidence is used to solve crimes. Begin at the point when investigators arrive at a crime scene. What procedures are used to avoid these errors? Choose an appropriate format for presenting your information.

Guided Inquiry • Skills Lab

Chapter 16 Lab Amino Acid Sequences: Indicators of Evolution

Problem

How can you use proteins to determine how closely organisms are related?

Introduction

Biologists have many ways to study evolution. They can use fossils to learn about ancient species. They can compare the anatomy of modern species. They can observe the order in which cells develop in embryos. All these clues reflect what took place over time at the molecular level. DNA and proteins, the genes and the products of genes, provide powerful evidence for descent with modification.

As DNA changes over time, the proteins that are produced by the DNA change too. The result is that many organisms have similar, but not identical, versions of a given protein. Differences among these homologous proteins provide clues to evolution.

In Part A of this lab, you will compare amino acid sequences of hemoglobin from seven mammals. In Part B, you will analyze data about sequences in a second protein—cytochrome c. In Part B, the organisms will be more varied.

Skills Focus

Analyze Data, Graph, Draw Conclusions

Build Vocabulary

Term	Definition
compare	To examine two or more things in order to discover ways in which they are alike, or *comparable,* and ways in which they are different
sequence	The order in which things are arranged, actions are carried out, or events happen
related	Connected by a common, or shared, origin; descended from a common ancestor
identical	Exactly the same or alike in every way

Materials

- highlighter pen, light-colored
- graph paper

Pre-Lab Questions

1. **Predict** Based only on their anatomy, rank gorillas, bears, chimpanzees, and mice from most recent common ancestor with humans to least recent common ancestor.

2. **Use Analogies** You tell a story to a second person who tells it to a third person, and so on. As the story is retold, changes are introduced. Over time, the number of changes increases. How is this process an analogy for what happens to DNA over time?

3. **Infer** Hemoglobin from two species is compared. On the long protein chains, there are three locations where the amino acids are different. Where would you place the common ancestor of the two species on the "tree of life," and why?

Procedure

Part A: Comparing Amino Acid Sequences in Hemoglobin

Hemoglobin is the molecule in blood that carries oxygen. This complex molecule contains four protein chains. Figure 1 shows the amino acid sequence for one of those chains in eight mammals. Each letter stands for a different amino acid. Each column is a location on the protein chain. **NOTE:** Locations where the amino acids are identical in all eight mammals are not shown.

Name ______________________ Class __________ Date __________

1. Use the row labeled Human as your control. Compare the sequence for the bear to the sequence for humans. When you find a difference in the bear sequence, highlight it.
2. Repeat Step 1 for each of the other mammals. Be sure to compare each sequence to the sequence for humans.

Figure 1 Comparison of amino acid sequences in hemoglobin from eight mammals

	4	5	6	9	10	12	13	20	25	33	41	43	50	51	52
Human	T	P	E	S	A	T	A	V	G	V	F	E	T	P	D
Bear	T	G	E	S	L	T	G	V	G	V	F	D	S	A	D
Chimpanzee	T	P	E	S	A	T	A	V	G	V	F	E	T	P	D
Gibbon	T	P	E	S	A	T	A	V	G	V	F	E	T	P	D
Gorilla	T	P	E	S	A	T	A	V	G	V	F	E	T	P	D
Monkey	T	P	E	N	A	T	T	V	G	L	F	E	S	P	D
Mouse	T	D	A	A	A	S	C	S	G	V	Y	D	S	A	S
Shrew	S	G	E	A	C	T	G	E	A	V	F	D	S	A	S

	54	56	58	68	69	70	71	72	73	75	76	77	80	87	104
Human	V	G	P	L	G	A	F	S	D	L	A	H	N	T	R
Bear	I	N	P	L	N	S	F	S	D	L	K	N	N	K	K
Chimpanzee	V	G	P	L	G	A	F	S	D	L	A	H	N	T	R
Gibbon	V	G	P	L	G	A	F	S	D	L	A	H	N	Q	R
Gorilla	V	G	P	L	G	A	F	S	D	L	A	H	N	T	K
Monkey	V	G	P	L	G	A	F	S	D	L	N	H	N	Q	K
Mouse	I	G	A	I	T	A	F	N	D	L	N	H	S	S	R
Shrew	V	G	P	L	H	S	L	G	E	V	A	N	N	K	R

	109	110	112	115	116	117	118	121	125	126	130	139
Human	V	L	C	A	H	H	F	E	P	V	Y	N
Bear	V	L	C	A	H	H	F	E	Q	V	Y	N
Chimpanzee	V	L	C	A	H	H	F	E	P	V	Y	N
Gibbon	V	L	C	A	H	H	F	E	Q	V	Y	N
Gorilla	V	L	C	A	H	H	F	E	P	V	Y	N
Monkey	V	L	C	A	H	H	F	E	Q	V	Y	N
Mouse	M	I	I	G	H	H	L	D	A	A	F	T
Shrew	V	L	V	A	S	K	F	E	P	V	F	N

3. Use the data table to record the number of differences you found for each mammal in comparison to humans.

Data Table	
Mammal	**Number of Differences in Hemoglobin**
Bear	
Chimpanzee	
Gibbon	
Gorilla	
Monkey	
Mouse	
Shrew	

Part B: Differences in Cytochrome *c*

Cytochrome c takes part in electron transport during the last stage of cellular respiration. This enzyme can be found in yeasts, bacteria, fungi, plants, and animals. The human cytochrome c molecule is relatively small. Its single strand of protein has 104 amino acids.

4. In Figure 2, human cytochrome c is the standard. Column 1 lists the species that are being compared to humans. Column 2 lists the number of differences for each pairing. Use the data to make a bar graph on a separate sheet of graph paper. Select an order for the bars that will best reveal a pattern in the number of differences.

Figure 2 How human cytochrome c differs from cytochrome c found in other species

Species	Number of Differences
Chimpanzee	0
Fruit fly	29
Horse	12
Pigeon	12
Rattlesnake	14
Red bread mold	48
Rhesus monkey	1
Snapping turtle	15
Tuna	21
Wheat	43

Analyze and Conclude

1. **Draw Conclusions** Based on the hemoglobin data, which mammal listed is most closely related to humans? What is the evidence for your conclusion?

2. **Analyze Data** Does the cytochrome c data support your conclusion in Question 1? Explain.

3. **Evaluate** Does the data support the rankings you made in Pre-Lab Question 1? If not, how would you explain any differences?

4. **Design an Experiment** The cytochrome c in both horses and pigeons differs from the human protein at 12 locations. Based on this data, you might infer that horses and pigeons are closely related. What could you do to support or reject this hypothesis?

5. **Communicate** In terms of descent, what does it mean to say that humans are more closely related to gorillas than to monkeys?

6. **Interpret Data** A student used the hemoglobin data to conclude that mice and shrews are more closely related than are mice and humans or shrews and humans. Was the student correct?

Build Science Skills

More than 100 locations were not listed in Figure 1 because the amino acid was the same in all eight species. One possible explanation is that no mutations occurred in the codons for those locations. Suggest another possible explanation. *Hint:* Think about why some mutations are harmful.

Guided Inquiry • Skills Lab

Chapter 17 Lab Competing for Resources

Problem

How can competition lead to speciation?

Introduction

At first Darwin did not pay much attention to the small brown birds he observed in the Galápagos Islands. Later, he realized that, despite their differences, all these birds were species of finches. Darwin suspected that the variation in beak shape and size among the species was related to the food they ate.

Darwin did not have time to gather the evidence to support his hypothesis. That task was left to Rosemary and Peter Grant, who spent years on the islands. The Grants were able to observe that finches tended to mate with finches that had similar beaks. This behavior was one of the factors leading to speciation among the Galápagos finches. Another factor was the competition for seeds.

In this lab, you will model variation in the size and shape of finch beaks. You will determine which "beaks" are better adapted to each type of food. You will also observe how competition and the amount of food affects survival.

Skills Focus

Use Models, Predict, Apply Concepts

Materials

- assorted tools
- seeds, large and small
- large paper plates
- small paper plates
- timer or clock with second hand

Build Vocabulary

Term	Definition
abundant	Very plentiful; more than enough; exists in large numbers, or *abounds*
scarce	Not common; hard to get; not able to meet the demand

Safety ⚠

Do not direct the sharp points of any tools toward yourself or others. Do not eat any of the seeds used in this lab.

Pre-Lab Questions

1. **Use Models** In this lab, what do the different types of tools represent?

 ____

2. **Predict** Which tools do you think will work best for picking up small seeds? Which will work best for picking up large seeds?

 ____

 ____

 ____

 ____

3. **Design an Experiment** Why will the time you have to collect seeds be limited?

 ____

 ____

 ____

Procedure

Round 1: Feeding Without Competition

In this round, you will model feeding when there is abundant food and no competition.

1. Choose a tool and obtain a large plate of small seeds and an empty small plate.
2. Each student in your group should practice using the tool to pick up seeds and transfer them to the empty plate. Pick up only one seed at a time.
3. Obtain a large plate of large seeds. Repeat Step 2.
4. Decide which type of seed you can pick up more easily with your tool. Return the other plate of seeds to your teacher. Record the type of tool and the type of seeds you will use in Step 5.

 Type of Tool: ______________________________

 Type of Seed: ______________________________

Get Ready! In Step 5, your goal will be to pick up as many seeds as possible in 15 seconds. Each student will do three 15-second trials. Assign each person in your group a letter code—A, B, C, and so on—to represent the order in which students will do the trials.

5. Your teacher will tell you when to start and end each trial. Use Data Table 1 to record the number of seeds picked up and placed in the small plate for each trial. Don't count seeds that do not land in the plate.
6. After each member of your group has done three trials, calculate the average number of seeds that were picked up in 15 seconds.

Data Table 1: Seeds Picked Up in Round 1

Trial	Number of Seeds	Trial	Number of Seeds	Trial	Number of Seeds
A1		C1		E1	
A2		C2		E2	
A3		C3		E3	
B1		D1		F1	
B2		D2		F2	
B3		D3		F3	
Average Number of Seeds Picked Up:					

Round 2: Feeding With Competition

In this round, you will model feeding when there is abundant food and competition. Use the same tool and type of seeds you used in Round 1. Your group will be paired with another group that used the same type of seeds.

Get Ready! In Round 2, each trial will involve competition with a member of the other group. The two competitors will pick up seeds from the same large plate at the same time.

7. Have each student do three 15-second trials. Your teacher will tell you when to start and end each trial. Record your group's results in Data Table 2 on page 106.
8. After each member of your group has done three trials, calculate the average number of seeds that were picked up in 15 seconds.

Data Table 2: Seeds Picked Up in Round 2					
Trial	Number of Seeds	Trial	Number of Seeds	Trial	Number of Seeds
A1		C1		E1	
A2		C2		E2	
A3		C3		E3	
B1		D1		F1	
B2		D2		F2	
B3		D3		F3	
Average Number of Seeds Picked Up:					

Round 3: Feeding When Food Is Scarce

In this round, you will repeat the procedure from Round 2. This time, however, there will be fewer seeds on the large plate to represent a time when food is scarce, which is a true test of your tool's ability to adapt. You will work with the same group you worked with in Round 2.

9. Count out 30 seeds and put them on the large plate. Return the rest of the seeds to your teacher.

10. Have each student do three 15-second trials. Your teacher will tell you when to start and end each trial. Record your group's results in Data Table 3.

11. After each member of your group has done three trials, calculate the average number of seeds that were picked up in 15 seconds.

Data Table 3: Seeds Picked Up in Round 3					
Trial	Number of Seeds	Trial	Number of Seeds	Trial	Number of Seeds
A1		C1		E1	
A2		C2		E2	
A3		C3		E3	
B1		D1		F1	
B2		D2		F2	
B3		D3		F3	
Average Number of Seeds Picked Up:					

Name ______________________ Class ________ Date ________

Analyze and Conclude

1. **Compare and Contrast** Look at all the tools that were used to pick up seeds. Identify at least one general difference between the tools that were better at picking up small seeds and those that were better at picking up large seeds.

2. **Analyze Data** In nature, a seed-eating bird would need to collect a minimum number of seeds to survive. For your model, assume that the minimum for survival is 14 seeds in 15 seconds. How many individuals in your group would have survived Round 1? How did the procedure in Round 1 help their survival?

3. **Relate Cause and Effect** When food was abundant, how did competition affect the survival rate? Why?

4. **Relate Cause and Effect** When food was scarce, how did competition affect the survival rate? Why?

5. **Use Analogies** How might a limited amount of food affect the size of a finch population?

6. **Predict** Within a gene pool, there will be alleles that result in beaks that are well adapted to the available food and beaks that are not well adapted. Use your results with the tools to predict how which birds survive can affect the alleles in the gene pool of the bird population.

7. **Apply Concepts** How might changes in the gene pool affect the ability of birds with beaks that are not well adapted to find mates?

Build Science Skills

Design an experiment to answer one of the following questions. Or pose your own question. (1) How would varying the depth and width of a seed container affect the ability of different "beaks" to collect seeds? (2) In nature, seeds are not found piled in one location, except in a bird feeder. How would scattering seeds affect a bird's ability to survive?

Chapter 18 Lab **Dichotomous Keys**

Problem

Can you construct a dichotomous key that could be used to identify organisms?

Introduction

In May 2007, scientists and other volunteers gathered in Rock Creek Park, Washington, D.C., to participate in a BioBlitz—a quick, 24-hour survey of species living in the park. Teams worked in 4-hour shifts throughout the park. By the time they were done, the teams had identified more than 650 species!

Teams included experts on different types of organisms such as birds, beetles, fungi, and plants. The experts used identification guides, or keys, to help them identify the organisms they found.

In this lab, you will first use a dichotomous key to identify sharks. A dichotomous key is built around pairs of statements that describe a visible trait. The reader must select the statement in each pair that best describes an organism. By following the steps in the key, the reader narrows down the list of choices and finally names the organism. After you have learned to use a dichotomous key, you will design your own key for a group of organisms.

Skills Focus

Observe, Classify, Compare and Contrast, Sequence

Materials

- reference materials

Build Vocabulary

Term	Definition
dorsal	On, in, or near the back or upper surface of an animal
projection	Something that juts out, or *projects,* beyond the rest of a surface
identify	To recognize or show to be the person or thing described; to figure out the *identity* of

Pre-Lab Questions

1. **Observe** Name three different physical traits that are used in the shark dichotomous key.

2. **Apply Concepts** After you make a list of physical traits that you can use in your dichotomous key, how will you decide which trait to pick for the first step?

Procedure

Part A: Use a Dichotomous Key

Before you try to identify sharks, you need to understand a bit about shark anatomy. Figure 1 is a general shark drawing with labels showing the possible locations of fins. Refer to Figure 1 as you use the dichotomous key to identify the sharks in Figure 2.

1. Tear out the sheet with the shark drawings (pages 115–116). Choose one shark from Figure 2.
2. Read statements 1a and 1b in the key. One of the statements describes the shark; the other does not. Choose the statement that describes the shark and follow the directions for that statement.
3. Continue following the steps in the key until you can identify the shark. Record the scientific and common name of the shark in the data table.
4. Repeat Steps 2 and 3 for the other sharks in Figure 2.

Figure 1 General external anatomy of shark

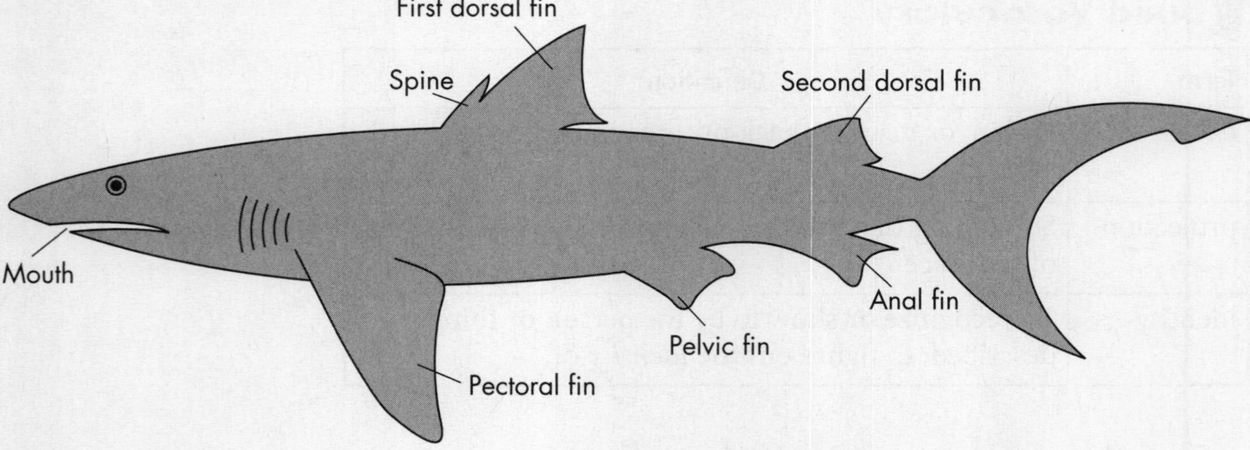

Dichotomous Key for Sharks		
Step	**Characteristic**	**Species**
1a	Anal fin present . . . *Go to Step 2*	
1b	No anal fin . . . *Go to Step 6*	
2a	One dorsal fin	*Notorynchus cepedianus*, Sevengill shark
2b	Two dorsal fins . . . *Go to Step 3*	
3a	Spines on dorsal fins	*Heterodontus francisci*, Horn shark
3b	No spines on dorsal fins . . . *Go to Step 4*	
4a	Mouth at front of head	*Rhincodon typus*, Whale shark
4b	Mouth at bottom of head . . . *Go to Step 5*	
5a	Eyes on ends of hammerlike projection	*Sphyrna zygaena*, Smooth hammerhead
5b	No hammerlike head	*Carcharodon carcharias*, Great white shark
6a	Flattened body (like ray)	*Squatina squatina*, Angel shark
6b	Body not flattened . . . *Go to Step 7*	
7a	Long sawlike projection from snout	*Pristiophorus schroederi*, Bahamas sawshark
7b	No sawlike projection	*Somniosus microcephalus*, Greenland shark

Data Table		
Shark	**Scientific Name**	**Common Name**
A		
B		
C		
D		
E		
F		

Part B: Construct a Dichotomous Key

You will be working with a group of organisms such as snails, birds, antelopes, rodents, or aquarium fish. You will need to consult reference books or Web sites that include illustrations.

5. Choose a group of organisms. Then make a list of visible physical traits that vary among the species in the group.

____

____

____

____

____

____

____

____

____

____

6. Choose six or eight species from the group. On a separate sheet of paper make a simple drawing of each species. Use a letter to label each drawing. Record the scientific name and common name of each species next to the appropriate letter below.

A: ____

B: ____

C: ____

D: ____

E: ____

F: ____

G: ____

H: ____

7. Use the space on page 113 to construct a dichotomous key for your group of organisms. Use the key for sharks as a model. Start by choosing a trait that divides your organisms into two smaller groups. Keep dividing each of the smaller groups with pairs of statements until you have a final identifying statement for each of your species.

8. Check the usefulness of your key by making a copy of your key and asking another student to use it to identify your drawings.

Dichotomous Key

Analyze and Conclude

1. **Predict** How would the dichotomous key for sharks need to change if you wanted to use it to identify ten different sharks?

2. **Evaluate** What was the most challenging part of making your own dichotomous key?

3. **Infer** Suppose you had actual samples instead of drawings. What other traits could you use to build a dichotomous key?

4. **Compare and Contrast** The shark dichotomous key groups three species that lack anal fins together. But a recent cladogram of sharks indicates that the Greenland shark is actually most closely related to the Sevengill shark, which has an anal fin. What does this tell you about the difference between a dichotomous key and a cladogram?

5. **Draw Conclusions** In what way are the characters used to design a dichotomous key more limited than the characters that are used to build a cladogram?

6. **Infer** The dichotomous keys in this lab are used to trace organisms to the species level. Could keys be designed which classify unknown organisms to higher levels of the Linnaean system—to a family or order, for example? Why or why not?

Build Science Skills

Find a cladogram in your textbook or other reference that lists derived characters. Which of the derived characters could be used as traits in a dichotomous key? Which of the traits could not be used, and why?

Figure 2 Shark species

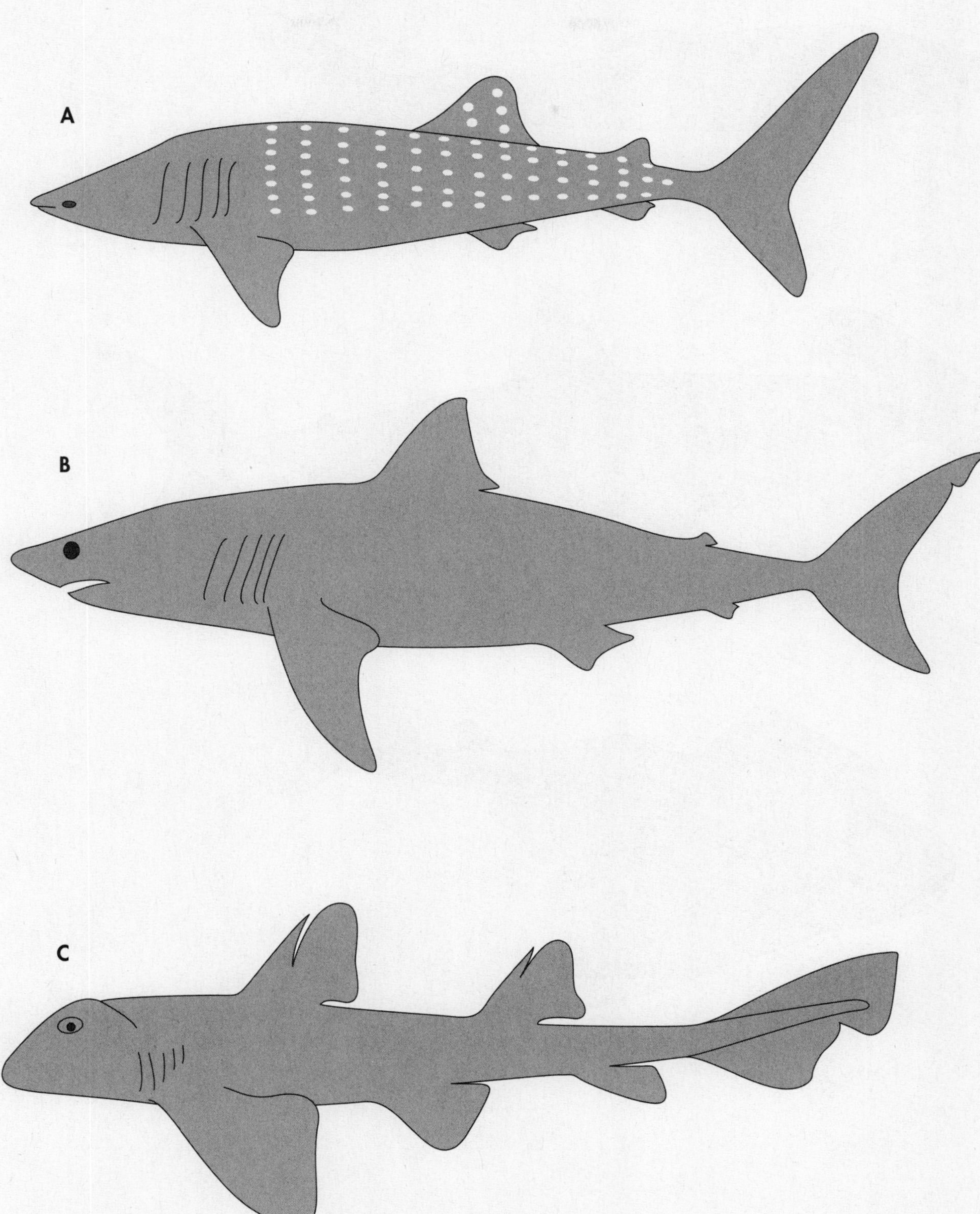

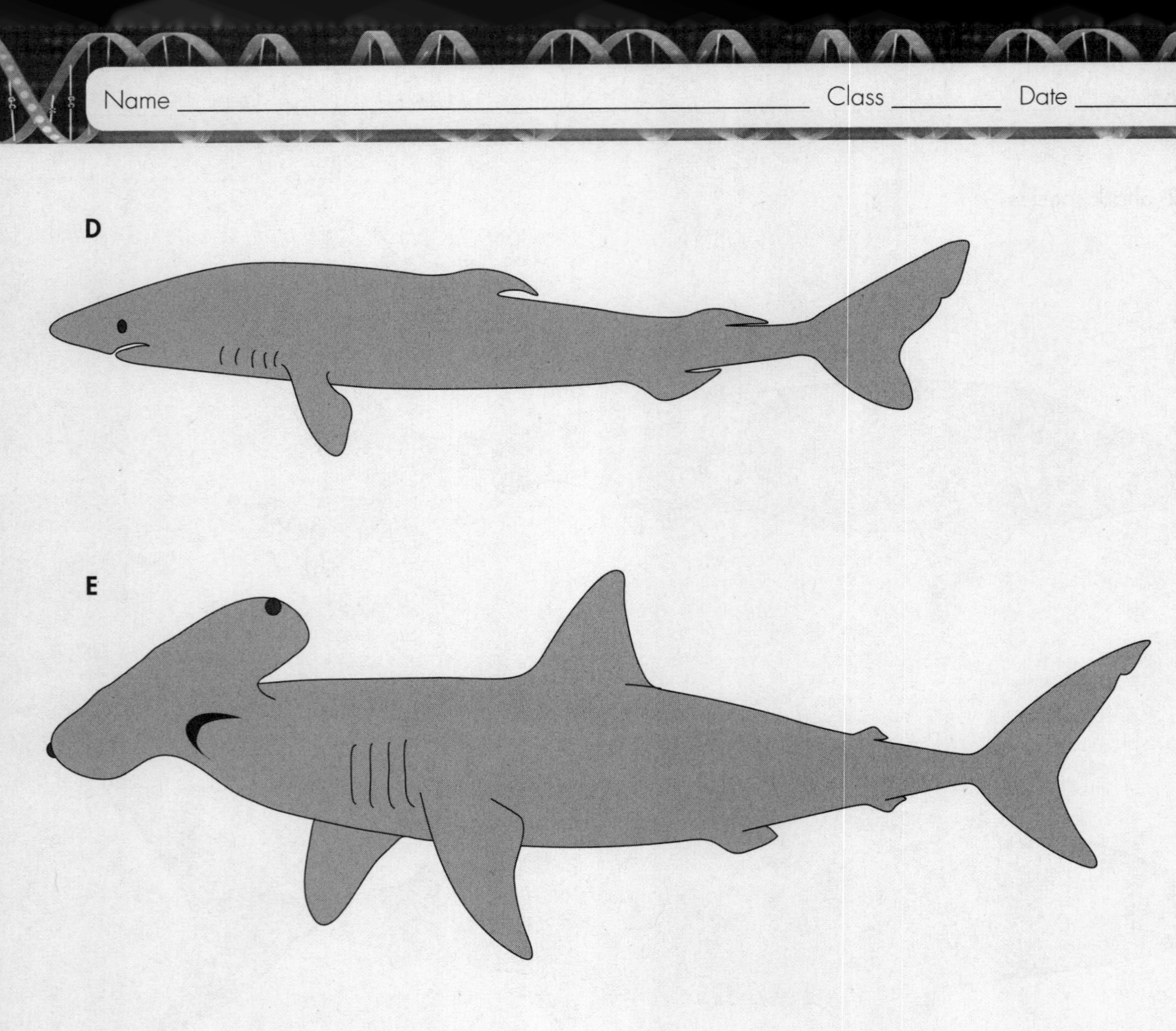
D
E
F

Guided Inquiry • Forensics Lab

Chapter 19 Lab Using Index Fossils

Problem

How can fossils be used to determine the relative ages of rock layers?

Introduction

It is easy to compare the ages of fossils found in sedimentary rocks at one location. Fossils found in an upper rock layer will be younger than fossils found in a lower layer, unless the layers have been overturned. It is not as easy to compare the ages of fossils found in rocks at different locations. Scientists use index fossils to determine the relative ages of rock layers. Scientists use the rate at which radioactive isotopes decay to find the actual age of rocks and fossils.

In this lab, you will work with drawings of rock layers from different locations. Each layer will contain at least two fossils. Using the fossils as clues, you will organize the layers from oldest to youngest.

Skills Focus

Interpret Visuals, Sequence, Draw Conclusions

Materials

- scissors

Build Vocabulary

Term	Definition
determine	To find out or come to a decision by investigation, thinking, or calculation
relative	Having a value that is not fixed, but depends on something else; *related* each to the other
index	Something that serves to guide, point out, or reveal; an indicator or sign
sequence	To arrange things or perform actions in a definite, specific order
scale	A ratio that relates the size of a model, such as a drawing, to the size of the object it represents

Safety

Do not direct the points of the scissors toward yourself or others. Use the scissors only as instructed.

Pre-Lab Questions

1. **Organize Data** After you cut out the drawings of the rock layers, how will you begin the process of sorting the layers by age?

2. **Infer** *Desmatosuchus* was a crocodile relative that lived only during the Triassic Period. Horsetails are plants that first appeared in the Triassic Period and still exist. Which of these organisms would be more useful as an index fossil for the Triassic Period? Why?

3. **Use Analogies** Luke found a box of photos labeled 1970–1995. Each photo shows his entire extended family. No dates appear on the photos. Luke knows that his grandmother died in 1985 and his uncle was born in 1975. Luke's sister was born in 1990. How can Luke use this information to sort the photos into four batches? How are Luke's relatives similar to index fossils?

Procedure

You will use fossils to order the rock layers pictured at the end of this lab. Nine of the layers represent periods from the Paleozoic and Mesozoic Eras. One layer represents the Cenozoic Era.

1. Tear out pages 123 and 125 at the end of this lab. Cut out each drawing of a rock layer. **NOTE:** The fossils are not drawn to scale.
2. Spread out the layers on a flat surface. Use the Key to Fossils to identify the fossils in each layer. Write the names of the fossils on the drawings. **NOTE:** Some of the drawings represent one species or one genus. Some represent a higher taxonomic level.
3. The oldest rock layer is from the Cambrian Period. Some organisms in this layer will not be found in any other layer. No organism in this layer still exists. Locate the layer that represents the Cambrian Period.
4. Look for fossils that are found in only two layers. Record their names below.

   ____

   ____

5. Use the information from Step 4 to pair up layers that must represent consecutive periods in the geologic record.
6. Use other fossils to determine which layer in each pair is older and the order of all the layers from oldest to youngest.
7. Each drawing has a letter in the upper left corner. Use the letters to record the correct sequence of layers in the data table on page 121. Record the letter for the youngest layer in the first row and the letter for the oldest layer in the last row. Also record the names of the fossils found in each layer.
8. If you have placed the layers in the right order, the letters will spell out the name of a geologic period.
9. Use pages 466–469 in your textbook to identify the geologic period that corresponds to each rock layer. Record the names of the periods in the data table.

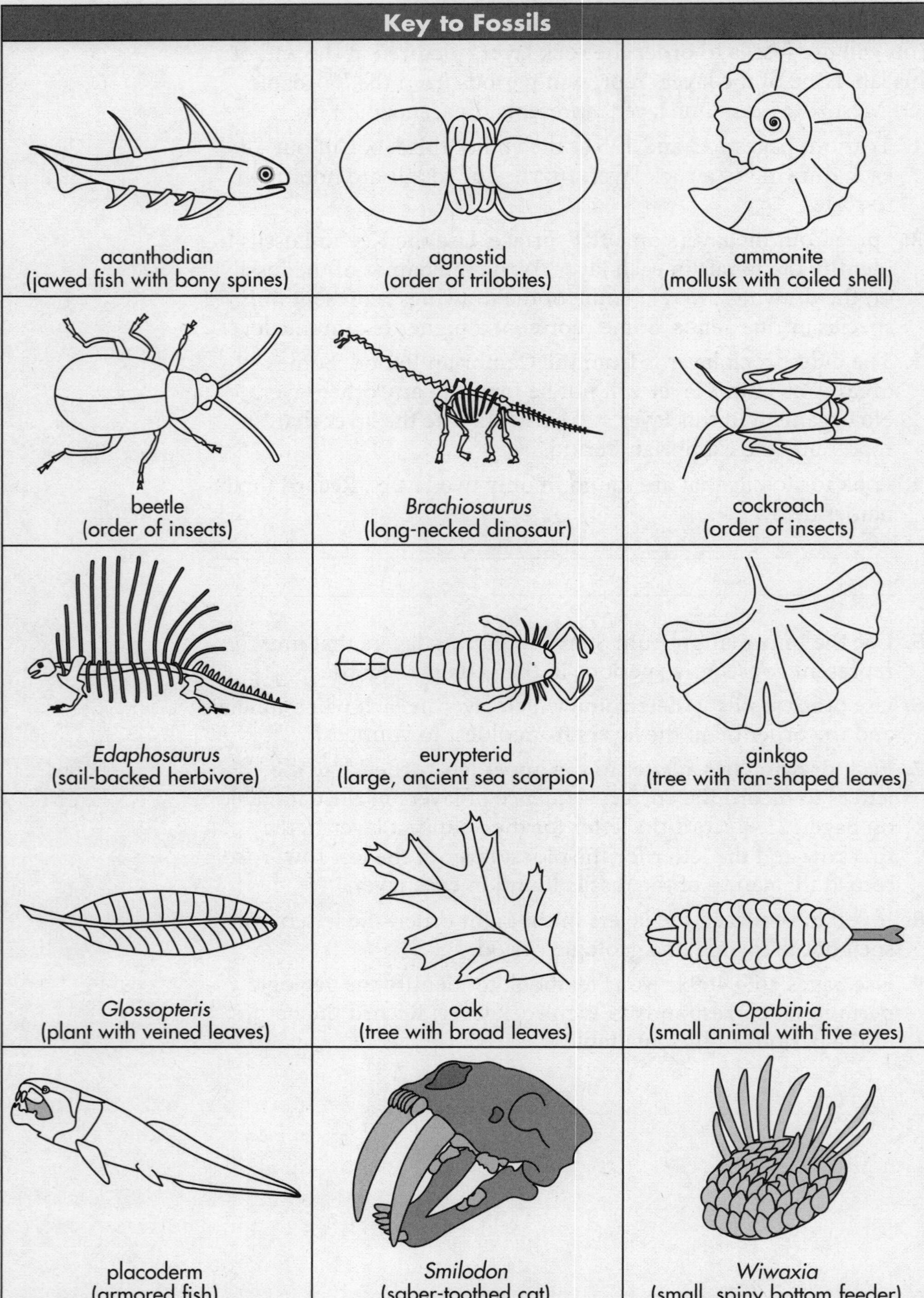
Key to Fossils
acanthodian
(jawed fish with bony spines)
agnostid
(order of trilobites)
ammonite
(mollusk with coiled shell)
beetle
(order of insects)
Brachiosaurus
(long-necked dinosaur)
cockroach
(order of insects)
Edaphosaurus
(sail-backed herbivore)
eurypterid
(large, ancient sea scorpion)
ginkgo
(tree with fan-shaped leaves)
Glossopteris
(plant with veined leaves)
oak
(tree with broad leaves)
Opabinia
(small animal with five eyes)
placoderm
(armored fish)
Smilodon
(saber-toothed cat)
Wiwaxia
(small, spiny bottom feeder)

Data Table		
Layer	Fossils Found	Geologic Period

youngest ↑ … ↓ oldest

Analyze and Conclude

1. **Analyze Data** How did you identify the layer from the Cambrian Period?

2. **Sequence** How did you identify the layer that belonged next to the Cambrian layer?

3. **Sequence** How were you able to determine which of the two layers containing a *Glossopteris* fossil was the older layer?

4. **Draw Conclusions** Why might a placoderm be a more useful index fossil than a cockroach?

5. **Infer** Ammonoids are found in rock layers from six different geologic periods. Yet ammonoids are considered excellent index fossils. Explain why this is possible. *Hint:* See the note in Step 2 of the procedure.

6. **Apply Concepts** Provide two explanations for why a species might disappear from the fossil record.

Build Science Skills

Mass extinctions occurred at the end of the Permian and Cretaceous Periods. Do research to find what scientists think may have caused these extinctions. Then decide whether any of these hypotheses could help to explain the current worldwide reduction in biodiversity.

A

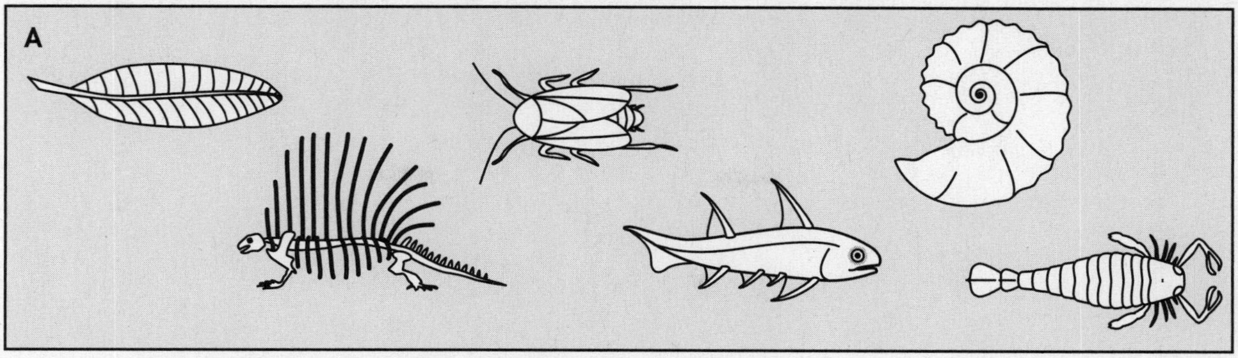

C

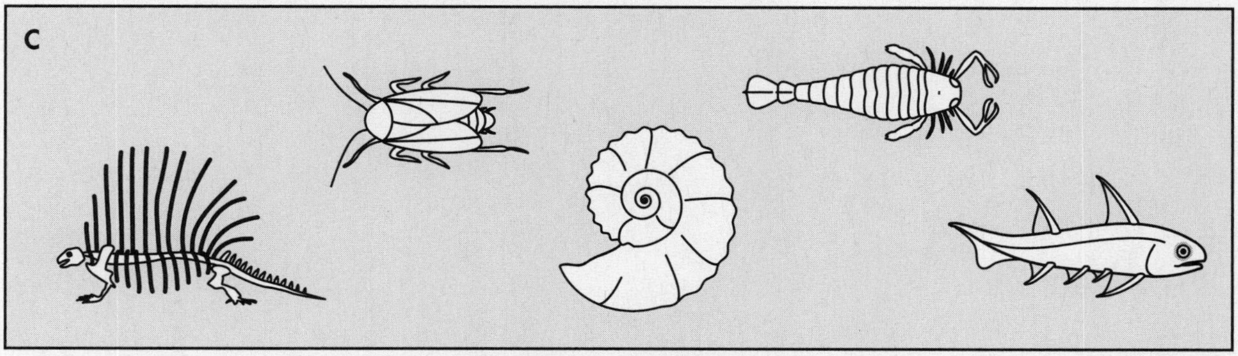

C

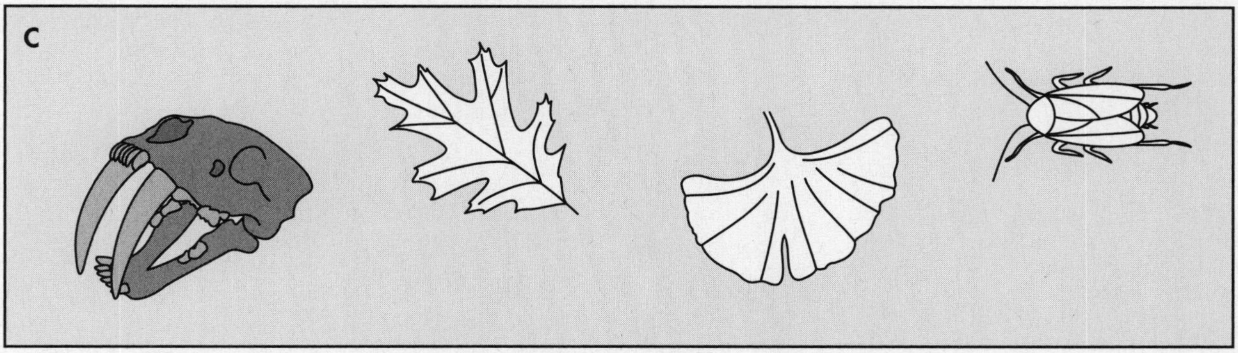

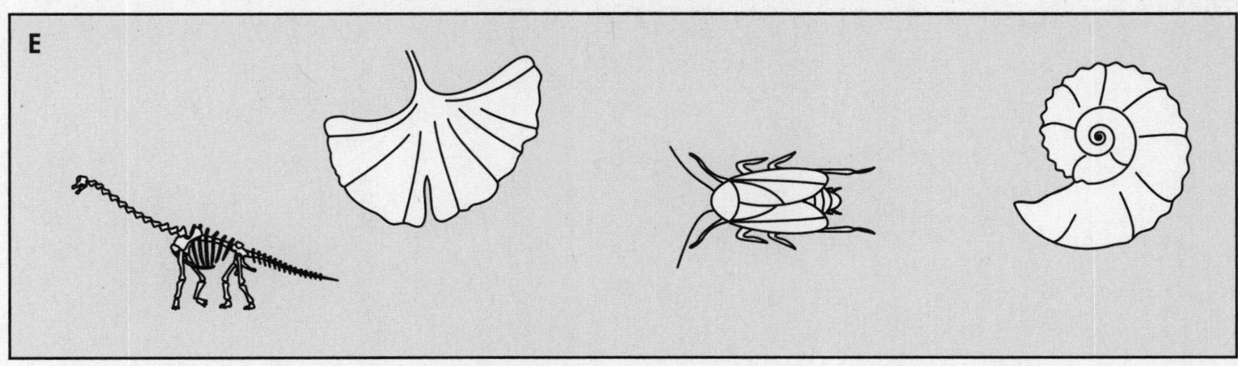

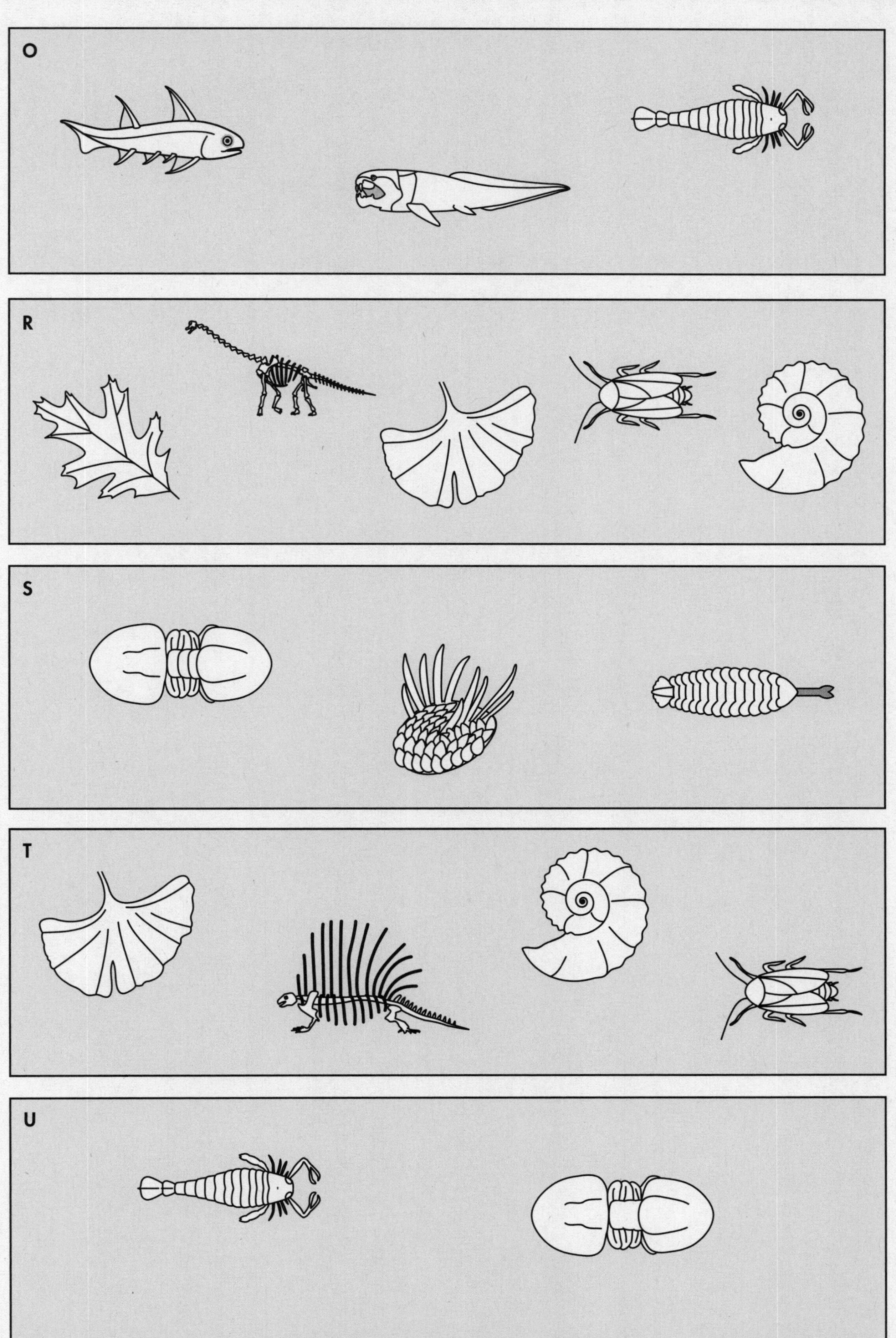
O
R
S
T
U

Guided Inquiry • **Real-World Lab**

Chapter 20 Lab **Controlling Bacterial Growth**

Problem

How can you determine the effectiveness of an antibiotic?

Introduction

Have you ever had an ear infection or strep throat? Did you use an antibiotic to treat the infection? Antibiotics can block a bacteria's ability to grow and reproduce. Not all antibiotics work on all types of bacteria. For example, some bacteria have an outer membrane that surrounds the cell wall. Antibiotics that cannot pass through this membrane have no effect on those species of bacteria.

Bacteria that are not affected by an antibiotic are said to be resistant to that antibiotic. Over time, there has been an increase in the resistance to antibiotics. Bacteria that used to be killed by certain antibiotics no longer respond to them. Some bacteria, such as MRSA, have built up many resistances. Scientists are trying to produce new drugs to kill these so-called "super bugs."

In this lab, you will test the effectiveness of antibiotics against two kinds of harmless bacteria. One of the bacteria has an outer membrane, and one does not.

Skills Focus

Observe, Measure, Draw Conclusions

Build Vocabulary

Term	Definition
resistant	In biology, being able to withstand, or *resist,* the effects of a harmful substance
effective	Having the desired result, or *effect*
minimize	To reduce to the lowest possible, or *minimum,* amount, size, or extent
incubate	To keep cells or microorganisms at a specific temperature in or on a medium, such as agar, so that the cells or microorganisms can multiply

Materials

- 2 agar plates
- glass-marking pencil
- 2 bacterial cultures
- 10 or more sterile glass beads
- disposal solution
- 2 sterile micropipettes
- 6 forceps
- 6 paper disks, 4 with antibiotics and 2 with distilled water
- masking tape
- metric ruler

Safety

Wear goggles and gloves while working with bacterial cultures. Even though you are working with harmless bacteria, follow your teacher's instructions about sterile techniques. For example, any item that touches the cultures should not touch your skin or your lab table. Follow your teacher's instructions about safe disposal of materials. Wash your hands thoroughly with soap and warm water before leaving the lab. Tell your teacher before the lab if you are allergic to penicillin or tetracycline.

Pre-Lab Questions

1. **Relate Cause and Effect** How will you know whether an antibiotic is able to control the growth of bacteria?

____

____

2. **Design an Experiment** Why is it important to leave space between the disks on the agar plates?

____

____

____

3. **Control Variables** Why must you avoid direct contact between your hands and the antibiotic disks?

____

____

____

____

Procedure

Part A: Setting Up the Experiment

When you add items to an agar plate, replace the lid as soon as you are done to minimize the time that the plates are exposed to the air.

1. Put on goggles and plastic gloves.
2. Obtain two agar plates. Use a glass-marking pencil to mark each lid with the name of one of the bacteria you will be testing.
3. Use the pencil to divide the bottom of each plate into thirds. In two of the sections, write the names of the antibiotics you will use. In the third section, write Distilled Water.
4. Obtain a bacterial culture. Pour about five sterile glass beads into the agar plate labeled with the name of that bacteria.
5. Use a micropipette to transfer a few drops of the culture to the agar plate.
6. Replace the lid and tilt the plate in different directions so that the beads spread the culture medium across the plate.
7. Remove the lid and carefully pour off the beads into the disposal solution. Put the lid back on the plate.
8. Repeat Steps 4 through 7 for the second culture.

   Get Ready! When you place an antibiotic disk on the agar, it is important not to touch the disk or the agar with your hands.
9. Take the lid off one agar plate. Use forceps to place the first antibiotic disk on the agar in the correct section of the plate. Press the disk flat so it sticks to the surface of the agar. Do not move the disk once it is in place.
10. Use a new forceps to place the second antibiotic disk on the agar in its section of the plate. Don't move the disk once it is in place.
11. Use a third forceps to add a disk that has been soaked in distilled water to the section marked Distilled Water.
12. Put the lid back on the plate. Tape the lid shut at two locations on opposite sides of the plate.
13. Repeat Steps 9 through 12 with the second agar plate.
14. Turn the plates upside down and incubate the cultures overnight at 37°C or for 2–3 days at room temperature.

Part B: Observing the Plates

During the incubation period, a milky film of bacteria should have formed on the agar.

15. Examine each plate. Look in particular at the areas immediately around the three disks. **CAUTION:** Do not uncover the plates.

16. Measure the distance across, or diameter, of any clear zones around the three disks. A clear zone is a zone without any noticeable bacteria. Record your data in the table below.

17. Follow your teacher's instructions for disposal of the cultures.

Data Table		
Name of Bacteria	**Material on Disk**	**Clear Zone Diameter (mm)**
	Distilled water	
	Distilled water	

Analyze and Conclude

1. **Design an Experiment** What is the purpose of the disk soaked in distilled water?

____

____

____

2. **Infer** Did you see any evidence of antibiotic-resistant bacteria on your plates? Explain.

____

____

____

3. **Draw Conclusions** Which antibiotic, or antibiotics, were effective against each type of bacteria?

____

____

____

4. **Apply Concepts** Some antibiotics are less effective against a specific type of bacteria after lengthy and repeated use. What do you think is responsible for this pattern? *Hint:* Think about the principle of natural selection.

5. **Infer** Suppose you are prescribed an antibiotic to treat a bacterial infection. Your doctor tells you to take the antibiotic for 10 days even if you feel better before then. Why should you continue taking the antibiotic for the full 10 days?

Build Science Skills

Antibiotics are not the only defense against bacteria. Household products often contain ingredients that can kill bacteria. Choose three household products and test their effectiveness against bacteria. Possible examples include alcohol, hand sanitizers, hand soap, dishwashing detergent, and mouthwash. Record the method you used and your results.

Guided Inquiry • Design Your Own Lab

Chapter 21 Lab **Mushroom Farming**

Problem

How does the amount of available light affect mushroom growth?

Introduction

Mushrooms are probably the type of fungus most familiar to you. You can find them in lawns, on rotting logs, or as an ingredient on pizza. The "mushroom" part of a fungus is the fruiting body, which is involved in reproduction. Spores are produced in the fruiting body. The largest part of a fungus, the mycelium, actually grows underground. The mycelium is the part of the fungus that absorbs water and nutrients from the soil. Under the right conditions, fruiting bodies grow from the mycelium.

In this lab, you will design an experiment to determine the effect of light on the growth of a fruiting body. The class will be divided into groups with each group assigned to monitor one of three experimental setups. The groups will share their results and then analyze the pooled data.

Skills Focus

Form a Hypothesis, Design an Experiment, Organize Data

Build Vocabulary

Term	Definition
nutrient	A chemical substance that an organism needs in order to survive
absorb	To soak up a liquid; to take in nutrients or other chemicals gradually
conditions	Factors that affect whether an event or process, such as the growth of a fungus, will take place
monitor	To keep close watch over something, such as an experimental setup
procedure	A list of steps that describe how to carry on, or *proceed,* with a task
medium	In biology, a material in which a specific organism can grow

Materials

- 3 mushroom-growing kits
- spray bottles with water
- metric rulers

Safety

Wear goggles and gloves if you are involved in the initial setup of a mushroom farm. Handle the mushrooms gently when you make measurements, and wash your hands thoroughly with soap and warm water when you are done. If you are sensitive to mold, don't handle the mushrooms. Don't eat the mushrooms grown in this lab.

Pre-Lab Questions

1. **Infer** Where will the mushrooms get the nutrients that they need to grow and develop?

____

____

____

2. **Relate Cause and Effect** Why will you have to wait about 10 days to observe the mushrooms?

____

____

____

____

3. **Apply Concepts** The mushrooms you will grow are a variety that is sold in food stores. Why do the instructions warn you not to eat the mushrooms?

____

____

____

____

Procedure

Part A: Design Your Experiment

You need to plan the experiment as a class to ensure that all the variables are controlled in each experimental setup, except for the amount of light.

1. **Form a Hypothesis** How do you think the amount of light will affect mushroom growth? Record your hypothesis as an if . . . then statement: If the amount of light . . . then the growth of the mushrooms will . . .

   Hypothesis: ______________________________

   ____

2. **Control Variables** Record the independent and dependent variables you will test as a class.

   Independent Variable: ______________________________

   Dependent Variable: ______________________________

3. **Design an Experiment** As a class, develop a procedure for testing how different light conditions affect the growth of mushrooms. Record the details of your plan, including how you will track changes in the dependent variable and how you will control other variables. Also record your expected outcome.

   Experimental Design: ______________________________

   ____

   ____

   ____

   ____

   ____

   ____

   ____

   ____

   Expected Outcome: ______________________________

   ____

   ____

   ____

4. **Organize Data** Make a data table in the space below. Include a column for each type of observation you will make to track the dependent variable. Include enough rows to record up to two weeks of observations. Choose a title for your table that includes a description of the setup your group will monitor.

Part B: Setting Up Your Mushroom Farm

The kit you will use should include a container, growth medium, and mushroom spores. The spores may come mixed with the growth medium, or you may need to add them to the medium. **NOTE:** Not everyone in your group will be able to do every task, but everyone in the group should do some tasks.

5. Follow your teacher's instructions for setting up your group's farm. **CAUTION:** Students who set up the kit should wash their hands thoroughly with soap and warm water when they are done.
6. Use the spray bottle to mist the growth medium and moisten the spores. Place the farm in your group's assigned location.
7. Mist the medium once a day. To control the amount of water, spray the medium 4 times at each misting. **CAUTION:** Make sure the nozzle on the spray bottle is set to "spray."

Part C: Observing Your Mushroom Farm

8. In about 10 days you should see bumpy growths forming on the surface of your farm. These bumps are the fruiting bodies. Inform your teacher when you notice the growths. Your farm will need to be misted twice a day from this point on.

   Get Ready! From the day you notice the first growths, the fruiting bodies will need about 4–6 days to mature. A fruiting body is mature when you can see fully formed gill ridges on the underside of the cap.

9. Once your mushrooms have matured, begin making daily observations. Record these observations in your data table. **CAUTION:** If you need to hold the mushrooms to make measurements, handle them gently. Wash your hands thoroughly with soap and warm water when you are done.

10. Once the experiment is complete, follow your teacher's instructions for cleanup and disposal of materials.

11. Post your results on the board for the rest of the class to see.

Analyze and Conclude

1. **Analyze Data** Did fruiting bodies appear in all three experimental setups?

   ____

   ____

2. **Form an Operational Definition** What standard did you use to decide which lighting condition was optimum? The word *optimum* means "the best out of a number of possible options."

   ____

   ____

   ____

3. **Draw Conclusions** Based on your answer to Question 2, which light condition was optimum for the growth of mushrooms?

   ____

   ____

4. **Perform Error Analysis** Was there a possible source of error in the design of the experiment? If so, how could you change the procedure to improve your results?

5. **Infer** Why might mushroom farmers be concerned about the overall appearance of their mushrooms?

Build Science Skills

How does the amount of moisture affect mushroom growth? Select the container that had the best growth. For three days, mist the mushrooms only once a day and observe what happens. After the third day, stop misting the mushrooms and observe what happens. Record your observations below.

Open-Ended Inquiry • **Real-World Lab**

Chapter 22 Lab **Exploring Plant Diversity**

Problem

How many different kinds of plants are in a small ecosystem?

Introduction

On your walk or ride to school, you may pass fields with crops, a dense forest, a city park with flowerbeds, or an overgrown vacant lot. In fields where a crop is growing, all the plants will look similar. But in most other areas, you should see a variety of plants—possibly tall shade trees, flowering shrubs, climbing vines, and grass. This variation tells you that many plant species can grow in the same area.

Ecologists often count the number of species in an ecosystem and note whether the species are native to the area. In general, a high degree of diversity is a sign of a healthy, balanced ecosystem. Sometimes nonnative plants compete so well that they crowd out native species and reduce diversity. Humans can lower natural diversity by clearing land for farms and buildings.

In this lab, you will explore a small, local ecosystem and survey its plant diversity. You will also identify as many plants as possible and infer the conditions in which these plants thrive.

Skills Focus

Observe, Measure, Classify, Infer

Build Vocabulary

Term	Definition
variation	The degree, or extent, to which a set of similar items differ, or *vary*
native	Belonging to an area by birth, production, or growth; describes a plant species that has its origin in a particular region
survey	To examine, or look at, for a specific purpose; to view or consider something as a whole
document	To make a record of something
summarize	To state briefly, or *sum* up; to prepare a brief statement or *summary*

Materials

- notepad or notebook
- protective work gloves
- measuring tape
- tweezers
- scissors
- small plastic bags
- labels
- hand lens
- field guides for plants
- camera (optional)

Safety

Be aware of dangerous plants that are common in your area. To avoid possible contact with poisonous or prickly plants, wear work gloves at all times. Alert your teacher to any allergies you may have. Do not disturb the nests of any animals you may encounter. Use scissors only as instructed. When you are done, wash your hands thoroughly with soap and warm water.

Pre-Lab Questions

1. **Design an Experiment** What are some ways that you can make sure that you survey all the plants in your ecosystem?

2. **Classify** What should you do if you are not sure that an organism is a plant?

3. **Infer** Why might you want to use a regional field guide rather than a national field guide when identifying plants?

Procedure

Part A: Survey Your Ecosystem

In Part A, you will work with a group to survey a local ecosystem. It may be a self-contained ecosystem or part of a larger ecosystem. You will be using the information you gather in Part A to help you identify the plants in Part B.

1. Decide as a group how you will ensure that you will survey the entire assigned area.
2. Record a general description of your site. Include information such as its location, whether it is sunny or shady, whether it is flat or sloped, and whether it is sheltered or windy.
3. Make a sketch of the area in your notepad. Note the location of any fences, paths, nearby buildings, or sources of water. **CAUTION:** Always wear protective work gloves when handling plants outdoors.
4. Following the plan you agreed on, document the plants you observe. Assign a number to each species. Use the number to record the location of the plant on your sketch of the ecosystem.
5. Make a drawing of each plant in your notepad. Include the assigned number with the drawing. Also include information that will help you identify the plant, such as its height, the shape and length of any leaves, and the color of any flowers.
6. If you have permission, collect pieces of plants in plastic bags. Label each bag with the plant's assigned number. Do not put samples from more than one plant in the same bag.

Part B: Classify the Plants

7. Use the data table to summarize your observations. For plant type, use the following categories: woody plant (trees, shrubs, and vines), herbaceous plant (grasses, weeds, small flowering plants), fern, or groundcover (mosses, lichens). If you found more species than will fit in the table, continue the table on a separate sheet of paper.

Data Table: Summary of Survey Results

Assigned Number	Plant Type	Observations	Name

8. Use print references and Web sites to identify the plants you observed. You may not be able to identify all the plants to the species level. Record the best information you can find. For example, you might identify a maple tree as genus *Acer* but not have enough information to decide which species of maple it is. For some plants, you may not be able to get more specific than the plant's family.
9. Add a key to your sketch of the ecosystem in which you identify each numbered species.
10. Display and compare your sketch with the sketches from other groups.

Analyze and Conclude

1. **Communicate** Describe the general nature of the area you surveyed.

2. **Design an Experiment** How did your group ensure that you surveyed the entire area?

3. **Form a Hypothesis** Why do you think your ecosystem contained as many (or as few) species as were present?

4. **Compare and Contrast** Did other groups find plants that you did not? If so, why do you think that happened?

5. **Predict** Would the survey results be different at another time of the year? Explain your answer?

Build Science Skills

An invasive species is one that is not native to a region and whose growth is uncontrolled. Invasive plant species generally spread easily, grow rapidly, and tolerate many different environments. Pick one local invasive plant species. Find out whether it was introduced accidentally or on purpose, what problems it has caused, and what is being done to control it. Explain why invasive species are hard to get rid of.

Guided Inquiry • Design Your Own Lab

Chapter 23 Lab Identifying Growth Zones in Roots

Problem

Where does growth occur in plant roots?

Introduction

The tissues in plant roots perform many different functions. Some tissues produce food, some provide support, and others absorb water and nutrients. As the root grows, the number of cells in these tissues increases. The new cells are formed from undifferentiated regions of cells called meristems.

In this lab, you will grow bean seedlings. You will use the seedlings to determine the location of a root's apical meristem, which is where lengthwise growth occurs in roots.

Skills Focus

Design an Experiment, Measure, Organize Data, Analyze Data

Materials

- 150-mL beaker
- paper towels
- 4 large bean seeds
- petri dish
- masking tape
- metric ruler
- fine-tip permanent marker

Build Vocabulary

Term	Definition
zone	An area viewed as separate or distinct from other areas based on a specific use or function
distribute	To place objects so that they are evenly spread throughout a given area
independent	Is not affected by, or does not *depend* on, another person or thing
initial	Coming first; related to or occurring at the beginning of an event or process

Safety

If you have glass petri dishes or beakers, check them for cracks and chips. Alert your teacher if you break a glass object. Handle the seedlings only as instructed. If you are allergic to certain plants or seeds, tell your teacher. Wash your hands thoroughly with soap and warm water before leaving the lab.

Pre-Lab Questions

1. **Predict** A root is marked at two points along its length. What will happen to the distance between these marks if the root grows longer only near the tip? What will happen if growth occurs evenly along the entire length of the root?

____

____

____

____

2. **Design an Experiment** The procedure in Part A asks you to use four seeds. Why not use two seeds instead?

____

____

____

____

3. **Design an Experiment** How will you keep track of which seedling is which?

____

____

____

Procedure

In Part A, you will grow plants from bean seeds. In Part B, you will design an experiment to determine where growth occurs along the roots of these plants.

Part A: Seed Germination

1. Fill the 150-mL beaker with loosely crumpled paper towels.
2. Dampen the towels with water until the water that collects in the bottom of the beaker is 1 cm deep.

3. Place four seeds between the damp towels and the sides of the beaker. Distribute the seeds evenly around the beaker. **CAUTION:** Do not allow any of the seeds to touch the water in the bottom of the beaker.
4. Cover the beaker with a petri dish.
5. After three days, water your seeds again.

Part B: Design an Experiment

Wait until the roots are at least 20 mm long to do Part B. While you are waiting, plan your procedure. To mark the roots, you will need to remove the seedlings from the beaker. **CAUTION:** You will need to handle the seedlings gently to avoid breaking the roots or separating them from either half of the bean.

6. **Form a Hypothesis** Where does the growth occur that causes a root to increase in length? Record the hypothesis you will test to answer this question.

   Hypothesis: ______________________________

   ____

   ____

7. **Describe Your Plan** Describe the procedure you will use to test your hypothesis.

   How many marks will you make on each root?

   ____

   ____

   How will you distribute the marks along the root?

   ____

   ____

   ____

   What measurements will you make initially?

   ____

   ____

   When will you make your final measurements?

   ____

   ____

   ____

8. **Control Variables** What will your independent variable be? What will your dependent variable be?

Independent Variable: ________________

Dependent Variable: ________________

9. Construct a data table in the space below to record your measurements of the distance from the root tip to each mark. Leave space to record both the initial and final measurements. Include a column for observations.

10. Review your procedure and your data table with your teacher before you do the experiment.

11. If you plan to do the Build Science Skills experiment, keep growing your seedlings. Otherwise, follow your teacher's instructions for cleanup and disposal of materials.

Analyze and Conclude

1. **Calculate** Use the data you collected to calculate the distances between marks for both the initial and final measurements. Record your results in Data Table 2.

Data Table 2: Distance Between Marks (mm)					
		Tip to Mark 1	Mark 1 to Mark 2	Mark 2 to Mark 3	Mark 3 to Mark 4
Seedling 1	Initial				
	Final				
Seedling 2	Initial				
	Final				
Seedling 3	Initial				
	Final				

2. **Interpret Tables** What patterns of growth are revealed by the data in Data Table 2?

3. **Draw Conclusions** In what region of the root is the apical meristem located? Give a reason for your answer.

4. **Infer** Do you think it would be adaptive for root growth to occur at the very tip of the root? Why or why not?

5. **Compare and Contrast** Which cells in animals are comparable to cells in plant meristems, and why?

Build Science Skills

A driver backed a car into a young tree, which left a scar in the bark one meter from the ground. Will the scar remain at the same distance from the ground as the tree grows? Design an experiment using your bean seedlings to determine where most stem growth occurs.

Guided Inquiry • Real-World Lab

Chapter 24 Lab **Plant Hormones and Leaves**

Problem

How does a plant hormone affect leaf loss?

Introduction

Seasonal leaf loss is an adaptation of plants to cold weather. Autumn in temperate biomes is a time of decreasing temperatures and light intensity. As the ground begins to freeze, water becomes more difficult to obtain. Each of these factors contributes to a decrease in the rate of photosynthesis. Deciduous plants respond to these changes by beginning to break down chlorophyll. In some plants, the colors of accessory pigments are visible for a short time before leaves drop for the winter.

Two classes of hormones, auxins and ethylene, are involved when trees lose their leaves in autumn. Changes in hormone concentrations cause cells near the base of the leaf petiole to break down. This area, called the abscission zone, becomes a weak point, which is vulnerable to, or open to, damage. A gust of wind, a heavy rain, even the weight of the leaf can cause the petiole to break off. In this lab, you will test the effect of auxins on petioles.

Skills Focus

Observe, Draw Conclusions, Apply Concepts

Materials

- leafy plant
- masking tape
- permanent marker
- scissors
- string
- toothpick
- auxin paste
- plastic container or tray

Build Vocabulary

Term	Definition
seasonal	Happening at or dependent on a specific *season*
accessory	Having a less-important function or providing added support
infer	To offer a reasoned opinion, or *inference,* based on observation and experience

Safety

Wear goggles while you are working with the auxin paste. Wear gloves to protect your skin against a possible reaction from the paste. Wash your hands thoroughly with soap and warm water immediately after you handle the paste. Use the scissors only as instructed. Do not direct the points of the scissors toward yourself or others. Alert your teacher if you suspect you are allergic to the plant species used in the lab.

Pre-Lab Questions

1. **Use Visuals** Draw a simple leaf. Label the blade and the petiole.

2. **Control Variables** What is the control in this experiment?

3. **Infer** How will auxins move from the paste to the base of the petiole?

Procedure

1. Obtain a leafy plant from your teacher. Apply a piece of masking tape to the plant's container and use a permanent marker to label the plant with your group number or initials.
2. Use the scissors to carefully cut off *only* the leaf blade from two leaves. **CAUTION:** Do not cut off any part of the petioles.
3. Loosely tie a small piece of string to one of the petioles that is missing a blade.
4. Use a toothpick to apply a small amount of the auxin paste to the cut end of the petiole with the string.

5. Set your plant in a plastic container or tray to catch water that may overflow, or run over, when you water your plant.
6. Place the plant in a sunny location and water it for the next two weeks as directed by your teacher.
7. Observe the petioles and the uncut leaves during each class period over the next two weeks. Make a data table in the space below to record your observations.

Analyze and Conclude

1. **Communicate** What happened to the petioles and the uncut leaves during the two weeks you observed the plant?

____

____

____

2. **Infer** What effect do auxins have on leaf loss in plants?

____

____

3. **Predict** In what part of a leaf are auxins produced? Explain your answer.

____

____

____

4. **Draw Conclusions** In autumn, the leaves of deciduous plants produce less auxin and more of another plant hormone, ethylene. What effect might ethylene have on leaf loss?

Build Science Skills

Is what happens in one leaf affected by what happens in other leaves? Design an experiment to determine whether the auxins produced by one leaf can affect other leaves. Obtain your teacher's approval for your procedure before doing your experiment.

Guided Inquiry • **Skills Lab**

Chapter 25 Lab **Comparing Invertebrate Body Plans**

Problem

What characteristics can be used to classify invertebrates?

Introduction

Biologists often consider the number of germ layers when they classify animals. Some animals have cells that are derived from only two germ layers—the endoderm and the ectoderm. Some also have cells that are derived from the mesoderm.

Most animals with cells derived from mesoderm have a fluid-filled body cavity located between the digestive tract and the body wall. In some animals, this cavity, called a coelom (SEE lum), is completely lined with cells derived from mesoderm. Some animals have a partially lined coelom, or pseudocoelom. *Pseudo* means "false." Animals that do not have a body cavity are acoelemates. The prefix *a-* means "not" or "without."

In this lab, you will compare the body plans and structures of invertebrates from three different phyla. The slides you will use will show a thin slice, or cross section, of each organism.

Skills Focus

Observe, Classify, Compare and Contrast

Materials

- compound microscope
- prepared slides with cnidarian, roundworm, and earthworm cross sections
- red, blue, and yellow colored pencils

Build Vocabulary

Term	Definition
derived	Obtained, formed, or made from something else
surround	To occupy the space all *around* something; to enclose or extend on all sides

 •

Safety

Review the rules for handling a microscope. To avoid electrical shocks, keep water away from cords and plugs, and make sure your hands are dry. Handle slides gently to avoid breaking them and cutting yourself.

Pre-Lab Questions

1. **Compare and Contrast** Which two features of animal body plans will you be comparing in this lab?

____

____

2. **Apply Concepts** Where will you look for tissue that formed from the ectoderm layer?

____

3. **Infer** Is a hydra smaller than, larger than, or about the same size as an earthworm? Base your answer on the procedure in this lab.

____

____

____

Procedure

Figure 1 shows general body plans for the three organisms you will observe. Before you begin Part A, look at the body plans and note ways in which they are different.

Figure 1 Body plans of cnidarian, roundworm, and earthworm

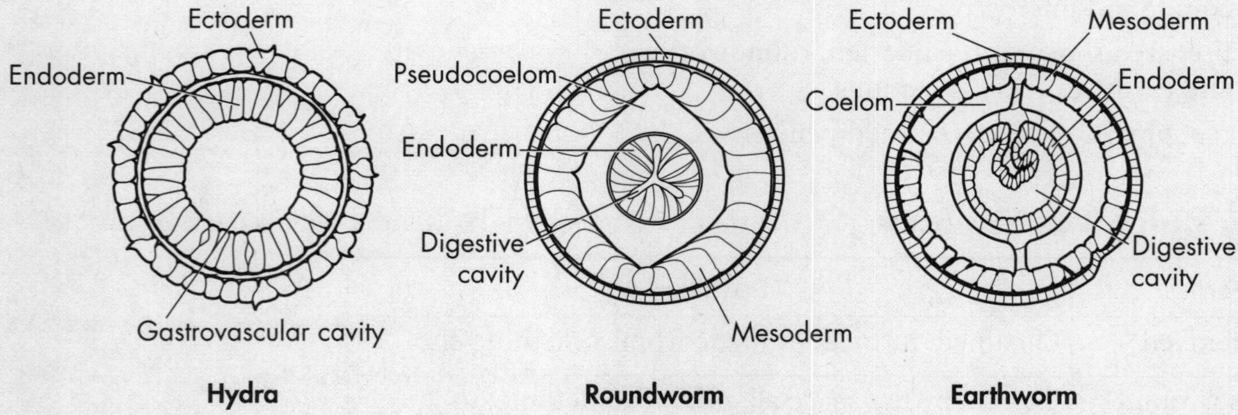

Part A: Observe the Body Plan of a Cnidarian

Organisms in the phylum Cnidaria (ny DAYR ee uh) include corals, jellyfish, sea anemones, and hydras. Your slide contains a cross section of a hydra.

1. Examine the slide under high power. Use the space below to make a labeled drawing of what you observe.
2. Start by locating the gastrovascular cavity in the center of the cross section. The name of this cavity reflects its two functions. It is the location where both digestion and circulation occur.
3. Locate the gastroderm, or inner cell layer.
4. You may see a whiplike structure sticking out of a cell in the inner cell layer. These whiplike structures are called flagella. They help circulate, or move, food and other materials throughout the cavity.
5. Locate the epidermis, or outer cell layer.
6. You may see a cell that has a sharp point, or barb, on its outer surface. The barbs are called nematocysts. The barbs can sting prey that come close to the hydra and inject a poison that can stun the prey.
7. In the area between the epidermis and the gastroderm, you may be able to see a noncellular, jellylike material called mesoglea (mez uh GLEE uh).
8. Your drawing should have labels for the gastrovascular cavity, gastroderm, and epidermis. It may also have labels for flagella, nematocysts, and mesoglea if you saw those structures.

Drawing of a Hydra

Part B: Observe the Body Plan of a Roundworm

The roundworm that you will observe is a parasite that lives in the digestive tract of animals and feeds on nutrients that flow by.

9. Examine the slide under medium power. Use the space below to make a labeled drawing of what you observe.
10. First find the thin outer layer called the cuticle. This tough coating keeps the roundworm from being digested by its host.
11. The cuticle consists mainly of proteins that are secreted by cells in the epidermis. Find the epidermis just inside the cuticle.
12. Find the thick layer of muscle tissue just inside the epidermis. The cells in this *longitudinal* muscle tissue run lengthwise along the body. Longitudinal muscle is responsible for moving the roundworm's body.
13. Now look for a space in the center of the roundworm. This space is the roundworm's digestive tract.
14. The thin layer of cells that surrounds the digestive tract is the roundworm's intestine. Cells in the intestine absorb nutrients from the digestive tract.
15. Find the thick layer of muscle tissue that is next to the intestine. This muscle tissue is called *radial* because its cells are arranged in rings. As these muscle cells contract, food moves through the digestive tract.
16. The fluid-filled space between the radial muscle tissue and the longitudinal muscle tissue is the pseudocoelom.
17. Make sure you have labeled the following structures in your drawing: cuticle, epidermis, longitudinal muscle, digestive tract, intestine, radial muscle, and pseudocoelom.

Drawing of a Roundworm

Part C: Observe the Body Plan of an Earthworm

People who garden are pleased to find earthworms in their soil. The tunnels that form as earthworms move through soil provide spaces through which air and water can circulate.

18. Examine the slide under low power. Use the space below to make a labeled drawing of what you observe.

19. First find the cuticle, which should be similar in appearance to the cuticle of a roundworm.

20. Just inside the cuticle, locate the first thin layer of cells. This is the earthworm's epidermis.

21. Beneath the epidermis are two layers of muscle tissue. In the thin outer layer, the cells circle around the earthworm. In the thick inner layer, the muscle tissue is longitudinal. The cells in the inner layer should appear branched and feathery.

22. Look for a round or horseshoe-shaped space in the center of the slide. This space is the digestive tract.

23. Three layers of cells surround the digestive tract. The thin innermost layer is the earthworm's intestine. The middle layer is smooth muscle, which moves food along the intestine. The outermost layer is called chloragogen tissue. Cells in this tissue help remove harmful waste products from the body.

24. The space between the chloragogen layer and the longitudinal muscle layer is the coelom.

25. Make sure you have labeled the following structures in your drawing: cuticle, epidermis, circular muscle, longitudinal muscle, digestive tract, intestine, smooth muscle, chloragogen tissue, and coelom.

Drawing of an Earthworm

Analyze and Conclude

1. **Compare and Contrast** What is the main difference between the cnidarian and the other two organisms?

2. **Infer** From which germ layer was the gastroderm in a cnidarian derived? From which germ layer was the epidermis derived?

3. **Apply Concepts** Which tissue layers line the coelom in an earthworm? From which germ layer were the cells in these layers derived? How do you know?

4. **Classify** The body plans table on page 614 in your textbook describes features of body plans for eight phyla of invertebrates. Is it possible to use only germ layers and type of body cavity to distinguish among all eight phyla? Explain.

Build Science Skills

On your drawings, color the tissues derived from ectoderm blue, the tissues derived from endoderm yellow, and the tissues derived from mesoderm red. Use Figure 1 and the information on page 612 of your textbook to help you decide which structures were derived from which germ layers.

Guided Inquiry • Forensics Lab

Chapter 26 Lab **Investigating Hominoid Fossils**

Problem

What can a comparison of skulls and hands reveal about the evolution of humans?

Introduction

A paleontologist takes photographs of a newly discovered fossil while it is in the ground and after it is removed. He or she also makes many measurements. These observations make it easier to compare the new fossil to fossils that have already been classified.

How can a scientist know whether a skeleton is typical of its species? For example, a scientist may find that one skeleton is much taller than another. Does this variation in height indicate that the individuals were members of two different species? Does it reflect a range of heights within the same species?

To deal with this problem, scientists use indexes. An index is a ratio that compares the value of one measurement in relation to another. Indexes are useful because they do not depend on overall size. Very tall and very short members of the same species should have similar indexes. With indexes, it is more likely that variations are related to differences in species, not just differences in size.

In this lab, you will measure the skulls and hands of different hominoid species. You will use your measurements to calculate indexes that will help you compare these species.

Skills Focus

Measure, Analyze Data, Compare and Contrast

Materials

- metric ruler

Build Vocabulary

Term	Definition
variation	The degree, or extent, to which a set of similar items differ, or *vary*
proportion	A part considered in relation to the whole

Pre-Lab Questions

1. **Use Models** What will you use instead of actual skulls and hands to make your measurements?

2. **Interpret Visuals** The bony cavities in a skull that protect the eyes are called orbits, or eye sockets. On the skulls, what does line AC measure? What does line BC measure?

3. **Use Analogies** Shoe sizes such as 9A and 11E (or 9 narrow and 11 extra-wide) are an example of an index. What two measurements are being compared in a shoe index?

Procedure

Part A: Supraorbital Height Index in Hominoids

Figure 1 shows side views of skulls from four hominoid species. You will use these drawings to determine distances from the top of the skull to the upper and lower edges of the eye socket. Then you will calculate the *supraorbital height index* (SHI). This index indicates the proportion of the skull that is above the eyes. The prefix *supra-* means "above."

1. Measure the distances AC and BC in centimeters for each skull. Record the measurements in Data Table 1.
2. For each species, divide the value of BC by the value of AC and multiply the result by 100. The result is the supraorbital height index (SHI). Round the answers to the nearest whole number, and record them in Data Table 1.

Data Table 1: Skull Measurements

Species	BC (cm)	AC (cm)	SHI
Pan troglodytes			
Australopithecus afarensis			
Homo erectus			
Homo sapiens			

Figure 1 Hominoid skulls

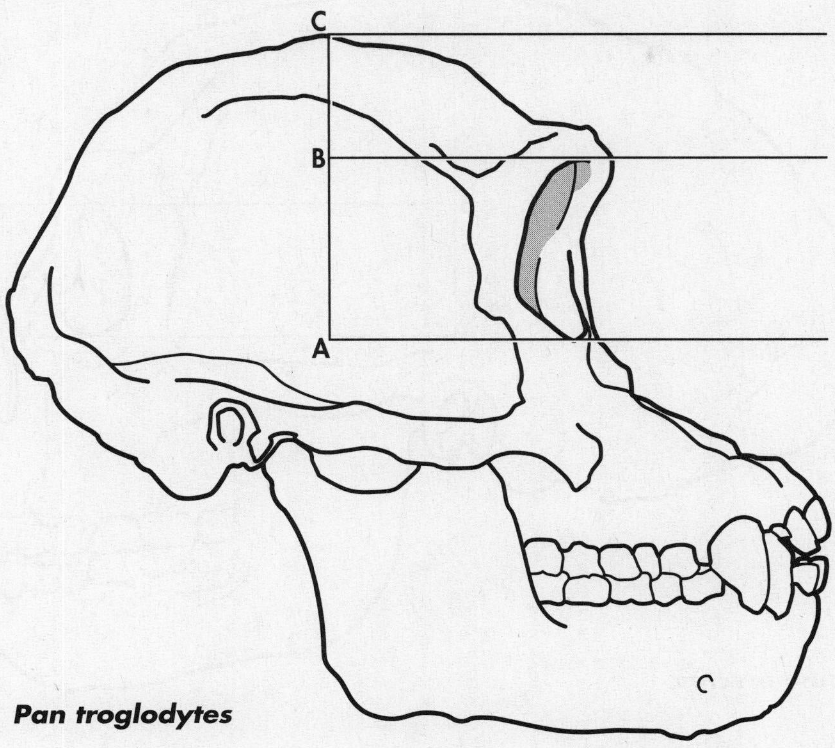

Pan troglodytes

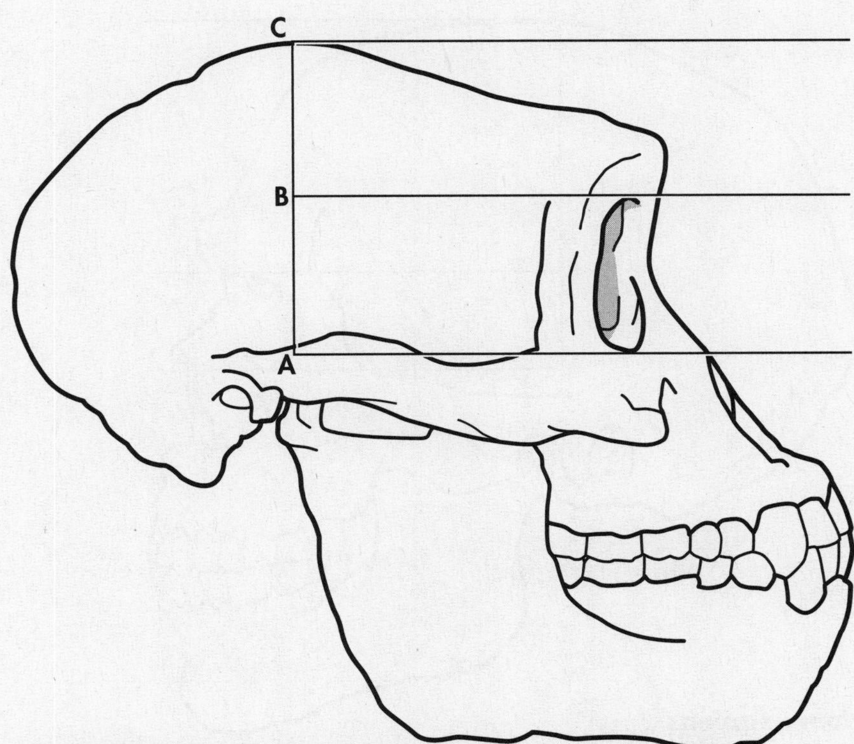

Australopithecus afarensis

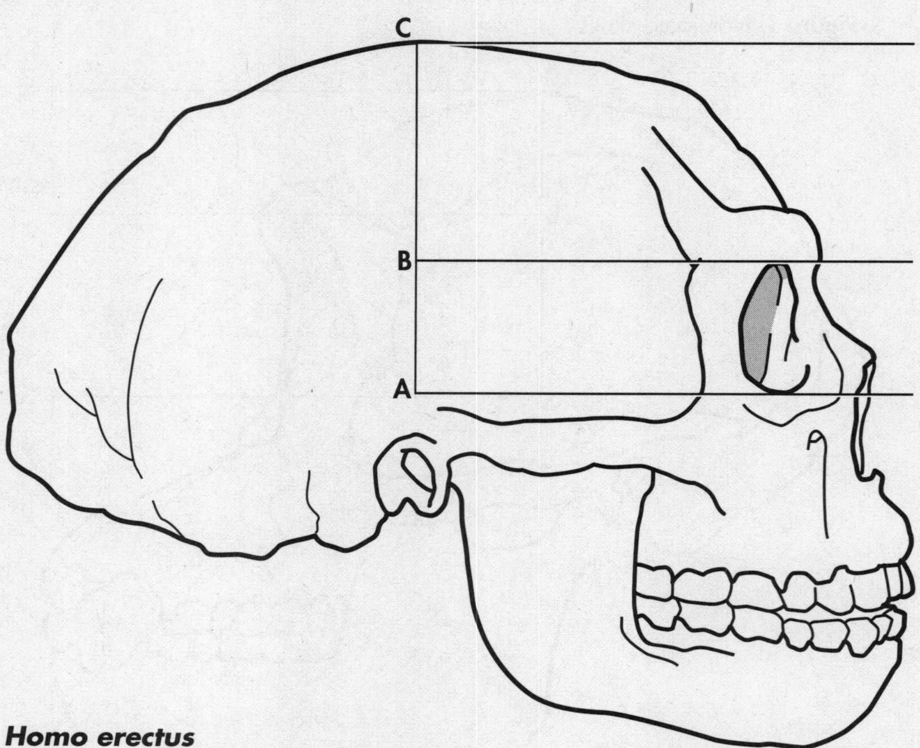

Homo erectus

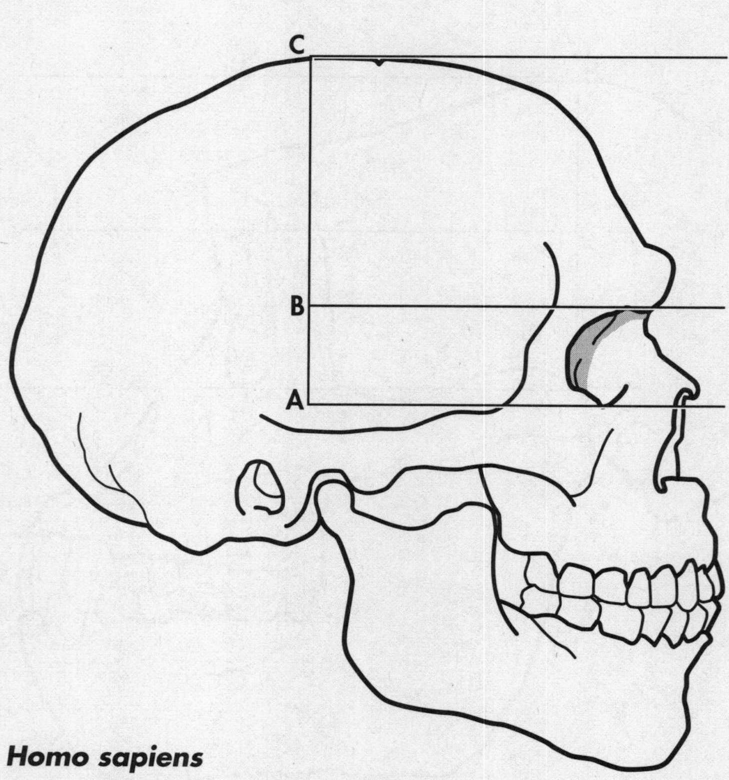

Homo sapiens

Part B: Thumb Index in Hominoids

Figure 2 depicts the thumb and index finger of *Pan troglodytes, Australopithecus afarensis,* and *Homo sapiens.* You will use these drawings to calculate a thumb index for each species. The thumb index compares the length of the thumb to the length of the hand.

3. For each species, measure the length of the thumb and the length of the index finger in centimeters. Make these measurements from the tip of the digit to the point where the finger and thumb meet at the wrist joint. Record your results in Data Table 2.
4. To calculate the thumb index, divide thumb length by index finger length and multiply the result by 100. Round the answer to the nearest whole number and record the result in the table.

Data Table 2: Hand Measurements

	Thumb Length (cm)	Index Finger Length (cm)	Thumb Index
Pan troglodytes			
Australopithecus afarensis			
Homo sapiens			

Figure 2 Hand bones of three hominoids

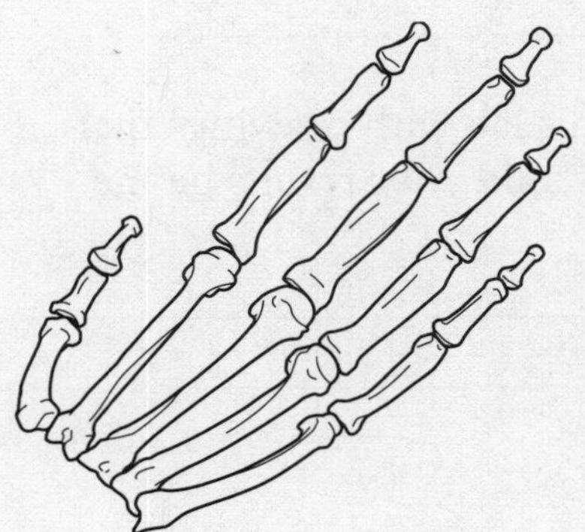

Pan troglodytes

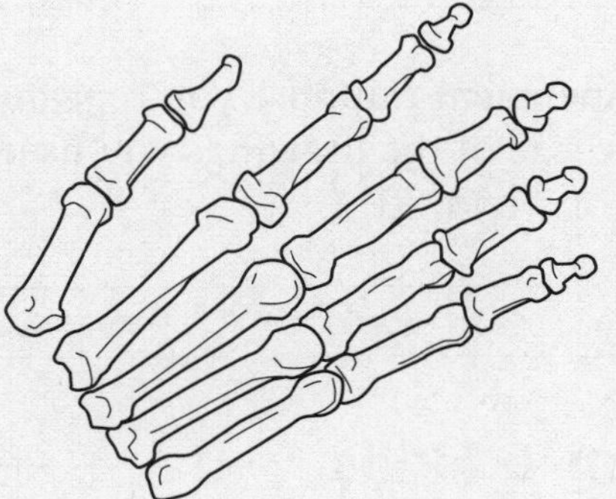

Australopithecus afarensis

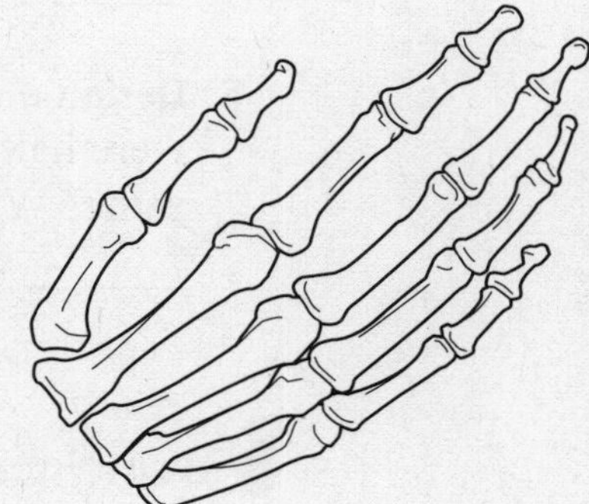

Homo sapiens

Analyze and Conclude

1. **Analyze Data** Of the species you investigated, which had the smallest SHI and which had the largest? What is the relationship between the SHI value and the shape of the skull?

2. **Infer** How might an increase in a hominoid's SHI value affect the size of its brain?

3. **Analyze Data** Does the data support the hypothesis that the thumb index increased as the opposable thumb hand evolved? Explain.

4. **Relate Cause and Effect** How could an increase in the thumb index affect a hominoid's ability to use its hands?

5. **Design an Experiment** Suppose you repeated this lab with drawings that were half the size of the drawings you used. Would your results be the same? Why or why not?

Build Science Skills

A skeleton retains clues about the life of its owner. How can fossils be used to determine a hominid skeleton's age, gender, or diet? How can fossils be used to tell how heavy or muscular an individual was?

Guided Inquiry • Skills Lab

Chapter 27 Lab Anatomy of a Squid

Problem

What structures does a squid use to obtain nutrients and eliminate wastes?

Introduction

A squid is an unusual mollusk. It doesn't have an external shell. Nor does it use a muscular foot to crawl, as snails do, or dig into the ocean bottom, as clams do. Instead, a squid uses a form of "jet propulsion." The squid expels water through an opening called the siphon, which pushes the squid through the water. By changing the siphon's position, the squid can swim forward or backward.

Unlike clams and oysters, which are filter feeders, squids are predators. They use their long tentacles to catch fish, crustaceans, and other mollusks. A squid uses its short arms to help hold the prey near its mouth and its beak to bite off pieces of the prey.

In this lab, you will dissect a squid. You will identify important structures and relate the structures to their functions.

Skills Focus

Observe, Infer, Sequence, Draw Conclusions

Build Vocabulary

Term	Definition
dissect	To cut apart or separate body tissues or organs
ventral	Refers to the front or lower surface of an animal
dorsal	Refers to the back or upper surface of an animal
external	Outside of or on the surface of an object, such as the *exterior* of a house
internal	Located within, or *inside;* in anatomy, refers to the inside of a body
primary	The main or most important item in a group of similar items

Materials

- squid
- dissecting tray
- hand lens
- forceps
- dissecting scissors
- dissecting pins
- dissecting probe

Safety

Wear your goggles, apron, and gloves while handling the squid. Use the dissecting tools only as instructed. Wash your hands thoroughly with soap and warm water before you leave the lab. Alert your teacher if you suspect you are allergic to squid.

Pre-Lab Questions

1. **Interpret Visuals** What structure can you use to distinguish the ventral side of a squid from the dorsal side?

____

____

2. **Infer** Why is it important to lift the mantle while cutting it?

____

____

____

3. **Predict** What do you expect the gills to look like, and why?

____

____

____

____

Procedure

Part A: Observe the External Structure of a Squid

Refer to Figure 1 as you examine the squid.

1. Put on goggles, a lab apron, and plastic gloves.
2. Obtain a squid specimen in a dissecting tray.
3. Examine both surfaces of the body thoroughly. Find the eyes and the lateral fins, which are located on the sides of the body.
4. Count the number of short arms and long tentacles. Use a hand lens to examine the suckers on the arms and tentacles.

   Number of arms: ______

   Number of tentacles: ______

5. Most of a squid's body has a fleshy covering called the mantle. Find the tubelike structure that extends from the mantle near the head of the squid. This structure is the siphon.

Figure 1 External anatomy of a squid

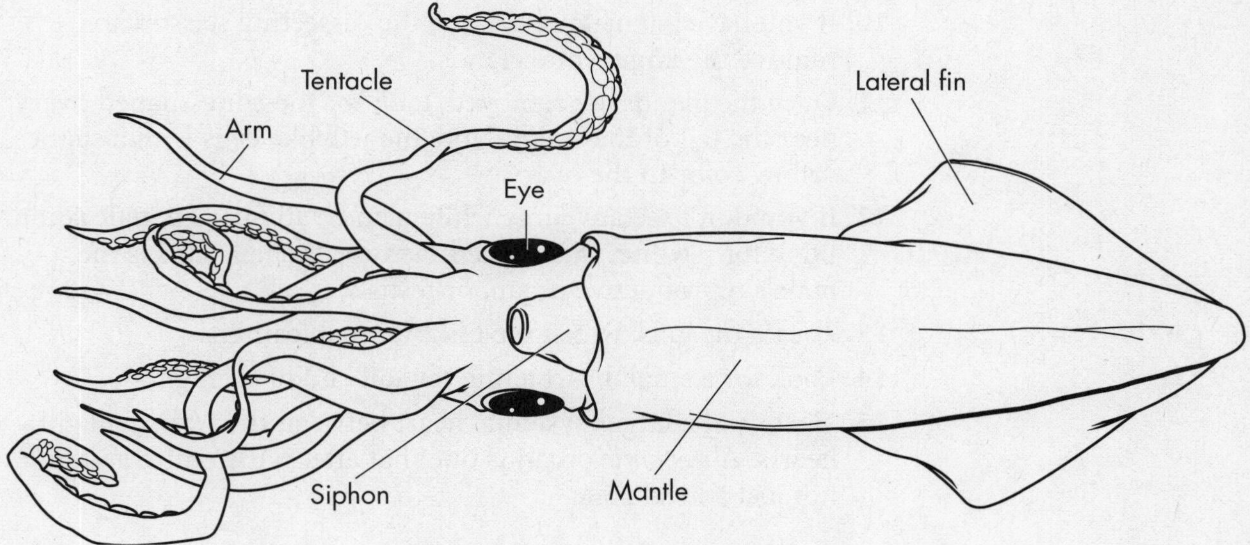

Part B: Observe the Internal Structure of a Squid

As you do the dissection, use the drawings to help you identify the squid's internal organs.

6. Position the squid with the ventral surface (the side with the siphon) facing up and the head facing toward you, as shown in Figure 2.
7. Use forceps to lift the free end of the mantle just above the siphon. Then, use the scissors to cut the mantle in a straight line to the tail end. **CAUTION:** Keep the ends of the scissors pointing up as you cut.
8. Spread the mantle and attach it to the tray with dissecting pins.
9. Use the probe to move aside the muscles that are attached to the siphon so that you can observe the entire length of the siphon.

   Get Ready! What you see next will depend on the sex of your squid. A female squid has two large white glands, which are attached to the ovary. These glands produce a gel that coats and hardens the eggs. If you do not see the large white glands, skip ahead to Step 12.
10. If you have a female squid, use the dissecting scissors to remove the large white glands.
11. Once the glands are removed, look for the cone-shaped ovary near the tail of the squid. Note the jellylike eggs with a slight yellow color in the ovary.
12. If you don't see any large white glands, you have a male squid. Look for a white, water-filled sac near the tail. This is the male's reproductive organ, or testis.
13. Locate the gills, which look like curved feathers.
14. Look for a small heart along the tail end of each gill.
15. Next, find a larger systemic heart between the two small gill hearts. A *systemic* organ is one that affects the entire system, not just a local area.

Figure 2 Internal anatomy of a squid, Part 1

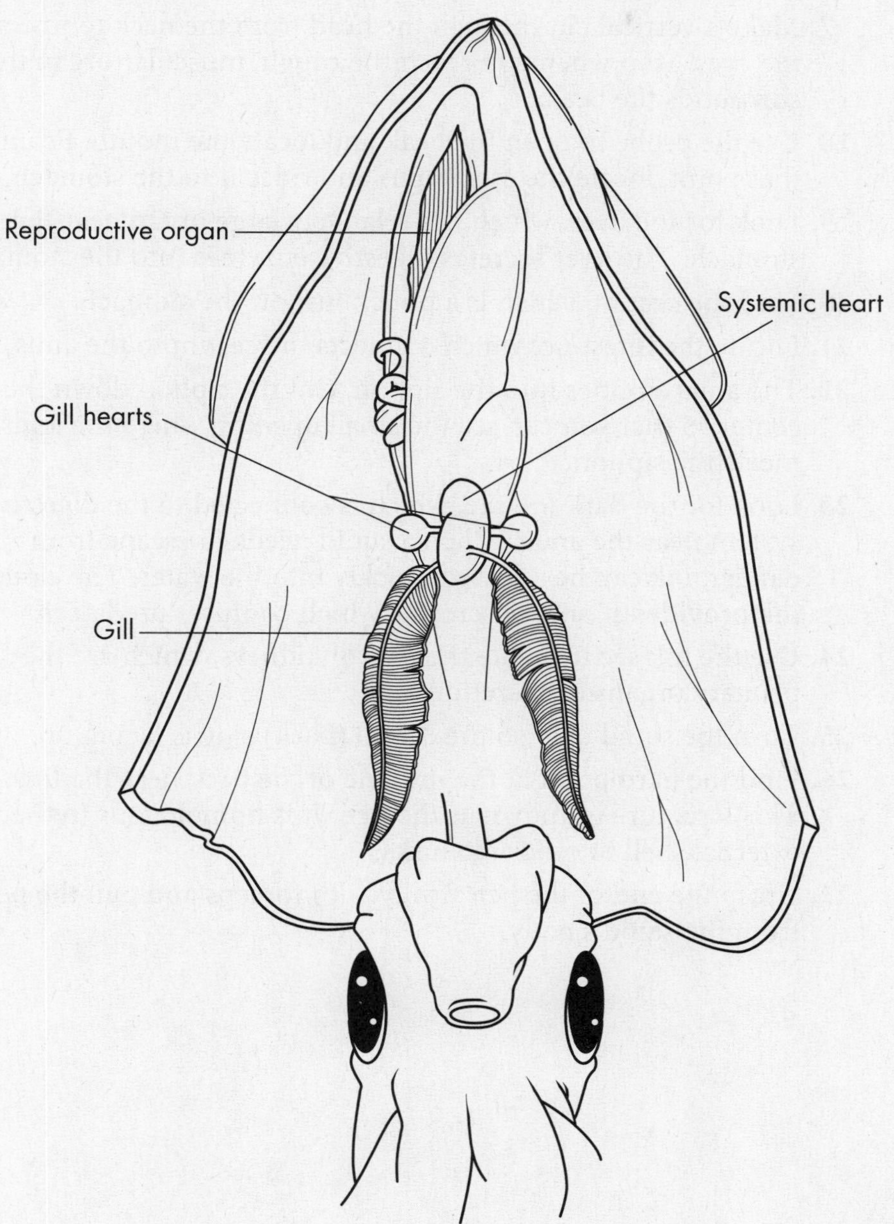

16. Turn the dissecting tray so the head is facing away from you, as shown in Figure 3.
17. Make a vertical cut through the head from the neck to just past the eyes. Stop when you reach the rough, muscular organ that surrounds the beak.
18. Use the probe to open the beak and locate the mouth. From that point, locate the esophagus and trace it to the stomach.
19. Look for the liver, which is a relatively large organ near the stomach. The liver secretes digestive enzymes into the stomach.
20. Find the cecum, which is a pouch just off the stomach.
21. Locate the intestine, which connects the cecum to the anus.
22. The anus empties into the siphon. Cut the siphon down the center so that you can see the small opening where the anus meets the siphon.
23. Look for the dark ink sac, which is connected to the digestive system near the anus. When a squid needs to escape from danger, ink can be released quickly into the water. The cloud of ink provides a "smoke screen," which confuses predators.
24. Use the ink sac to locate the pair of kidneys, which are the primary organs of excretion.
25. Turn the squid over so the dorsal (back) side is facing up.
26. Find the hard point at the midline of the back near the fins. This structure is known as the pen. It is homologous to the external shell in other mollusks.
27. Grasp the end of the pen firmly with forceps and pull the pen from the squid's body.

Figure 3 Internal anatomy of a squid, Part 2

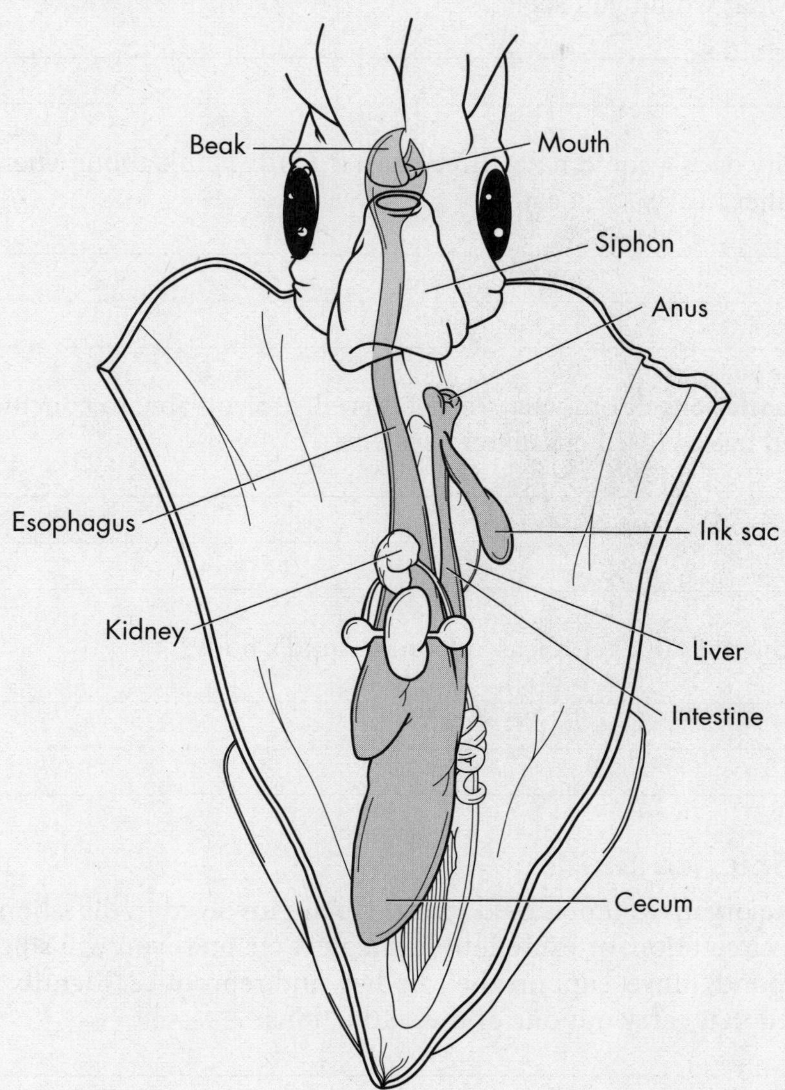

Analyze and Conclude

1. **Sequence** Trace the path of food through the digestive system. What happens to food that is not completely digested and absorbed?

____

____

____

____

2. **Infer** Based on its location, what function might the cecum have in the digestive system?

____

____

3. **Apply Concepts** If you viewed a piece of a gill under a microscope at high power, what would you see?

4. **Infer** Why does a squid have three hearts? *Hint:* Think about where the two smaller hearts are located.

5. **Draw Conclusions** From what you observed, are you able to conclude that the squid has a closed circulatory system?

6. **Infer** How does ink get released from a squid's body?

Build Science Skills

Not all of the organs you observed in this lab are involved in digestion, respiration, circulation, or excretion. In the next chapter, you will study how animals respond, move, support their bodies, and reproduce. Identify organs you observed that carry out one of these functions.

Open-Ended Inquiry • **Real-World Lab**

Chapter 28 Lab **Comparing Bird and Mammal Bones**

Problem

Is the density of an animal's bones related to the way the animal moves?

Introduction

When you hear the word *cattle,* do you see cows moving slowly across a pasture, or do you see a bull charging across a rodeo ring? Cattle are domesticated mammals that were bred to be large and muscular. The endoskeleton of cattle must be able to support a large animal standing, walking, or even running on four legs.

A duck's movement isn't limited to waddling, from place to place. Ducks can also swim and fly. Many species of wild ducks are capable of long, sustained flights as they migrate. By contrast, chickens spend most of their time on the ground pecking for food. At most, a chicken may take flight for a few seconds.

In this lab, you will compare cross sections of bones from cows, ducks, and chickens. You will use your observations to form a hypothesis about the density of the bones. Then, you will design an experiment to test your hypothesis.

Skills Focus

Form a Hypothesis, Design an Experiment, Measure

Materials

- cross sections of chicken, duck, and cow bones
- hand lens
- small chicken, duck, and cow bones
- balance

Build Vocabulary

Term	Definition
relative	Viewed in comparison to other similar values; *related* each to the other
support	To provide evidence for the accuracy of a statement; to argue in favor of

Safety

If you use glass containers in Part B, check them for cracks or chips. After you finish handling the bones, dispose of the gloves and wash your hands thoroughly with soap and warm water.

Pre-Lab Questions

1. **Compare and Contrast** Compare the type of data you will collect in Part A to the type of data you will collect in Part B.

2. **Predict** How might looking at cross sections of bones help you form a hypothesis about the relative density of the bones?

3. **Design an Experiment** Will you need to use samples with the same mass in Part B? Why or why not?

Procedure

Part A: Examine Cross Sections of Bones

By looking at cross sections cut from bones, you will be able to observe the interior, or inside, of the bones.

1. Put on a pair of disposable plastic gloves.
2. Use a hand lens to examine each cross section. Record your observations in Data Table 1. Include a drawing of each cross section.

Data Table 1: Observations		
Animal	**Drawing**	**Observations**
Chicken		
Duck		
Cow		

3. **Predict** Do bird bones and mammal bones have the same density? Give a reason for your prediction.

   Prediction: ______________________________

Part B: Design an Experiment

In Part B, you will use small bones instead of cross sections. You will measure the mass and volume of the bones and calculate the density. The density of a sample is the ratio of the sample's mass to its volume.

$$\text{Density} = \frac{\text{Mass (g)}}{\text{Volume (mL)}}$$

4. **Describe Your Plan** You can use a balance to measure the mass of your samples. You must decide how you will measure the volume of the samples. Record your approach below.

   Experimental Plan: ______________________________

5. Construct a data table in the space below to record your measurements and calculations.
6. Have your teacher review your plan and your data table before you do your procedure. Then, gather the required materials. Put on an apron before you begin the experiment.

Analyze and Conclude

1. **Analyze Data** Did your results support your prediction in Step 3?

2. **Relate Cause and Effect** How could the density of cow bones be adaptive (improve the chance of survival) for cattle?

3. **Relate Cause and Effect** How could the density of bird bones be adaptive for species, such as ducks, that fly long distances?

4. **Draw Conclusions** Is bone density the factor that prevents chickens from flying long distances? Why or why not?

5. **Form a Hypothesis** What factors other than bone density may prevent or limit the ability of chickens to fly? *Hint:* How does the ecological niche of chickens differ from that of their wild ancestors?

Build Science Skills

From your results, you might conclude that bone density is related more to the size of an animal than to its mode of movement. To test this conclusion, choose one of the following activities: determine the bone density of small mammals; read about a dinosaur called *Quetzalcoatlus.*

Chapter 29 Lab **Termite Tracks**

Problem

How can you determine the type of stimulus that triggers a particular response?

Introduction

Termites are insects that live in large colonies. They are known for the damage they cause to trees and wooden buildings. Termites are able to eat wood because symbiotic microorganisms living in a termite's gut digest the wood. Within a colony, most termites are workers. Their tasks include hunting for food and building the structures that protect the colony and queen. As the termites work, they communicate with one another.

Insects use visual cues, sound signals, and chemical signals as methods of communication. In this lab, you will observe a termite's reaction to a line drawing. You will then design an experiment to determine which type of stimulus caused the reaction.

Skills Focus

Form a Hypothesis, Design an Experiment, Draw Conclusions

Materials

- petri dishes
- paper
- scissors
- termite
- small paintbrush
- forceps
- ballpoint pens
- rollerball pens
- felt-tip pens

Build Vocabulary

Term	Definition
pattern	A predictable, orderly arrangement of objects; a way of acting or doing that does not vary
reliability	The quality of being dependable or *reliable;* an experiment that is highly reliable will produce similar results in each trial

Safety

To avoid injuring the termite, use a forceps and small paintbrush to gently handle the termite. If you have glass petri dishes, check for cracks or chips. Do not direct the points of the scissors toward yourself or others. Use the scissors only as directed.

Pre-Lab Questions

1. **Control Variables** Why do you think the instructions ask you to draw a figure eight rather than a straight line?

2. **Draw Conclusions** How will you decide whether a termite has a positive reaction, a negative reaction, or no reaction to a stimulus?

3. **Predict** Read pages 703–704 of your textbook. Which of the signals described could be a stimulus for the termite in this lab? Explain your answer.

Procedure

Part A: Observing Termite Behavior

1. You need to make a paper circle that will fit inside a petri dish. Use the dish to trace a circle on a piece of white paper. Then cut just inside the line as you cut out the circle.
2. Use the red ballpoint pen supplied by your teacher to draw a large figure eight on the paper. Retrace the figure three or four times so that the line is dark and thick.
3. Then place the circle inside the petri dish.
4. Select a termite that seems active from the central supply. Use the forceps and small paintbrush to gently transfer the termite onto the paper in the petri dish.

5. Observe the termite's behavior. Record your observations.

6. Move the termite to a second petri dish where it can remain until you are ready to do Part B. **CAUTION:** Make sure the termite does not escape from the dish.

Part B: Design an Experiment

7. **Communicate** Discuss the behavior you observed in Part A with your partner. Identify two stimuli that might have caused the termite's reaction.

8. **Form a Hypothesis** What stimulus caused the behavior you observed in Part A? Record your hypothesis as an if . . . then statement: If the termite is responding to . . . then it will . . .

   Hypothesis: ______________________

9. **Control Variables** What will your independent variable be? What will your dependent variable be?

   Independent Variable: ______________________

   Dependent Variable: ______________________

10. Describe Your Plan Describe the procedure you will use to test your hypothesis. Focus on how your plan will vary from the experiment you did in Part A. Explain how you will make sure that the termite is responding to the independent variable and not to a different variable. Before you begin, have your teacher review your plan.

Experimental Plan: ______________________________

11. Organize Data Construct a data table in the space below to record the results of your tests.

12. Disposal When you are done with your trials, follow your teacher's instructions for cleanup and disposal of materials.

Analyze and Conclude

1. **Analyze Data** Look at both your results and the results from other groups. Describe any patterns you see.

2. **Draw Conclusions** Termite workers are blind. Use this fact and your data to explain the behavior of the termites.

3. **Perform Error Analysis** How could testing only one or two termites affect the reliability of the results? How could pooling your data with other groups affect the reliability of the results?

4. **Infer** How could the type of behavior you observed help a termite colony to survive? *Hint:* When might it be useful for a termite to follow the path of another termite?

5. **Apply Concepts** Termites can cause considerable damage to buildings that are constructed from wood. Based on your observations, how might owners protect wooden buildings without having to use insecticides?

Build Science Skills

Design an experiment to determine whether the shape of the drawn path affects the behavior of the termite.

Guided Inquiry • Real-World Lab

Chapter 30 Lab **Digestion of Dairy Products**

Problem

How can an enzyme deficiency affect digestion?

Introduction

Milk is an important source of nutrients, especially calcium, which is needed for healthy bones and teeth. Suppliers of milk often add vitamin D, which helps the body absorb calcium and phosphorus. Unfortunately, some people cannot digest lactose, a sugar that is found in milk. The condition is known as lactose intolerance.

People with this condition do not produce enough of the enzyme lactase. This enzyme speeds up the breakdown of lactose into the simple sugars glucose and galactose. Lactose that is not digested moves into the large intestine, where it can cause bloating and cramps. Thus, people who are lactose intolerant try to avoid drinking milk and eating products made from milk.

Lactose, however, can be difficult to avoid. Milk is used to make yogurt, ice cream, sour cream, and cheeses. Milk is also found in foods such as instant breakfast drinks, prepared puddings, and pancake mixes. Also, avoiding all dairy products puts people at risk of having too little calcium and vitamin D in their diets.

Is avoiding diary products the only way to solve the problem of lactose intolerance? In this lab, you will test an over-the-counter product that claims to aid in lactose digestion.

Skills Focus

Control Variables, Infer, Draw Conclusions

Build Vocabulary

Term	Definition
intolerant	Not able to put up with, or *tolerate;* in medicine, easily affected in a negative way by a drug, food, or other substance
claim	To state that something is true, especially without proof or evidence
control	The setup used to test the results of a managed, or *controlled,* experiment

Materials

- spot plate
- sheet of paper
- glucose solution
- milk
- milk-digestion aid
- toothpicks
- glucose test strips
- timer or clock

Safety

If one of the dropper bottles breaks or the contents spill, follow your teacher's instructions for cleanup. Do not taste any of the materials used in the lab. Wash your hands thoroughly with soap and warm water before you leave the lab.

Pre-Lab Questions

1. **Design an Experiment** What is the purpose of the glucose solution?

2. **Control Variables** What is the control in this lab?

3. **Communicate** Read the instructions on the package of glucose test strips. Then briefly describe how you will test your samples for the presence of glucose.

Procedure

1. Put on your goggles and apron.
2. Place your spot plate on a sheet of paper and label four of the wells 1–4.
3. Add 2 drops of the glucose solution to Well 1.
4. Add 2 drops of milk to Well 2.
5. Add 2 drops of the milk-digestion aid to Well 3.
6. Place 2 drops of milk in Well 4. Then, add 1 drop of the milk-digestion aid.
7. After 2 minutes, test all four samples for glucose.

8. Use the data table to record your results.

Data Table: Glucose Test Results		
Well	Sample	Test Result
1	Glucose	
2	Milk	
3	Digestion aid	
4	Milk and digestion	

Analyze and Conclude

1. **Relate Cause and Effect** How could you tell when glucose was present in one of the wells?

2. **Draw Conclusions** What evidence do you have to support the claim that the digestion aid you used actually breaks down lactose?

3. **Control Variables** Why was it necessary to test the digestion aid for glucose?

4. **Apply Concepts** Describe two different ways that the digestion aid could be used to help people that are lactose intolerant.

5. **Predict** Would you expect milk that is labeled "lactose-free" to taste sweeter than untreated milk? Why or why not?

6. **Infer** Suggest a reason why people who are lactose intolerant can tolerate yogurt that contains "live cultures" or "active cultures" of bacteria.

7. **Infer** Scientists now think that lactose intolerance can sometimes "run in families." What does this mean, and what does it suggest about the nature of lactose intolerance?

Build Science Skills

Does lactase work only on lactose, or will it digest other sugars? Design an experiment to determine the effect of lactase on a disaccharide other than lactose.

Guided Inquiry • Real-World Lab

Chapter 31 Lab Testing Sensory Receptors for Touch

Problem

What factors affect a person's ability to detect gentle pressure on skin?

Introduction

Your skin is the boundary between your body and the physical world that surrounds you. So it is not surprising that your skin has many different sensory receptors. Some of those receptors detect changes in temperature. Others respond to tissue injury or damage. Still others are mechanoreceptors that respond when you touch an object or when an object touches you. The receptors for touch are more concentrated in some areas of your skin than in others.

In this lab, you will use a bent paper clip to infer the relative concentration, or density, of receptors for touch in three different areas of your skin. When the density is high, you should be able to sense two touches that are close together. When the density is low, it will be harder to distinguish two touches that are close together.

Skills Focus

Measure, Analyze Data, Draw Conclusions

Materials

- bent paper clips
- metric ruler

Build Vocabulary

Term	Definition
detect	To notice or become aware of
distinguish	To tell apart; to sense as different or *distinct*
density	The quality of being crowded together, closely packed, or dense; a measure of the number of items in a given area
sensitivity	The quality of being able to feel, or *sense,* a stimulus

Safety

Use the paper clip only as instructed. The ends of the clip will be sharp. Use only gentle pressure when applying the ends to skin.

Pre-Lab Questions

1. **Predict** Which area will have the highest density of receptors for gentle pressure—your fingertips, the back of your hand, or your forearm?

   ____

2. **Control Variables** Why must you have your eyes closed while your partner touches your skin with the bent paper clip?

   ____

   ____

3. **Predict** Will you and your partner have the same density of touch receptors in a given area of skin? Give a reason for your prediction.

   ____

   ____

Procedure

You will be working with a partner. Your partner will test your skin and record your data. You will test your partner's skin and record your partner's data. CAUTION: You and your partner should use different paper clips.

1. Practice gently touching the ends of your paper clip to your arm. Note the difference in the sensation when you use both ends of the clip and when you use only one end. CAUTION: Do not apply enough pressure to pierce the skin.
2. Squeeze your partner's paper clip until the ends are 2 cm apart. Then use Steps 3–5 to test the skin on the back of your partner's hand. Choose an area in the center of your partner's hand.

   Get Ready! In Step 3, you will touch the paper clip to your partner's skin 10 times—5 times with two ends and 5 times with one end. You will need to mix up the two-end and one-end touches so that your partner cannot identify a pattern.
3. Make sure your partner's eyes are closed. Touch the paper clip to the back of your partner's hand. After each touch, ask whether your partner felt one end or two. Record the responses in Data Table 1.

4. Decrease the distance between the ends of the paper clip to 1.5 cm and repeat Step 3. Record the responses in Data Table 1.
5. Repeat Step 4 with the distance between the ends at 1 cm, 0.5 cm, and 0.3 cm.

Data Table 1: Back of Hand

	2 cm		1.5 cm		1.0 cm		0.5 cm		0.3 cm	
Touch	Ends Used	Ends Felt	Ends Used	Ends Felt	Ends Used	Ends Felt	Ends Used	Ends Felt	Ends Used	Ends Felt
1										
2										
3										
4										
5										
6										
7										
8										
9										
10										

6. Use the procedure in Steps 2–5 to test the skin on the tip of your partner's index finger. Record the responses in Data Table 2.

Data Table 2: Fingertip

	2 cm		1.5 cm		1.0 cm		0.5 cm		0.3 cm	
Touch	Ends Used	Ends Felt	Ends Used	Ends Felt	Ends Used	Ends Felt	Ends Used	Ends Felt	Ends Used	Ends Felt
1										
2										
3										
4										
5										
6										
7										
8										
9										
10										

7. Repeat the procedure in Steps 2–5 for your partner's forearm. Pick a location halfway between the wrist and the elbow. Record the responses in Data Table 3. Then, return the paper clip to your teacher.

Data Table 3: Forearm

	2 cm		1.5 cm		1.0 cm		0.5 cm		0.3 cm	
Touch	Ends Used	Ends Felt	Ends Used	Ends Felt	Ends Used	Ends Felt	Ends Used	Ends Felt	Ends Used	Ends Felt
1										
2										
3										
4										
5										
6										
7										
8										
9										
10										

8. What was the shortest distance at which your partner could detect two ends of the clip at least three times?

   Back of hand: ______

   Fingertip: ______

   Forearm: ______

9. What was the shortest distance at which you could detect two ends of the clip at least three times?

   Back of hand: ______

   Fingertip: ______

   Forearm: ______

10. Record the class results for Steps 8 and 9 on the board.

Analyze and Conclude

1. **Evaluate** Do your results support the prediction you made in Pre-Lab Question 1 about which area of skin would have the highest density of sense receptors? Explain.

2. **Form a Hypothesis** Why do you think that humans have a higher density of receptors for touch in some areas of skin than in other areas?

3. **Evaluate** Do your results and those of your partner support the prediction you made in Pre-Lab Question 3? Explain.

4. **Form a Hypothesis** What factors could account for variation in sensitivity to touch from one person to another?

5. **Form a Hypothesis** How might activities such as playing a guitar, laying bricks, preparing food, or playing video games affect a person's sensitivity to touch?

6. **Use an Analogy** The phrase *thick skinned* is used to describe people who are not easily affected by other people's criticisms. Relate this meaning of *thick skinned* to how areas of thickened skin could affect a person's sense of touch.

7. **Apply Concepts** Automobile dashboards have many control knobs and buttons. Drivers might have fewer accidents if they did not have to look at these controls to adjust the temperature or change the station on the radio. What could dashboard designers do to make it easier for drivers to keep their eyes on the road?

Build Science Skills

Design an experiment to answer the following question. How does temperature affect the sensitivity to touch?

Guided Inquiry • Skills Lab

Chapter 32 Lab **Comparing Limbs**

Problem

How is the structure of skeletal muscles and bones related to the functions of these body parts?

Introduction

Although humans sometimes use all four limbs to move around, most of the time humans use their legs and arms for distinctly different functions. Legs support the body and carry it from place to place, while arms lift and carry objects.

Despite these differences in tasks, arms and legs have similar overall structures. The upper part of each limb is supported by a single bone, and the lower part of each limb is supported by two bones. Pairs of opposing muscles move the bones around their joints.

Do the limbs of other vertebrates have similar arrangements of bones and muscles? For example, is the wing of a bird similar to a human arm? In this lab, you will begin by comparing the motion of arms and legs. Then, you will dissect a chicken wing and compare its internal structure to that of a human arm.

Skills Focus

Observe, Infer, Compare and Contrast

Materials

- disposable plastic gloves
- chicken wing
- disposable dissection tray
- dissecting scissors
- forceps
- colored pencils or markers

Build Vocabulary

Term	Definition
opposing	Used to describe two objects whose positions or actions are the reverse, or *opposite,* of one another
arrangement	A group of things organized, or *arranged,* in a specific way
extend	To unbend, or straighten out, an object to its full *extent*

Safety

Disease-causing species of *Salmonella* bacteria may be present on raw chicken. To avoid infection, wear gloves and avoid touching your eyes, nose, and mouth. Use the dissecting scissors only as instructed to avoid injuring yourself and others. Wash your hands thoroughly with soap and warm water before leaving the lab.

Pre-Lab Questions

1. **Observe** How will you observe the structure and function of your elbow and knee joints?

2. **Relate Cause and Effect** Why is it important to wear goggles and disposable gloves while examining the chicken wing?

3. **Predict** Will the arrangement of bones and muscles in a chicken wing be similar to the arrangement in a human arm? Why or why not?

Procedure

Part A: Observe the Motion of Human Limbs

1. Extend your right arm with the palm facing down and place two fingers of your left hand on the tip of your right elbow. Bend your right arm and then straighten it out. Describe any movement at the tip of your elbow.

2. Extend your right arm with the palm facing down and place two fingers of your left hand on the tip of your right elbow. Keep your arm straight while you rotate your hand so that your palm faces up, and then rotate your hand back to its original position. Describe any movement at the tip of your elbow.

3. Keep your right arm extended with the palm facing down. Place the fingers of your left hand under your right forearm just above the wrist. Rotate your hand so that your palm faces up, and then rotate your hand back to its original position. Describe what you feel.

____

____

____

4. Sit in a chair with your feet flat on the floor. Place the fingertips of your right hand on the middle of your kneecap. Raise your lower leg. Describe what happens to your kneecap.

____

____

5. Raise your lower leg again. Try to turn your foot so that the sole of the foot is facing up. Describe what happens.

____

____

6. Look at the drawings in Figure 1. Identify the muscles that bend and straighten the elbow and knee joints.

____

____

Figure 1 Muscles in a human arm and leg

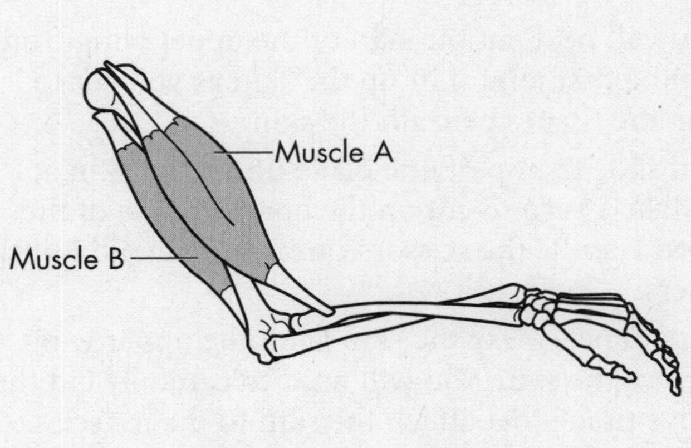

Part B: Observe the Structure of a Chicken Wing

7. Put on goggles and gloves.
8. Place a chicken wing in the dissecting tray and observe its structure. On the drawing in Figure 2, label the upper wing, lower wing, joints, and wing tip.

Figure 2 External Anatomy of a Chicken Wing

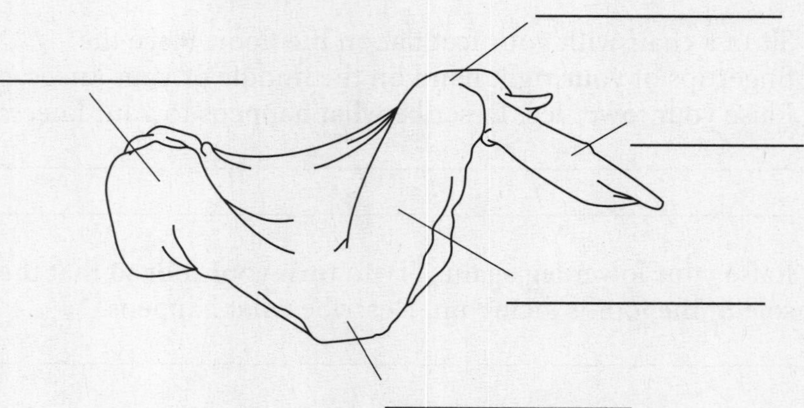

9. Bend and straighten the joint between the upper wing and the lower wing. Bend the joint between the lower wing and the wing tip. Describe the motion you observe.

____

____

____

____

Get Ready! You will next cut the skin of the upper wing from the shoulder to the first joint. Lift up the skin as you cut to avoid damaging the tissues beneath the skin.

10. To start the cut, slide the tip of one blade under the skin at the shoulder. Make a second cut on the opposite side of the wing. **CAUTION:** Handle the scissors carefully to avoid injuring yourself or others.
11. Use your fingers to peel away the skin from the upper wing. To completely remove the skin, you will need to carefully cut the bits of connective tissue that attach the skin to the muscles.
12. Repeat Steps 10 and 11 to remove the skin from the lower wing.

13. After you remove the skin, use the forceps or your fingers to gently separate the muscles from one another. Use the space below to make a sketch that shows the muscles.

14. Pull on each muscle, one at a time, to see whether the muscle bends or straightens a joint. Identify the opposing pairs of muscles and color-code these pairs on your drawing.
15. Trace each muscle to the joint between the upper and lower wing. Cut the shiny white tendons that connect the muscles to the joint and peel back the muscles.
16. In the space below, sketch the arrangement of the bones around the joint.

17. Follow your teacher's instructions for disposal of the chicken wings, dissecting trays, gloves, and paper towels. Wash the scissors and forceps and any surfaces you might have touched while doing the dissection. When you are done, wash your hands thoroughly with soap and warm water.

Analyze and Conclude

1. **Compare and Contrast** How was the motion at your elbow joint similar to the motion at your knee joint? How was it different?

2. **Infer** How is the ability to rotate the bones in the forearm an advantage for humans?

3. **Infer** How is it an advantage for the human knee to have a smaller range of motion than the human elbow?

4. **Observe** In the chicken wing, where were the muscles that bend and straighten the joint between the upper and lower wing located?

5. **Compare and Contrast** Identify structures in the chicken wing that are homologous to bones and joints in the human arm. Use the drawings in your textbook, Figure 1 in this lab, and your observations of the chicken wing.

Build Science Skills

View prepared slides of skeletal muscle and bone. On a separate sheet of paper, draw a sketch for each type of tissue. Then, write a paragraph explaining how the structure of each type of tissue is adapted to its function.

Guided Inquiry • Design Your Own Lab

Chapter 33 Lab Tidal Volume and Lung Capacity

Problem

What factors can affect lung capacity?

Introduction

When you inhale, air rushes into your lungs. The amount of air that rushes in during a normal breath is called the *tidal volume.* Your lungs have the capacity to accept a much larger volume of air than you typically inhale. For example, you might be asked to take a deep breath during a medical exam. Scientists use the term *vital capacity* to describe the largest volume of air that you can exhale after you take a deep breath.

In this lab, you will measure tidal volume and vital capacity. Then you will design an experiment to investigate a factor that can affect vital capacity.

Skills Focus

Measure, Design an Experiment, Interpret Graphs

Materials

- round balloons
- metric ruler
- meterstick

Build Vocabulary

Term	Definition
capacity	The amount of space that can be filled
estimate	A close, but not exact, measurement or calculation
correspond	To have a clearly defined relationship; such as between an object's diameter and volume
convert	To change from one form to another
ratio	The relationship between two numbers expressed as the quotient of one divided by the other

Safety ⚠

Do not test your vital capacity if you are ill or if you have difficulty breathing. If at any point you feel faint or dizzy, stop what you are doing and sit down. Ask your partner to inform your teacher of the problem. If you have an allergy to latex, do not handle the balloons. Make sure you and your partner use different balloons.

Pre-Lab Questions

1. **Control Variables** What is the one difference between the procedures in Part A and Part B?

____

____

2. **Design an Experiment** Why must you use round balloons for this experiment?

____

____

3. **Predict** Which do you think will be greater—your estimated vital capacity or your measured vital capacity? Why?

____

____

____

____

Procedure

Part A: Measuring Tidal Volume

1. Stretch a round balloon lengthwise several times.
2. Inhale normally, and then exhale normally into the balloon. Immediately pinch the balloon shut so that no air escapes.

   Get Ready! You will hold the balloon while your partner measures its diameter.
3. Keep pinching the balloon as you place it on a flat surface. Have your partner measure the diameter of the balloon at its widest point as shown in Figure 1 on the next page.
4. Record the measurement in Data Table 1.
5. Allow the air out of the balloon. Then, repeat Steps 2–4 two more times.
6. Calculate the mean for the measurements from the three trials. Add the volumes and divide by three. Record your answer in Data Table 1.

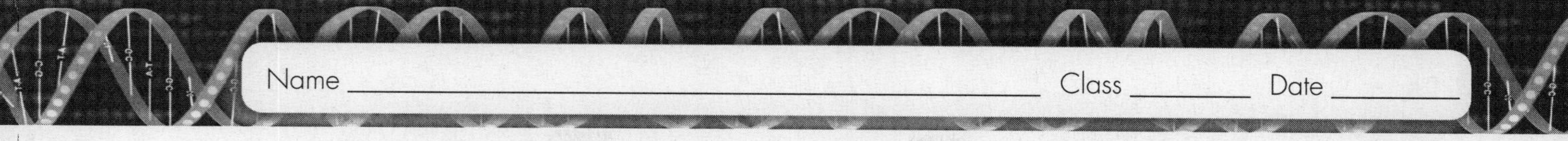

Figure 1 How to measure the diameter of the balloon

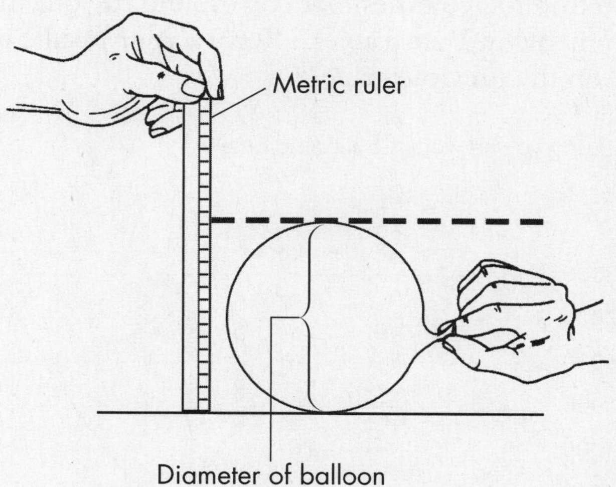

Part B: Measuring Vital Capacity

7. Take as deep a breath as possible. Then, exhale as much air as you can from your lungs into the balloon. Immediately pinch the balloon shut so that no air escapes.
8. Keep pinching the balloon as you place it on a flat surface. Have your partner measure the diameter of the balloon at its widest point. Record the measurement in Data Table 1.
9. Allow the air out of the balloon. Then, repeat Steps 7 and 8 two more times.
10. Calculate the mean for the measurements from the three trials and record your answer in Data Table 1.

Data Table 1: Balloon Diameter (cm)		
Trial	Tidal Volume	Vital Capacity
1		
2		
3		
Mean		

Data Table 2: Volume (cm^3)		
Trial	Tidal Volume	Vital Capacity
1		
2		
3		
Mean		

11. On the graph in Figure 2, balloon diameter in centimeters is plotted against volume in cubic centimeters (cm^3). Use the graph to find the volumes that correspond to your diameter measurements in Data Table 1. Record your results in Data Table 2 on the previous page.

Figure 2 Lung volume versus balloon diameter

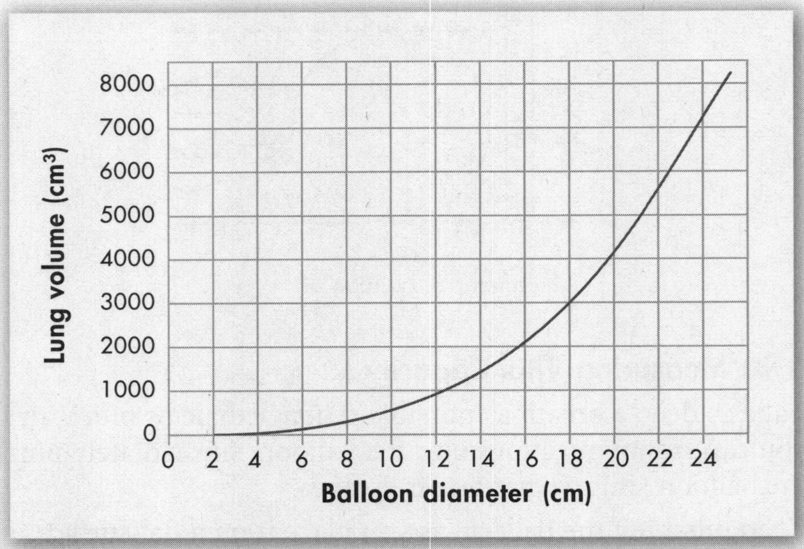

Part C: Estimating Vital Capacity

Research has shown that vital capacity is related to the surface area of a person's body. You can estimate your surface area if you know your height and your mass.

12. You can use the meterstick to measure your height in centimeters. Or you can convert your height in inches to centimeters by multiplying the number of inches by 2.54.

Height: ______________________

13. To convert your mass in pounds to kilograms, multiply the number of pounds by 0.454.

Mass: ______________________

14. Use Figure 3 to estimate the surface area of your body. Find your height on the scale on the left. Find your mass on the scale on the right. Use a ruler to draw a straight line between those points. The location where the line crosses the middle scale is your estimated surface area.

Surface area: ______________________

Figure 3 Estimated surface area based on height and mass

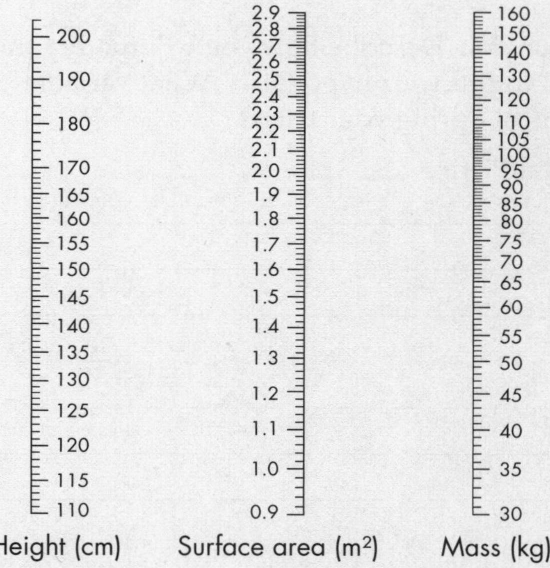

Get Ready! To calculate the estimated vital capacity of your lungs, you will multiply your surface area in square meters by the ratio of vital capacity to surface area. The ratio is 2000 cubic centimeters per square meter for females. For males, the ratio is 2500 cubic centimeters per square meter.

15. Use the correct ratio to calculate and record your answer.

Estimated vital capacity = surface area (m^2) × ratio $\left(\frac{cm^3}{m^2}\right)$

Estimated vital capacity: ______________________

Part D: Design Your Own Lab

You were probably standing up when you measured your vital capacity. Would the results have been different if you were seated? Would your posture when seated affect the results?

16. Form a Hypothesis How will changing the position of your body affect your vital capacity? Record the hypothesis you will test to answer this question.

Hypothesis: ____

____

17. Describe Your Plan Describe how you will modify the procedure from Part B to test your hypothesis. What variables will you need to control during your trials?

Experimental Plan: ____

____

____

____

____

____

____

____

18. Construct a data table in the space below. Make as many rows for recording data as the number of trials you plan to do. Include a row for recording the mean of your trials.

Name ______________________ Class ________ Date ________

Analyze and Conclude

1. **Analyze Data** How did your estimated vital capacity compare with your measured vital capacity? Was your prediction in Pre-Lab Question 3 correct?

2. **Draw Conclusions** What could have caused any difference between the estimated value and the measured value?

3. **Design an Experiment** Why is it important to do more than one trial when making measurements?

4. **Infer** In Step 15, why did females and males use different ratios to calculate estimated vital capacity?

5. **Analyze Data** How did your position affect the vital capacity of your lungs? Suggest an explanation for any difference you found.

6. **Perform Error Analysis** In Part A, why might the volume in the first trial be smaller than in the second and third trials? How could the procedure be adjusted to avoid this result.

7. **Predict** How would smoking affect lung capacity, and why?

Build Science Skills

Use the class data to determine whether aerobic exercise affects vital capacity. As a class, determine which information you need about each data point to rule out the effect of other variables.

Guided Inquiry • Forensics Lab

Chapter 34 Lab Diagnosing Endocrine Disorders

Problem

Can you diagnose an endocrine disorder based on a patient's symptoms?

Introduction

Glands in the endocrine system secrete chemical messengers called hormones. Feedback mechanisms regulate the amounts of hormones released. When the levels of hormones in the blood are normal, reactions in the body take place at a normal rate and homeostasis is maintained.

Sometimes, however, endocrine glands do not respond properly to feedback mechanisms. A gland might produce too much of a hormone, or it might produce too little. Or, a receptor might not respond to a hormone as expected. Either way, some reactions do not occur at a normal rate. As a result, a person may experience certain symptoms, which prompt a visit to a primary care doctor.

The doctor will ask the patient some questions and do a brief medical exam. If the doctor suspects an endocrine disorder, he or she will refer the patient to a specialist. A doctor who diagnoses and treats disorders of the endocrine system is an endocrinologist. In this lab, you will play the role of an endocrinologist. Based on a patient's symptoms, you will form a hypothesis about the cause and consider what should be done to confirm the diagnosis.

Skills Focus

Analyze Data, Draw Conclusions, Relate Cause and Effect

Build Vocabulary

Term	Definition
normal	Behaving in an expected way; typical
symptom	A sign that something is present or exists
diagnose	To identify a disease or disorder in a patient through an interview, physical exam, or tests
confirm	To support or establish the truth

Pre-Lab Questions

1. **Interpret Tables** When patients complain of fatigue they are usually referring to a lack of energy or motivation. Which conditions listed in the table have fatigue as a symptom?

2. **Apply Concepts** Why do doctors typically use blood tests to diagnose endocrine disorders?

Procedure

You will use your knowledge of hormones and the table provided to diagnose the patients described in four case studies. Column 2 in the table lists common complaints that a patient might make. Column 3 lists the results of tests that a doctor could order to confirm or rule out an initial diagnosis. Most lab tests involve the analysis of blood or urine. If you do not recall the functions of any hormones mentioned in the table, look up this information in your textbook.

Case Study 1

A woman complains of muscle weakness, anxiety, and depression. Which disorders listed in the table could account for these symptoms? What other symptoms might you look for or ask about to distinguish between these disorders?

Case Study 2

A man broke a bone in his arm. The doctor who set his arm was concerned that the man's bones were unusually weak. The man also complained of fatigue and nausea. What disorder could this patient have? What could you do to confirm this diagnosis?

Name ______________________ Class ________ Date ________

Case Study 3

A man complains of fatigue. He has lost weight, although he is not trying to. His blood glucose level is normal, but the level of sodium in his blood is low. What test would you order next, and why?

____

____

____

Case Study 4

A patient has a swollen thyroid gland, which is a symptom of both hyperthyroidism and hypothyroidism. Before you order any tests, what two measurements could you make during an exam to help determine the cause. Why would these measurements be helpful?

____

____

____

Endocrine Disorders		
Disorder	**Symptoms**	**Lab Test Results**
Addison's Disease	Fatigue, muscle weakness, weight loss, increased pigment in the skin	High potassium and low sodium levels in blood; high ACTH level in blood, low cortisol level in blood
Cushing's Syndrome	Muscle weakness, backache, anxiety, depression, extra fat deposits on the back of the neck and upper back, irregular menstrual cycle in females	High levels of cortisol in blood
Hyperparathyroidism	Excessive thirst, weakened or broken bones, fatigue, nausea	High calcium levels in blood; high parathyroid hormone levels in blood
Hyperthyroidism	Nervousness, rapid heart rate, high body temperature, excessive sweating, weight loss, irregular menstrual cycle in females	High thyroxine level in blood, low TSH level in blood
Hypothyroidism	Muscle weakness, depression, fatigue, weight gain, slow heart rate, low body temperature and intolerance of cold	Low thyroxine level in blood, high TSH level in blood
Type I Diabetes Mellitus	Frequent urination, excessive thirst, weight loss	Glucose present in urine, high blood glucose level, islet cell antibody in blood
Type II Diabetes Mellitus	Frequent urination, excessive thirst	Glucose present in urine, high blood glucose level, no islet cell antibodies in blood

Name ______________________ Class ________ Date ________

Analyze and Conclude

1. **Draw Conclusions** Why is it important for a doctor to ask a patient questions in addition to doing a physical exam?

2. **Relate Cause and Effect** Why would a doctor expect to see low levels of TSH in the blood of a patient with hyperthyroidism?

3. **Compare and Contrast** How are Type I and Type II diabetes similar?

4. **Compare and Contrast** How are Type I and Type II diabetes different?

5. **Infer** A patient is told not to eat or drink anything for 12 hours before having blood drawn to test the level of glucose. Why do you think it is necessary for the patient to fast before the test?

Build Science Skills

On a separate sheet of paper, write your own case study of a patient with an endocrine disorder. Use the case studies in the lab as models. Give your description to a classmate who will try to diagnose the disorder.

Guided Inquiry • Forensics Lab

Chapter 35 Lab Detecting Lyme Disease

Problem

How can a blood test be used to detect Lyme disease?

Introduction

Lyme disease is caused by the bacterium *Borrelia burgdorferi*. The bacteria can be spread through the bite of a tiny organism called a deer tick. Campers, hikers, and gardeners all risk exposure to these disease-carrying ticks. One possible early sign of Lyme disease is a bull's-eye-shaped rash that appears around the site of the tick bite. Other possible symptoms include fever, fatigue, muscle and joint pain, sore throat, and headache.

Many of these symptoms are very common and can be caused by multiple illnesses. In addition, not everyone who has Lyme disease shows all these symptoms. Thus, Lyme disease can be difficult to diagnose.

There is no direct test for the presence of the bacteria that cause Lyme disease. Instead, doctors will order a blood test to see if there are antibodies to the bacteria in a patient's blood. This test is called an Enzyme-Linked Immunosorbent Assay (ELISA). There are several steps in an ELISA. If the technician sees a color change after the final step, the test is considered positive. Once the diagnosis is confirmed, Lyme disease can be treated with antibiotics.

In this lab, you will not be doing an actual ELISA, nor will you be testing actual blood samples. Instead, you will use a procedure that simulates, or imitates, the steps in an ELISA.

Build Vocabulary

Term	Definition
detect	To notice or become aware of
solution	A mixture in which all the substances are spread evenly throughout the mixture
infer	To offer a reasoned opinion, or *inference,* based on observations and experience
flush	To clean or wash out an object by pouring water (or another liquid) into, on, or through it

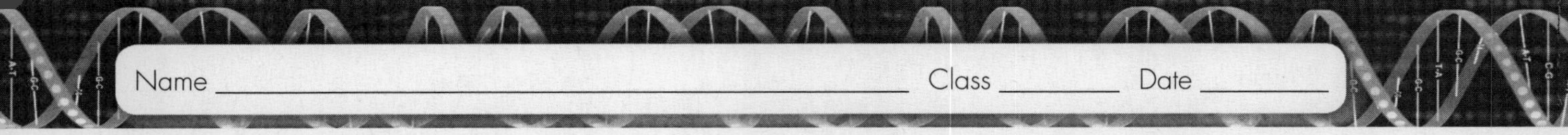

Skills Focus

Control Variables, Analyze Data, Draw Conclusions

Materials

- well plate
- permanent marker
- sheet of white paper
- 400-mL beaker
- 100-mL beaker
- distilled water
- 2 micropipettes
- test solutions

Safety

Whenever you are working with unknown solutions, you should wear goggles and gloves. Wash your hands thoroughly with soap and warm water before leaving the lab.

Pre-Lab Questions

1. **Sequence** Use a flowchart to show the order in which the solutions will be added to the well plate.

2. **Infer** What is the advantage of having a control for a positive test and a control for a negative test?

3. **Control Variables** Why must you rinse the micropipette with distilled water before using it to add a different solution to the well plate?

 •

Procedure

The test solutions that you will use come in small bottles, which your group will need to share with other groups. Your teacher will decide the order in which groups will receive the solutions.

If you are the first group to receive the test solutions, use your flowchart to line the bottles up in the order that you will use them in the procedure. As soon as you are done with a bottle, carefully pass it along to the next group. The last group to receive the bottles should return them to your teacher at the end of the lab.

1. Label your well plate as shown in Figure 1. S1 and S2 stand for Sample 1 and Sample 2.
2. Place the plate on a sheet of white paper. The paper will provide a clean spot to set down a micropipette, if necessary.

Figure 1 Labeled well plate

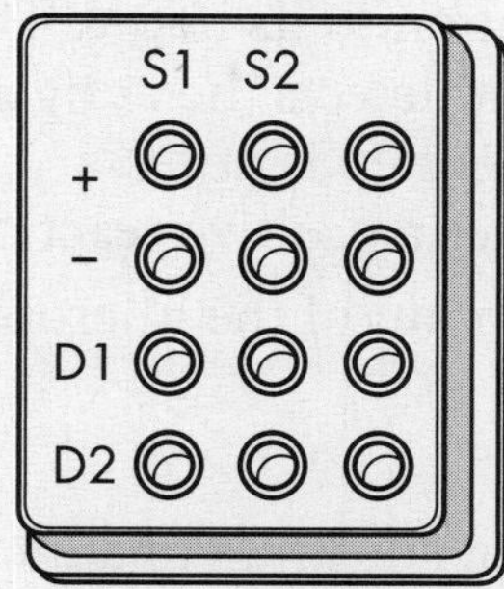

3. Put on your safety goggles and gloves.
4. Pour about 250 mL of distilled water into a large beaker. Pour about 30 mL of water from the large beaker into a small beaker.
5. Use a micropipette to place 2 drops of antigen in all 8 marked wells. Return any unused solution to its bottle.
   CAUTION: Never let the micropipette touch any of the solutions in the wells.
6. Use the distilled water in the small beaker to flush the antigen solution out of the micropipette.
7. Discard the water in the small beaker. Replace it with water from the large beaker.
8. Let the well plate sit for 5 minutes, which will allow time for the antigen to attach to the walls of the wells.
9. Use the micropipette to add 2 drops of the negative control to the wells next to the minus sign (–). Return any unused solution to its bottle.
10. Use the distilled water in the small beaker to flush the negative control solution out of the micropipette.
11. Discard the water in the small beaker and replace it with water from the large beaker.

12. Use the micropipette to add 2 drops of the positive control to the wells next to the plus sign (+). Return any unused solution to its bottle.
13. Flush the positive control solution out of the micropipette with distilled water. Discard and replace the water.
14. Use the micropipette to add 2 drops of Donor 1 solution to the D1 wells. Return any unused solution to its bottle.
15. Flush the Donor 1 solution out of the micropipette. Discard and replace the water.
16. Use the micropipette to add 2 drops of the Donor 2 solution to the D2 wells. Return any unused solution to its bottle.
17. Discard the micropipette.
18. Let the well plate sit for 5 minutes.
19. Use a new micropipette to add 2 drops of secondary antibody to all 8 wells. Return any unused solution to its bottle. The secondary antibody is a substance that detects the antigen-antibody complex and binds to it. This step is necessary to produce the color change that indicates a positive reaction.
20. Flush the secondary antibody solution out of the micropipette. Discard and replace the water.
21. Let the well plate sit for 5 minutes.
22. Use the micropipette to add 2 drops of substrate to all 8 wells. Return any unused solution to its bottle.
23. In wells where the secondary antibody combined with an antigen-antibody complex, a reaction occurs when the substrate is added. This reaction will produce a color change. Observe the wells, and record your results in the data table.

Data Table: Results of ELISA Simulation

Sample	Column S1	Column S2
Negative Control		
Positive Control		
Donor 1		
Donor 2		

Analyze and Conclude

1. **Control Variables** Why was it important to keep the micropipette from touching any of the solutions in the wells?

2. **Design an Experiment** What was the purpose of having two sets of wells with exactly the same contents?

3. **Draw Conclusions** Donor 1 and Donor 2 are patients who were bitten by deer ticks. Which patient has Lyme disease? How do you know?

4. **Infer** Why did you have to wait 5 minutes in Step 18?

5. **Infer** Why did you have to wait 5 minutes in Step 21?

6. **Infer** A hiker removes a deer tick from his leg and develops a bull's-eye-shaped rash four days later. An ELISA run on blood drawn the next day is negative. An ELISA run on blood drawn a few weeks later is positive. The hiker was not exposed to ticks during the time between the two tests. Suggest a reason for the initial negative test.

Build Science Skills

Research whether Lyme disease is a problem in your area. If so, find out at what time of year and in what kinds of locations the risk is greatest.

Data Analysis 1 Picturing Data

Goal

Explore different types of graphs and draw a line of best fit.

Skills Focus

Interpret Graphs, Analyze Data

Build Connections

A graph can be thought of as a "picture" of data. Graphs are useful for scientists because they can reveal patterns or trends that words and tables cannot. Three types of graphs typically used to display scientific data are circle graphs, bar graphs, and line graphs.

Circle graphs, or pie charts, display data as part of a whole. Each "slice" represents a distinct category. Circle graphs can be used only when you have data for all categories you are comparing. You could use a circle to compare the amount of time you spent sleeping, being active, or being inactive during a 24-hour period.

Bar graphs are used to compare data from different categories. In a bar graph, the dependent variable represents a category that is not represented by a number. For example, you could use a bar graph to compare extinction rates for different types of animals. The animal groups are marked along the *x*-axis. The rate of extinction, the independent variable, is plotted along the *y*-axis.

Line graphs are used when you have numerical data for both the dependent and independent variables. A line graph shows how one variable changes in response to another variable. The independent, or manipulated, variable is plotted along the *y*-axis. The dependent, or responding, variable is plotted along the *x*-axis. By drawing a line from point to point on the graph, you may notice a trend that will allow you to make a prediction. Sometimes, if the data are scattered, you will need to draw a line of best fit to help you see a trend. A line of best fit is a straight line drawn through the data points so the same number of points are above the line as below the line.

In this four-part activity, you will convert data tables into graphs. In Parts A and B, you will need to decide which type of graph to make.

Name ______________________ Class __________ Date __________

Part A: Trees of the Rain Forest

A rain forest is divided into four layers. The bottom layer is the *forest floor,* which gets almost no light because of the trees. The next three layers are characterized by different types of trees and the height they reach above the forest floor. The *understory* is 0–10 meters above the forest floor. It has young trees, shrubs, and other plants. It also includes some species of trees that are short when full grown. The *canopy* is a dense layer that forms 10–40 meters above the forest floor.

Most species of the rain forest live in the canopy. The leaves of canopy trees spread out, forming a "roof" over the rain forest. The canopy lets in very little light and tends to spread raindrops from tropical downpours. The uppermost layer is the *emergent layer,* which is 40–70 meters above the forest floor. A few trees grow above the canopy. They either get full sun or drenching rain. Use the grid on page 221 to make an appropriate graph.

Trees of the Rain Forest

Tree	Full Height (m)
Kapok	70
Teak	46
Ebony	30
African yellowwood	20
African oil palm	18
Raffia palm	12
Cape fig	7

Analyze and Conclude

1. **Evaluate** What type of graph did you use and why? Identify the dependent and independent variables.

____

____

2. **Interpret Data** How many and what types of trees are found in each of the rain-forest layers? Suggest a way to highlight this information on your graph.

____

____

____

____

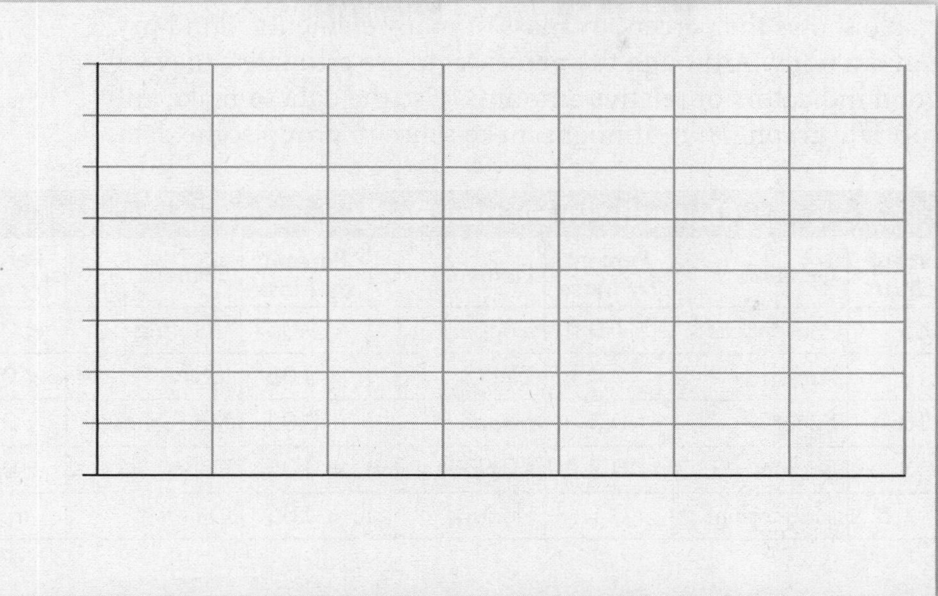

Build Science Skills

Monkeys, flying squirrels, tree frogs, and anteaters are common to the rain forest. Each one occupies a different layer. Based on the information given, match each animal to a layer of the rain forest and explain your choice.

____

____

____

____

____

Name ______________________ Class __________ Date __________

Part B: Elements in the Human Body

The table shows the percent by mass of many elements found in the human body. Although the percentages are estimates, they are good indicators of relative amounts. Use the data to make an appropriate graph. *Hint:* It might make sense to group some data.

Elements in Human Body

Element	Percent by Mass	Element	Percent by Mass	Element	Percent by Mass	Element	Percent by Mass
Oxygen	65	Phosphorus	1.0	Copper	< 0.05	Chlorine	< 0.05
Carbon	18	Potassium	0.4	Zinc	< 0.05	Iodine	< 0.05
Hydrogen	10	Sulfur	0.3	Selenium	< 0.05	Manganese	< 0.05
Nitrogen	3	Sodium	0.2	Molybdenum	< 0.05	Cobalt	< 0.05
Calcium	1.5	Magnesium	0.1	Fluorine	< 0.05	Others	trace

Analyze and Conclude

1. **Evaluate** What type of graph did you use and why? Are there variables in this graph? Explain.

____

____

2. **Interpret Data** List the elements in the human body that are at least 1 percent of mass. Overall, what percent of body mass do these elements add up to?

____

____

____

Build Science Skills

Most of the mass of the human body is water. The mass of water can vary from 60 to 90 percent. Do the data support this fact? *Hint:* Think of the chemical formula for water.

___

___

___

___

Part C: Hare and Lynx Pelts

One of the best-known examples of a population study came from the records of a fur-trading company in Canada. The Hudson's Bay Company (HBC) kept records of its catches of hare and lynx over a long period of time. Charles Elton, an English ecologist, used the records to hypothesize about cycles in animal populations. The table shows the HBC data for hares and lynx pelts taken between 1845 and 1899.

Comparison of HBC Hare and Lynx Pelts

Year	Hare	Lynx	Year	Hare	Lynx
1845	20	32	1873	70	20
1847	20	50	1875	100	34
1849	52	12	1877	92	45
1851	83	10	1879	70	40
1853	64	13	1881	10	15
1855	68	36	1883	11	15
1857	83	15	1885	137	60
1859	12	12	1887	137	80
1861	36	6	1889	18	26
1863	150	6	1891	22	18
1865	110	65	1893	52	37
1867	60	70	1895	83	50
1869	7	40	1897	18	35
1871	10	9	1899	10	12

Name ______________________ Class __________ Date __________

Analyze and Conclude

1. **Analyze Data** Assume that the number of hare pelts taken between 1845 and 1899 are representative of the larger population of hare in the wild. What pattern do you see in the graph of the data for hare pelts? Think about patterns in numbers and time.

____

____

____

2. **Graph** Add a line to the graph for lynx pelts taken between 1845 and 1899. Describe the trend you see.

____

____

____

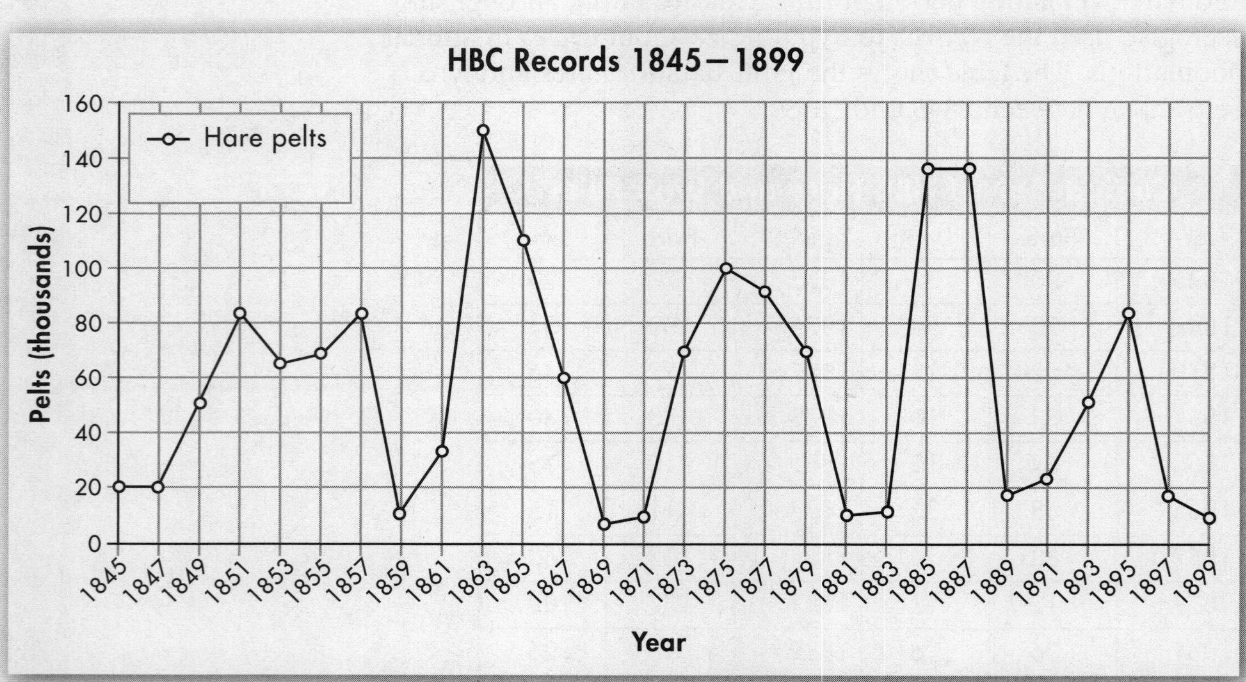

Build Science Skills

Write a hypothesis that accounts for the trend you identified in Question 2. *Hint:* Think in terms of a food chain.

____

____

____

____

Part D: Fat Content of Sandwiches

The table compares the fat content and number of Calories in some common sandwiches. Although the serving sizes vary, you should be able to draw some conclusions about the relationship between fat content and number of Calories. You will use the data to make a graph with a line of best fit.

Sandwich	Fat (g)	Calories
Ham and cheese	15.5	352
Roast beef	18.8	346
Peanut butter and jelly	20.3	439
Turkey	5.0	297
Steak	14.1	459
Cheeseburger	22.7	451
Tuna salad	19.0	383
Egg salad	16.0	380

Analyze and Conclude

1. **Organize Data** Before you plot the data points, you need to choose a dependent and independent variable. Explain your choice.

______

______

2. **Graph** Plot the data points. Then draw a line of best fit.

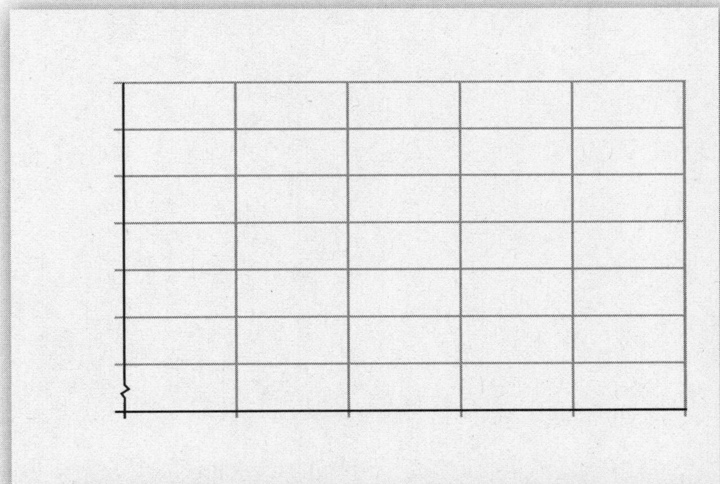

3. **Interpret Graphs** What trend do you see when comparing fat content in the sandwiches to number of Calories?

____

____

Build Science Skills

The data in the table is not dependent on the serving size of the sandwich. Do you think data based on equal serving sizes would change the overall trend in the graph? Why or why not?

____

____

____

Name ______________________ Class ________ Date ________

Data Analysis 2 **What's in a Diet?**

Goal

Interpret and draw circle graphs.

Skills Focus

Interpret Graphs, Analyze Data

Build Connections

The siamang gibbon is an ape that lives in the rain forests of Southeast Asia. These gibbons depend on more than 160 species of rain-forest trees and other plants for food. Many acres of rain forests are being cleared for palm-oil and coffee plantations. The circle graph below provides a picture of the diet of siamangs that live in Malaysia. Use the graph to answer the Analyze and Conclude questions.

Diet of Siamang Gibbons in Malaysia

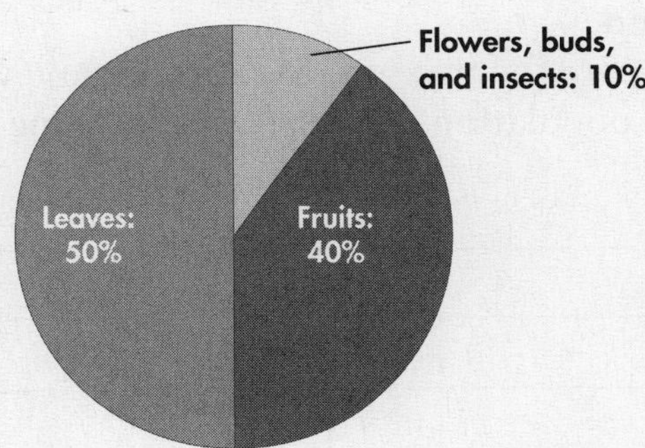

Analyze and Conclude

1. **Interpret Graphs** Food is a source of energy. What is the biggest source of energy for the siamang gibbons of Malaysia? How do you know?

____

____

2. **Analyze Data** Insects make up a small part of the diet of the Malaysian siamangs' diet. Is it 10 percent, less than 10 percent, or greater than 10 percent? How do you know?

____

____

3. Infer Fruit grows from the flowers of fruit trees. After insects pollinate the flowers, the fruit can develop. Suppose a flower-eating insect species invades the gibbon's rain-forest habitat. What are two possible ways the insect invasion could change the siamangs' diet?

____

____

____

____

4. Predict What might happen to the siamang gibbons if the trees in the rain forests were cut down? Explain.

____

____

____

Build Science Skills

The siamangs that live in Sumatra eat more fruit than the siamangs that live in Malaysia. Fruit makes up 60 percent of their diet, and leaves make up 30 percent. The remaining 10 percent is made up of flowers, buds, and insects. Use the space below to make a circle graph that shows the diet of the siamang gibbons that live in Sumatra. Remember to include a title. Use the circle graph on the previous page as a model.

When you are done, compare the two graphs. Identify one way in which the diets of the two siamang populations are the same and one way in which they are different.

____

____

____

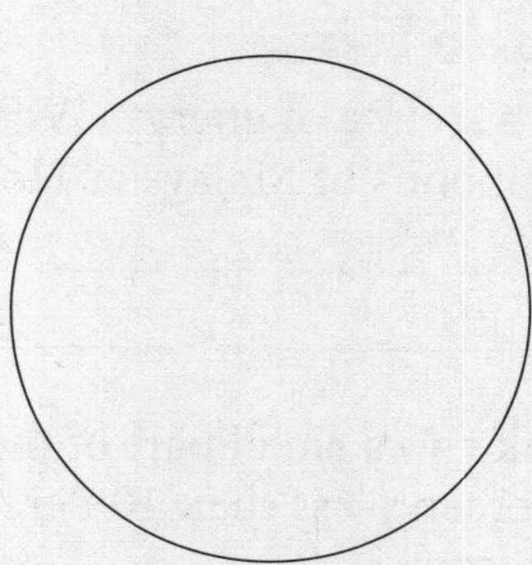

Lesson 2.3

Data Analysis 3 Comparing Fatty Acids

Goal

Analyze data to understand properties of fatty acids.

Skills Focus

Analyze Data, Classify, Compare and Contrast

Build Connections

To stay healthy, you need *some* fat in your diet, but not too much. Fat is a good source of energy, acts as a shock absorber for your organs, and helps your body retain heat. Many parts of your body, such as your brain, are rich in fat.

The type of fat you eat is as important as the amount of fat you eat. Fish, nuts, vegetable oils, and seeds tend to be high in *unsaturated* fats. A molecule of unsaturated fat has at least some double bonds between its carbon atoms. Animal products, such as butter, tend to be higher in *saturated* fats. A molecule of saturated fat has only single bonds between its carbon atoms.

Fats are formed from glycerol and fatty acids. The table compares some properties of fatty acids with 18 carbon atoms. Use the table to explore those properties.

Effect of Carbon Bonds on Melting Point

Fatty Acid	Number of Carbons	Number of Double Bonds	Melting Point (°C)
Stearic acid	18	0	69.6
Oleic acid	18	1	14
Linoleic acid	18	2	–5
Linolenic acid	18	3	–11

Analyze and Conclude

1. **Read Tables** What properties of fatty acids does the table provide data on?

____

____

2. **Interpret Tables** Which property was used to organize the list of fatty acids? Explain.

____

3. **Classify** One of the fatty acids is saturated. Which one is it? How do you know?

4. **Relate Cause and Effect** A melting point is the temperature at which a substance changes from a solid to a liquid. As the number of carbon-carbon double bonds increases, what happens to the melting point of the fatty acids?

5. **Compare and Contrast** Average room temperature is described as 70°F, which is 22°C. Which of the fatty acids in the table would be solid at this temperature? Which would be liquid?

6. **Analyze Data** The oils and fats that people cook with usually have a combination of fatty acids. Human body temperature is about 37°C. Fatty acids with a melting point higher than 37°C are less healthy than other fatty acids for most people. Which of the four fatty acids have a melting point lower than 37°C?

7. **Apply Concepts** Safflower oil is about 78 percent linoleic acid. Butter fat melts at 35°C (95°F). Shortening is 100 percent saturated fat. For health reasons, which of these items should you avoid when possible? Explain your reasoning.

Build Science Skills

Suppose you get a job as a cook at a science research base in Antarctica. It's −9°C outside, and you're bored. You want to show a fellow kitchen worker the difference between the *linoleic* acid in safflower oil and the *linolenic* acid in fish oil. Design a simple experiment that will show how their properties differ.

Data Analysis 4 The 10-Percent Rule

Goal

Relate a food web to an energy pyramid.

Skills Focus

Interpret Visuals, Calculate, Predict

Build Connections

All organisms need energy. Energy enters most ecosystems from the sun and flows through the ecosystem by way of food webs. Pyramids of energy show the energy flow. Energy flows from one level to the next when organisms at a higher level eat organisms from a lower one. Humans tend to be at the top of the pyramid.

Primary producers are the base, or bottom level, of a pyramid of energy. Most primary producers turn light energy into food through photosynthesis. When a first-level consumer eats a primary producer, that consumer gets energy from the producer. Only 10 percent of the energy in the organisms at one level gets stored as energy in the bodies of the animals that eat them. Most of the energy is lost as heat or is used up by the body processes of the organism. This rule is called the "10-percent rule."

Analyze and Conclude

Use this energy pyramid to answer Analyze and Conclude Questions 1–6.

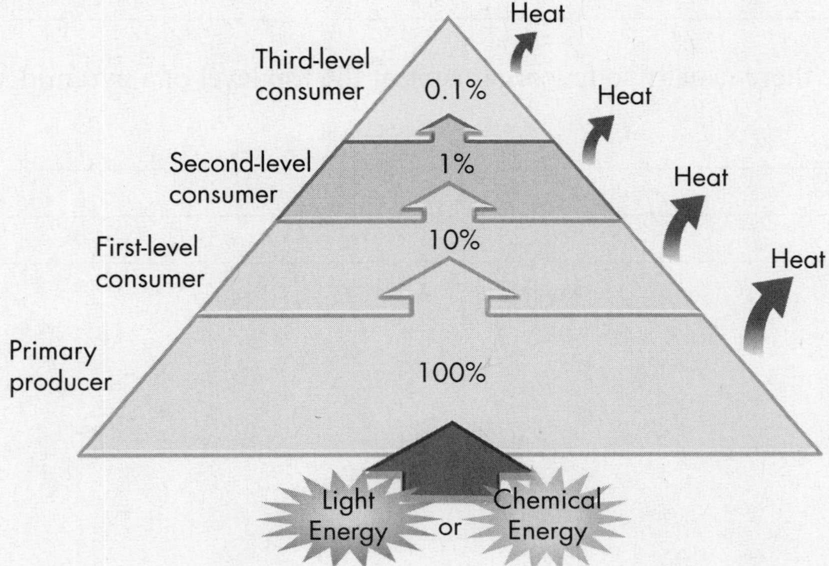

1. **Interpret Visuals** What is the original source of the energy that flows through most ecosystems? What would happen without this source?

2. **Calculate** If 10 percent of energy moves up to the next level of the ecosystem, what percentage of energy is lost as heat?

3. **Calculate** Remember that percentages are based on one-hundredths. The value 100% is equal to 100 one-hundredths or 100/100. The value 50% equals 50/100, which can also be written as the decimal 0.50. The value 5% equals 5/100 or 0.05. The value 0.5% equals 0.5/100 or 5/1000 or 0.005. Convert the following percentages into one-hundredths and then into a decimal: 75%, 20%, 0.8%.

4. **Calculate** Assume there are 1000 units of energy in the producer level of the energy pyramid. How many units of energy are available at each of the three consumer levels? Show your calculations. *Hint:* First, change the percentages to decimals.

5. **Calculate** Suppose there are 500 units of energy available at the base of a pyramid of energy. How many units of that energy will the first-level consumers store? How many units will the second-level consumers store?

6. **Infer** Why are there usually so few organisms at the top level of a pyramid of energy?

Use this diagram of an antarctic food web to answer Questions 7–9 and Build Science Skills.

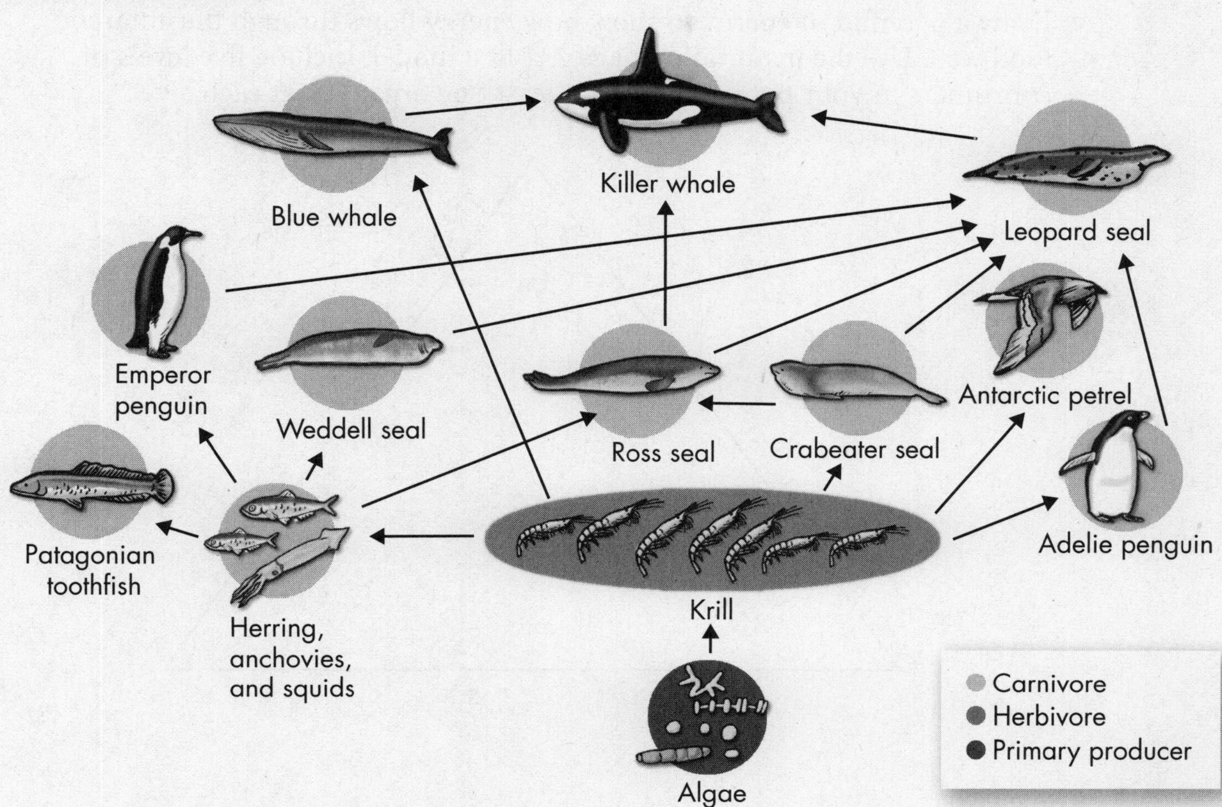

7. **Interpret Visuals** How are the blue whale and Adelie penguin alike as consumers?

____

____

8. **Draw Conclusions** What effect would a drop in the size of the krill population have on the antarctic food web and why?

____

____

____

9. **Predict** Adult krill feed on algae found in open water. Their larvae feed on algae found under the sea ice. More and more sea ice is melting. Will melting sea ice affect the killer whale? Explain.

____

____

____

____

____

Build Science Skills

Draw a pyramid of energy to show how energy flows through the antarctic food web. Use the pyramid on page 231 as a model. Include five levels of consumers in your pyramid. Place at least one organism at each level.

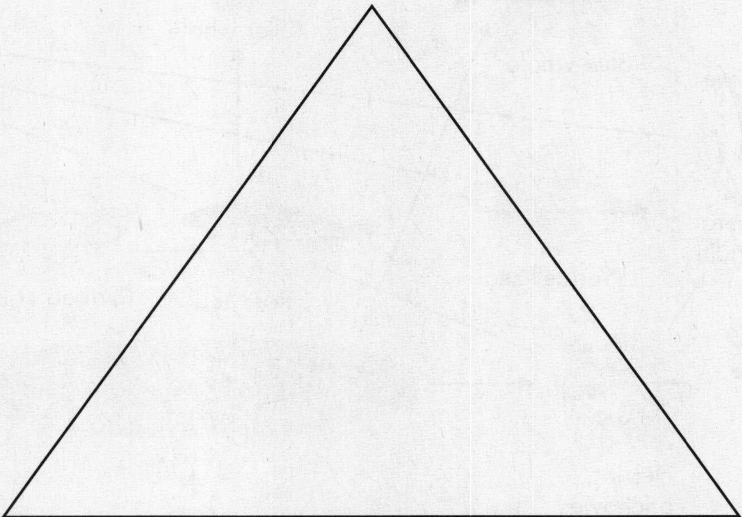

Lesson 4.2

Data Analysis 5 Predator-Prey Dynamics

Goal

Model interactions between predators and prey.

Skills Focus

Interpret Graphs, Relate Cause and Effect

Build Connections

When something is dynamic, that means it is always changing. A predator and prey relationship is dynamic. For example, a growing population of mice can support a growing population of owls. But, as an owl population increases, it will need more and more mice.

The graph models a typical relationship between predator and prey populations. The lines are called population growth curves.

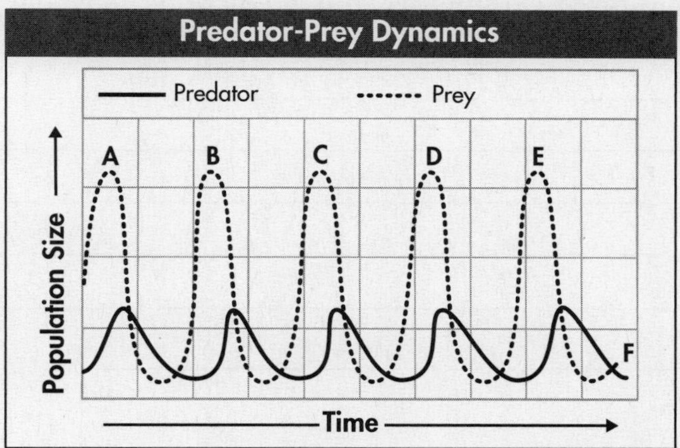

Analyze and Conclude

1. **Read Graphs** What does the *x*-axis show? What does the *y*-axis show?

____

2. **Interpret Graphs** Describe the pattern of the growth curves over time. What does this pattern tell you about population size?

____

____

3. **Interpret Graphs** Identify two characteristics of predator-prey growth curves other than the general pattern.

____

____

4. **Relate Cause and Effect** When the predator population starts to increase in size, what begins to happen to the prey population? How can you tell?

____

____

5. **Compare and Contrast** Compare the drop in a prey's population curve to that of a predator. What do the curves suggest about what happens to each population?

____

____

____

Build Science Skills

Suppose a long period of cold weather destroys almost the entire predator population at point B on the graph. Briefly describe what you think will happen to the prey population. Assume the predator population does not recover until point D. Think about what factor, other than a predator, could affect the size of the prey population. Then, extend the lines on the graph from point B to beyond point D to model your predictions. Give the graph a new title.

____

____

____

____

____

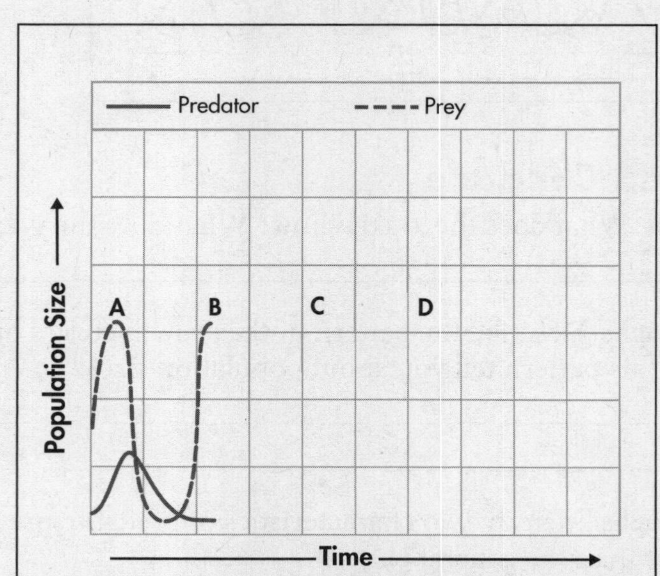

Data Analysis 6 Which Biome?

Goal

Classify biomes according to climate data and make a climate diagram.

Skills Focus

Interpret Graphs, Analyze Data, Draw Conclusions

Build Connections

You may think of biomes as a scientific idea, with little connection to you. But how you experience life is connected to the biome in which you live. Are your winters warm or cold? Are your summers so hot that it's hard to stay outside? What kinds of plants and animals do you find in your environment? All these aspects of your life are related to the biome in which you live. Three numbers help define your biome. The first number indicates where you are in the world, the latitude of where you live. The second is the amount of precipitation. The third is temperature.

Ecologists typically work with temperature and precipitation when they study climate. The graph shows monthly average temperatures over the course of a year for two locations. In Location A, the total precipitation for the year was 273 cm. The total precipitation for the year was 11 cm in Location B.

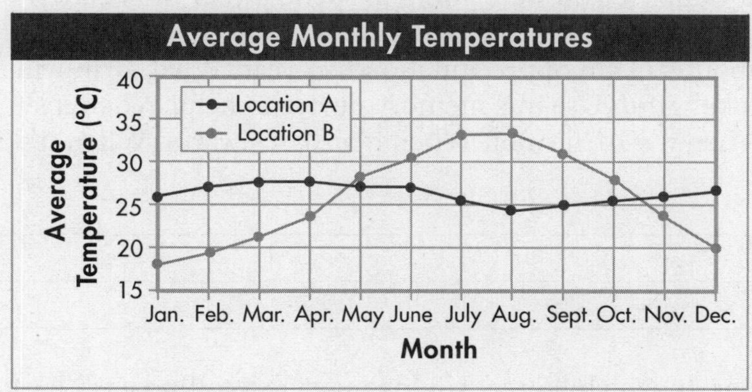

Analyze and Conclude

1. **Read Graphs** Which variable is plotted on the horizontal axis? Which variable is plotted on the vertical axis?

2. **Interpret Graphs** During which months do both locations have almost the same average temperature? How can you tell?

3. **Analyze Data** When are the highest and lowest average temperatures in Location A? In Location B? What are these temperatures?

4. **Analyze Data** How would your understanding of the climate be different if the only temperature data you had was a yearly average. *Hint:* Use the graph to estimate the average yearly temperature. Compare that temperature with the highest and lowest temperatures from Question 3.

5. **Apply Concepts** Suppose you were going to spend a year in Location A. What type of clothes would you pack and why? Recall that this location gets about 273 cm of precipitation in a year. What form will this precipitation take? *Hint:* Use this memory device to help: When it's 0, it's freezing. When it's 10, it's not. When it's 20, it's warm. When it's 30, it's hot.

6. **Draw Conclusions** In which biome would you expect to find each location? Why?

Build Science Skills

You are going to use the graph grid on the next page to make a climate diagram that shows the monthly averages for both temperature and precipitation. Ask your teacher whether you should (1) collect temperature and precipitation data for your area and record it in the table below or (2) use the data provided for Austin, Texas. Remember to include a title for your diagram. *Hint:* Use the climate diagrams in your textbook as a model.

After you are done, answer the following questions. What biome do you live in? What does the biome tell you about the plants and animals you share the environment with?

____

____

____

____

____

Location:												
	Jan	**Feb**	**Mar**	**Apr**	**May**	**Jun**	**Jul**	**Aug**	**Sep**	**Oct**	**Nov**	**Dec**
Average Temperature (°C)												
Average Precipitation (mm)												

Location: Austin, Texas												
	Jan	**Feb**	**Mar**	**Apr**	**May**	**Jun**	**Jul**	**Aug**	**Sep**	**Oct**	**Nov**	**Dec**
Average Temperature (°C)	10	13	17	21	24	27	29	29	27	21	15	11
Average Precipitation (mm)	48	51	54	64	128	97	50	59	74	101	68	62

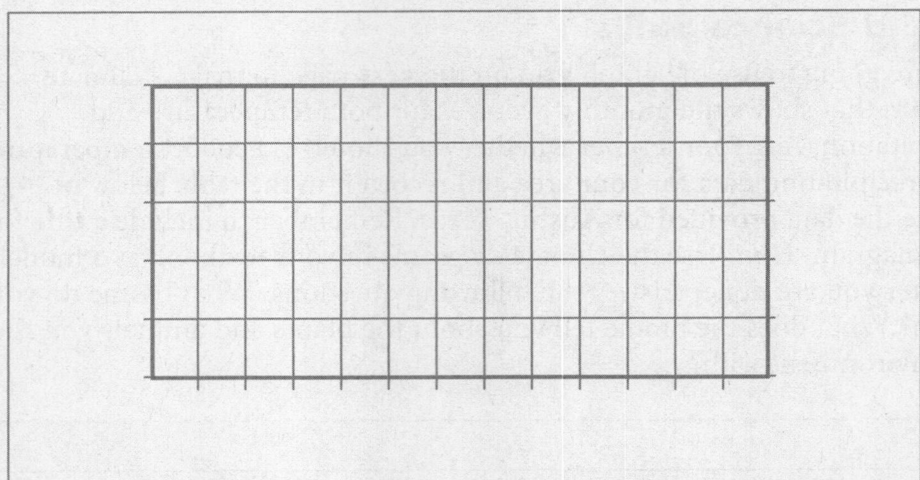

Lesson 5.1

Data Analysis 7 Multiplying Rabbits

Goal

Organize and graph data to reveal patterns in population growth.

Skills Focus

Analyze Data, Graph, Calculate

Build Connections

Some people use the expression "multiplying like rabbits" to describe a rapid growth in number. The Chapter 5 Mystery tells the story of what happened when a farmer introduced a few rabbits into the Australian countryside. Let's assume that a farmer with an empty barn wants to find out what the expression really means.

Analyze and Conclude

1. **Organize Data** The farmer plans to start with a single pair of rabbits, the parents. The first generation of offspring consists of 6 rabbits: 3 males and 3 females. What if the pattern were to continue and each pair of rabbits were to breed only once? To find out, use the data table to continue the pattern for four more generations.

Rabbit Population Data

Generation	Number of Pairs	Number of Offspring
Parents	1	6
1	3	18
2	9	
3		
4		
5		

2. **Calculate** How many rabbits would the farmer have after five generations? *Hint:* Remember to include all the rabbits in your final count.

____

____

3. Graph Use the data table from Question 1 to make a graph, starting with generation 1. Plot generations on the x-axis and population size on the y-axis. Compare the size of the smallest data point (generation 1) with the largest data point (generation 5) before deciding what units to use on the y-axis. Title your graph.

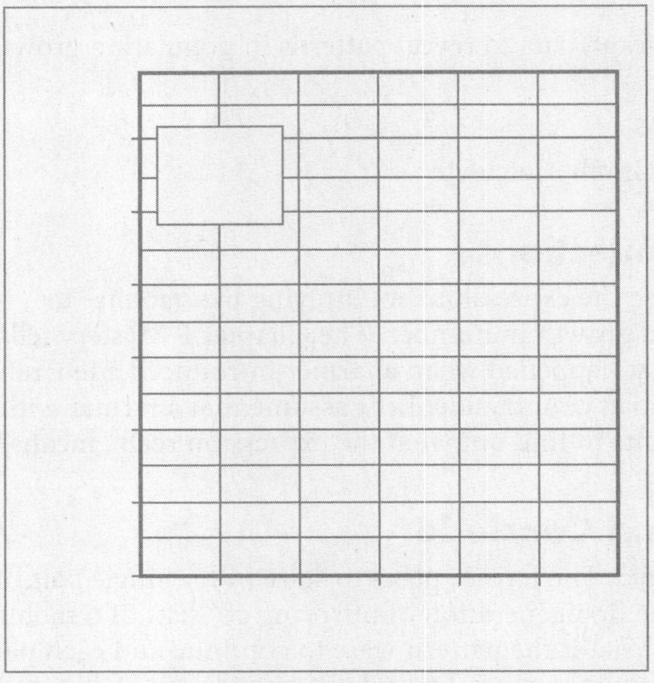

4. Interpret Graphs Is your graph J-shaped or S-shaped? What does the shape indicate about the type of population growth?

____

____

5. Analyze Data You can use a mathematical formula to represent the increase in the number of rabbit pairs for each generation.

The formula is N^x.

The variable x is an exponent. As an exponent, it indicates the number of times the number N is multiplied by itself. In this example, N is the number of rabbit pairs in generation 1 and x is the number of generations. Use the formula to calculate the number of pairs for generations 2, 3, 4, and 5.

____

____

6. **Calculate** Write a formula to calculate the number of offspring that would be produced for any generation of rabbits. Base your formula on the data from Question 1. Let *y* be the number of offspring for each generation. Use N^x to represent the number of pairs. Use your formula to determine the number of rabbit offspring in generation 10. *Hint:* Many calculators have an exponential function.

______

______

______

Build Science Skills

The number N in the formula N^x is called the base. For any base greater than 1, there is always growth as the exponent *x* increases. How is the rate of growth affected when there are 2 pairs of rabbits in generation 1 (N = 2) and when there are 4 pairs of rabbits in generation 1 (N = 4)? In each case, assume 5 generations of offspring.

As before, each pair of rabbits will produce 6 offspring. Organize the data in two data tables. Plot the results on the graph for Question 3. Use a different color for each line and add a key to the graph. When you are done, describe the differences between the data sets in terms of the slope of the curves and the size of N.

______

______

______

Rabbit Population Data, N= 2		

Rabbit Population Data, N= 4		

Data Analysis 8 Vehicle Emission Trends

Goal

Draw conclusions from trends shown in a graph.

Skills Focus

Interpret Graphs, Compare and Contrast, Draw Conclusions

Build Connections

The United States is often described as a nation in love with cars. For a population of around 300 million people, there are typically about 136 million registered cars on the road. Each year, the U.S. Environmental Protection Agency (EPA) estimates emissions from vehicles, including automobiles. Vehicles emit six common pollutants: carbon monoxide, lead, nitrogen oxide, organic compounds, particulates, and sulfur dioxide.

On the graph, all six pollutants are lumped together as *aggregate emissions*. The graph also shows *vehicle miles traveled* and *energy consumption*. The graph was drawn using EPA data collected from 1980 to 2007. The values shown are the total percent change.

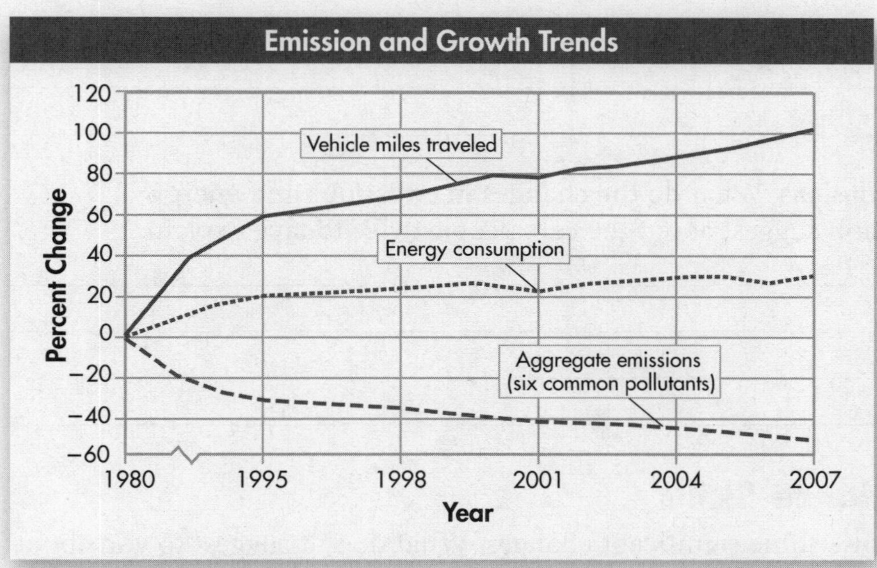

Analyze and Conclude

1. **Interpret Graphs** This graph shows *relative* values for emissions. How would a graph that showed *absolute* values for emissions differ from this one?

2. **Compare and Contrast** Look at the percent change in energy consumption and in automobile travel since 1980. How have they both changed overall? How can you tell?

3. **Interpret Graphs** Describe the overall trend in aggregate emissions since 1980. By how much have they changed? Is this trend what you would have expected? Explain.

4. **Interpret Graphs** Look at the percent change from 2001 to 2007. What is increasing? What is decreasing? What is staying about the same? How can you tell?

5. **Draw Conclusions** What do the changes in emissions and energy consumption suggest about the cars people drive today? Explain.

Build Science Skills

The graph shows some significant changes. What does it suggest to you about the impact humans can have on their environment?

Data Analysis 9 Saving the Golden Lion Tamarin

Goal

Interpret line graphs to understand population changes.

Skills Focus

Organize Data, Calculate, Analyze Data

Build Connections

Zoos are no longer just a place to house animals for display and public education. Many zoos participate in programs to assist in the survival of endangered species, such as the golden lion tamarin. This primate is native to the coastal regions of the Amazon rain forest. The tamarins are threatened because their habitat is being split into small pieces and destroyed.

In the early 1970s, there were 91 golden lion tamarins in 26 different zoos. Biologists made a plan to help the species survive. The goal was to increase the number and genetic diversity of golden lion tamarins. As of 2007, there were 496 golden lion tamarins in 145 zoos around the world. Further, about 153 tamarins from the program have been reintroduced to the wild since 1984. These tamarins are part of a healthy wild population of more than 650.

Analyze and Conclude

1. **Organize Data** Use this data table to help you organize the data from Build Connections.

	Number of Captive Golden Lion Tamarins	Number of Participating Zoos
1970s		
2007		

2. **Calculate** Use the formula below to find the percent by which the captive population of golden lion tamarins has increased since 1970.

$$\text{percent increase} = \frac{\text{original population}}{\text{new population}} \times 100$$

____

3. Analyze Data Until the captive population had reached a target size, biologists limited the number of tamarins that were reintroduced into the wild. What do you think the target size for the captive population is? Use the graph to explain your answer.

____

____

____

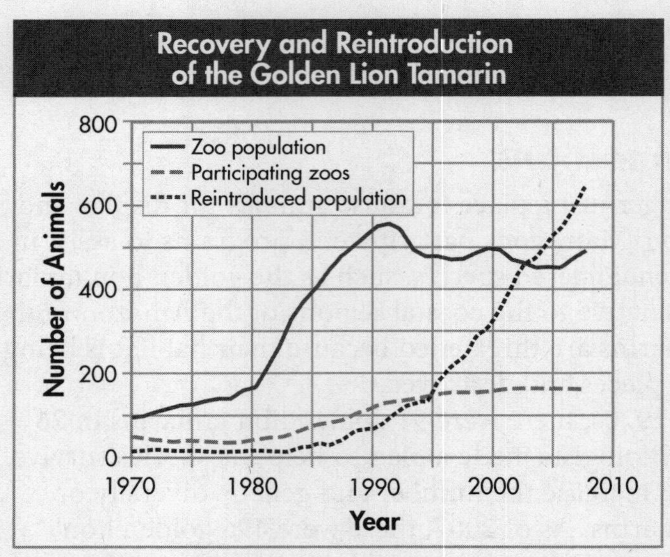

4. Infer Only 153 golden lion tamarins have been reintroduced from captivity. However, there is now a reintroduced population of about 650. Where did the other 497 come from?

____

____

Build Connections

When populations of wild animals become very small, do you think that they should be removed from the wild and brought into zoos? Why or why not?

____

____

____

____

____

____

Lesson 7.4

Data Analysis 10 Mitochondria Distribution in the Mouse

Goal

Interpret bar graphs to learn about cell activities.

Skills Focus

Interpret Graphs, Analyze Data, Infer

Build Connections

Medical researchers have a particular interest in mice because the mouse carries almost the same set of genes as humans. Studying mice is one way to learn about the function of human genes and body systems. Thus, the laboratory mouse can open a window into a greater understanding of the human body.

Researchers have studied the makeup of several organs in mice. They found that some organs and tissues have more mitochondria than others. The mitochondrion is the organelle that provides a cell with energy. Researchers measured the volume of mitochondria and compared that to the total volume of the cells. In the bar graph below, that comparison is shown as a percentage. In areas where there were more mitochondria, the mitochondria made up a higher percentage of the total volume of the cell.

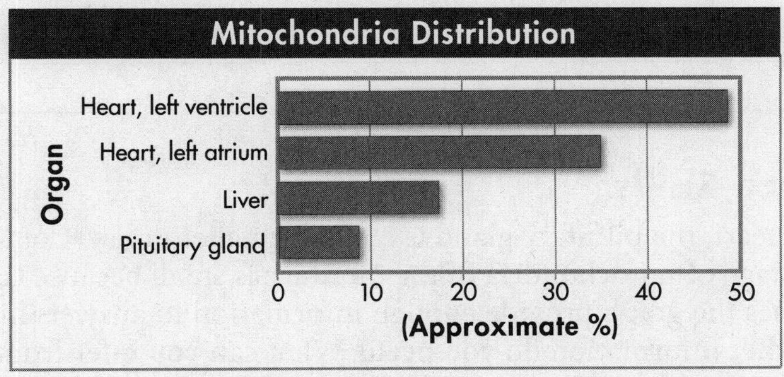

Analyze and Conclude

1. **Interpret Graphs** What kind of information does the bar graph provide? Put into words what the graph indicates about the cells in a mouse liver.

2. **Interpret Graphs** Of the organs studied, which organ in a mouse has the most mitochondria in its cells? Which has the least? About what percentage of the total cell volume is made up of mitochondria in these two organs?

3. **Calculate** About how much more of the total cell volume is made up of mitochondria in the liver than in the pituitary gland?

4. **Infer** There are four chambers in the mouse heart—two ventricles and two atria. Remember that mitochondria supply cells with energy. Based on this fact and on information from the graph, do you think the left ventricle or the left atrium pumps blood from the heart to the rest of the body? Explain your answer.

Build Science Skills

Compared to the heart, the pituitary gland is a much smaller organ. Could it be that the percentage of mitochondria in the pituitary is small because the organ is small? Does the graph provide enough information to answer this question? What other information do you need? What can you infer from the information supplied.

Lesson 8.3

Data Analysis 11 Rates of Photosynthesis

Goal

Interpret graphs to explore factors that affect the rate of photosynthesis.

Skills Focus

Interpret Graphs, Analyze Data, Compare and Contrast

Build Connections

If you go to a nursery to buy plants, you'll notice that each plant has a tag listing the amount of sun needed for the plant to thrive. Different plant species are adapted for different growing conditions. Shade plants typically have leaves with a larger surface area and contain more chlorophyll than plants that are adapted for full sun.

The graph compares the average rate of photosynthesis of sun plants and shade plants. The intensity of the light shining on the plants affects these rates. Direct, overhead sunlight is more intense than light that comes through tree branches or at an angle. Other factors also affect the rate of photosynthesis. Two examples are the amount of water the plant receives and the temperature.

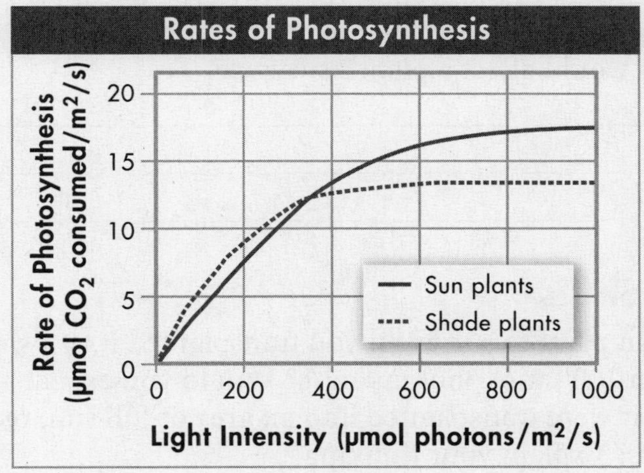

Analyze and Conclude

1. **Interpret Graphs** What factor is being used to measure the rate of photosynthesis? What does this factor have to do with what is happening in the plant cells? *Hint:* Look at the units on the *y*-axis.

2. **Interpret Graphs** As you move up the *y*-axis, is the rate of photosynthesis increasing or decreasing? As you move along the *x*-axis to the right, is the light intensity increasing or decreasing?

3. **Interpret Graphs** What happens to the rate of photosynthesis in both sun and shade plants as light intensity increases?

4. **Compare and Contrast** Which kind of plant—a sun plant or a shade plant—has a higher rate of photosynthesis when light intensity is below 200 μmol photons/m^2/s? When light intensity is above 400 μmol photons/m^2/s?

5. **Infer** Light intensity in the Sonoran Desert averages about 400 μmol photons/m^2/s. According to the graph, what would be the approximate rate of photosynthesis for plants that grow in this environment? What other factors would affect a plant's survival?

Build Science Skills

Would you expect a sun plant to survive if you transplanted it to a shaded area receiving no more than 200 μmol photons/m^2/s? Would you expect a shade plant to grow better if it were transplanted into an area of full sun, receiving 400 μmol photons/m^2/s? Explain your thinking.

Lesson 9.1

Data Analysis 12 You Are What You Eat

Goal
Use information about the type of food to calculate Calories.

Skills Focus
Interpret Tables, Calculate

Build Connections
The unit of measure for the energy stored in food is a calorie. A Calorie with a capital C is another name for a kilocalorie and is equal to 1000 calories. The Calorie is the unit you find on food labels. Why should people care how many Calories food contains? The problem is that the human body can be very efficient at storing the unused energy in food as fat.

The foods you eat are made up of different combinations of proteins, carbohydrates, and fats. Each kind of molecule gives your body a certain amount of energy. One gram of carbohydrate or protein has about 4 Calories. One gram of fat has about 9 Calories. Use the table to explore the Calorie content of some foods.

Composition of Some Common Foods

Food	Protein (g)	Carbohydrate (g)	Fat (g)
Apple, 1 medium	0	22	0
Bacon, 2 slices	5	0	5
Chocolate, 1 bar	3	23	13
Eggs, 2 whole	12	0	9
2% milk, 1 cup	8	12	5
Potato chips, 15 chips	2	14	10
Skinless roast turkey, 3 slices	11	3	1

Analyze and Conclude

1. **Read Tables** What type of information does the table provide?

____

____

2. **Interpret Tables** Which of the foods listed in the table has the most protein? Which has the most carbohydrates? Which has the most fat?

3. **Apply Concepts** How can you use the information in the table to find the number of Calories in each serving? *Hint:* See the second paragraph in Build Connections.

4. **Calculate** How many Calories are in 2 slices of bacon and 3 slices of roast turkey? Use the table to show your work.

	Bacon	Turkey
Protein		
Carbohydrate		
Fat		
Total		

5. **Analyze Data** What is the difference in total Calories between the servings of bacon and turkey? What is the main reason for this difference?

6. **Calculate** Your body uses about 5 Calories per minute when you are walking. At that rate, how many minutes would you have to walk to burn the Calories in one bar of chocolate? Show your work.

Build Science Skills

Potato chips are one of the most popular snack foods in the United States, based on the volume of chips sold. Apples are the most popular fruit. Use the data table on the first page of this activity to calculate the number of Calories in a single chip and in a single medium apple. Use the table below to show your work.

	15 Potato Chips	1 Apple
Protein		
Carbohydrate		
Fat		
Total		

This table lists the daily Calorie requirement for males and females in your age range based on level of physical activity.

Daily Calorie Requirement Based on Activity Level

	Age	Low	Medium	High
Female	14–18	1800	2000	2400
Male	14–18	2200	2600	3000

How many of each type of food (apples and chips) would a male who has a medium level of activity have to eat to meet his daily Calorie requirement? Show your work.

____

____

____

____

Name ______ Class ______ Date ______

Lesson 10.3

Data Analysis 13 **The Rise and Fall of Cyclins**

Goal

Interpret data related to cyclin levels during the cell cycle.

Skills Focus

Interpret Graphs, Predict

Build Connections

Because of the universal nature of the genetic code, many of the same processes that occur in simple organisms are also found in more complex ones. This idea is referred to as *conservation.*

Cyclins are a family of proteins that regulate the timing of the cell cycle in eukaryotes. Research has shown that cyclins play an important role in the cells of the simplest eukaryotes, such as yeasts, and the most complex, such as humans. Cyclins are made and destroyed throughout the cell cycle. To explore how the cyclin level changes during mitosis, scientists measured the cylin level in the dividing cells of clam eggs. The data are shown in the graph.

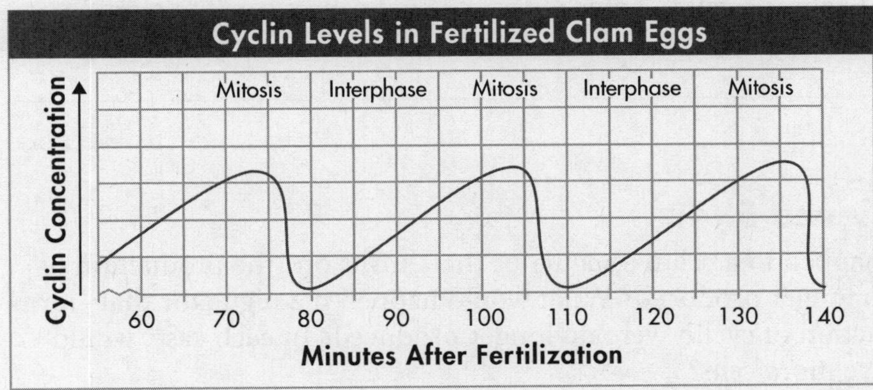

Analyze and Conclude

1. **Interpret Graphs** What does the *x*-axis on the graph show? How does the interval before the first label on the *x*-axis compare to the other intervals. *Hint:* What does the jagged line tell you?

____

____

____

2. **Interpret Graphs** What does the *y*-axis show?

3. **Interpret Graphs** What do the labels at the top of the graph show and why are those labels important?

4. **Interpret Graphs** In which part of the cell cycle does cyclin production begin? During which part of the cell cycle is cyclin destroyed?

5. **Interpret Graphs** Does it take longer for the cell to produce cyclin or to destroy it? How does the shape of the graph help you answer this question?

6. **Infer** What causes a cell to enter mitosis? What causes a cell to stop dividing and enter interphase?

Build Science Skills

What would happen to a cell if a regulator that "turns on" the production of cyclin were no longer produced? What would happen if a regulator that "turns off" the production of cyclin were no longer produced? In each case, would the cell produce more cells?

Lesson 10.4

Data Analysis 14 Cellular Differentiation of *C. elegans*

Goal

Practice math and analysis skills on data from *C. elegans* research.

Skills Focus

Calculate, Organize Data, Draw Conclusions

Build Connections

The microscopic worm *C. elegans* is a very simple organism. Biologists are using this worm to help them understand how an organism develops from an egg to an adult. A simple organism that is used as a model for more complex ones is called a *model organism.* By accepting *C. elegans* as a model, the scientific community agrees to focus on this organism.

C. elegans has just 959 cells as an adult, many of which are visible through its transparent cuticle. It goes through an entire life cycle in just three days. The drawing shows the worm's anatomy.

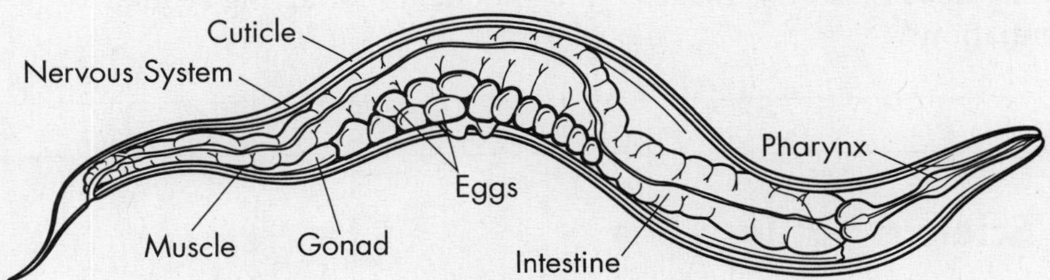

The table shows the distribution of cells in an adult worm. You will complete the table as you answer the questions on the next page.

Cellular Differentiation of *C. elegans*		
Cell Type	**Number of Cells in Adult**	**Percent of Total**
Cuticle	213	22%
Gonad	143	
Mesoderm muscle	81	
Pharynx	80	
Other		

Analyze and Conclude

1. **Calculate** Use the formula below to find the percentages of the total number of *C. elegans* cells in the gonad, the mesoderm muscle, and the pharynx. Round your answers to the nearest percent and record them in the table on the previous page. Show your work.

$$\frac{\text{Number of cells in adult}}{\text{Total number of cells}} \times 100$$

2. **Calculate** How many cells are in tissues not listed in the table? What is the percent of these "other" cells? Show your work. Enter your answers in the data table. *Hint:* Start by subtracting the number of cells listed from the total number of cells.

3. **Organize Data** Which kind of graph would best represent the data in the table—a line graph, a bar graph, or a circle graph? Explain.

4. **Infer** Why does *C. elegans* make an ideal model for studying cellular differentiation?

Build Science Skills

What cellular process are scientists using *C. elegans* to study? Why would it be more difficult to study this process in more complex animals, such as humans?

Data Analysis 15 Human Blood Types

Goal

Analyze data and make inferences about human blood type alleles.

Skills Focus

Infer, Interpret Graphs

Build Connections

Antigens are molecules that can trigger an immune reaction in the body. Red blood cells carry antigens on their surfaces. Human blood type A has an A antigen. Blood type B has a B antigen. Type AB has both antigens. Human blood type O carries neither antigen. The gene for blood type antigens has three alleles—A, B, and O.

Sometimes a patient is given blood during surgery or after a serious injury. The donated blood must not introduce a new antigen into the body. Otherwise, the patient's body will respond to the donated blood just as it would to a pathogen. So a person with type A blood can be given type O, but a person with type O blood cannot be given type A.

Human red blood cells may also carry another antigen, known as Rh factor. Rh^+ individuals carry this antigen. Rh^- patients do not. Blood with a positive Rh factor can be given to other patients with a positive Rh factor only. Rh^- can be given to patients with a positive or negative Rh factor. The circle graph below shows the percentage of each blood type in the U.S. population.

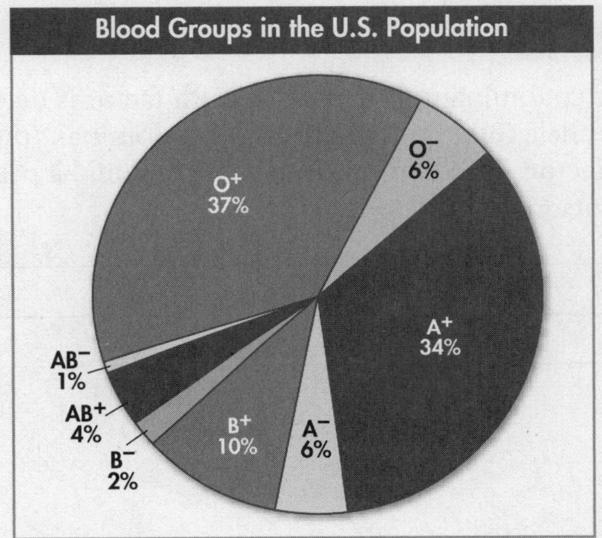

Name ______________________ Class ________ Date ________

Analyze and Conclude

1. **Infer** People with blood type O^- are sometimes called universal donors. Why?

2. **Infer** What blood type would a universal acceptor—a person who can receive any blood type—have?

3. **Interpret Graphs** Study the circle graph. Which blood type is most common in the U.S. population? What percentage of the population has that blood type?

4. **Interpret Graphs** Find all of the parts of the circle graph that represent a positive Rh factor. What percentage of the U.S. population has a positive Rh factor?

5. **Interpret Graphs** What percentage of the U.S. population has a negative Rh factor?

6. **Infer** Which blood type can be donated to the largest percentage of people? Which type can be donated to the smallest percentage of people? Explain your answer.

Build Science Skills

Blood types A and B are codominant. O is recessive. Rh factor is determined by a different gene. The allele for a positive Rh factor is dominant over the allele for a negative Rh factor. Based on this information, could a person with O^+ blood have two parents with O^- blood?

Data Analysis 16 Calculating Haploid and Diploid Numbers

Goal

Explore the relationship between haploid and diploid numbers.

Skills Focus

Interpret Tables, Apply Concepts, Organize Data

Build Connections

One characteristic shared among members of a species is the number of chromosomes in its body cells. Because chromosomes in body cells exist as pairs, this number is referred to as the diploid number. It is represented by the term 2N, which means "two times N." The haploid number, N, represents the chromosomes that contain a full, single set of genes.

The number of chromosomes varies widely among organisms. The record for the smallest chromosome number goes to a subspecies of the ant *Myrmecia pilosula.* The females have just a single pair of chromosomes (2N = 2, N = 1). The male ants have only a single chromosome. The record for the largest chromosome number goes to the fern *Ophioglossum reticulatum.* It has 630 pairs of chromosomes or 1260 chromosomes per body cell.

If you know either the haploid or diploid number, you can calculate the other. For example, if the haploid number (N) is 3, the diploid number (2N) is 2 × 3, or 6. If the diploid number (2N) is 12, the haploid number (N) is 12/2, or 6. The table shows haploid or diploid numbers for several types of organisms. Complete the table. Then use it to answer the Analyze and Conclude questions.

Trait Survey

Organism	Haploid Number	Diploid Number
Amoeba	N = 25	
Chimpanzee	N = 24	
Earthworm	N = 18	
Fern		2N = 1010
Hamster	N = 22	
Human		2N = 46
Onion		2N = 16

Analyze and Conclude

1. **Interpret Tables** Which organism in the table has the most chromosomes? Which has the fewest?

2. **Apply Concepts** Which cells in a body will have the haploid number of chromosomes?

3. **Analyze Data** How many chromosomes are in a chimpanzee's body cells? How many chromosomes are in a chimpanzee's gametes?

4. **Apply Concepts** Why is a diploid number always even?

5. **Organize Data** If you were asked to organize the data from this table into a graph, which kind of graph would you choose? Explain your choice.

Build Science Skills

Compare the number of chromosomes for the different types of organisms in the table. What can you conclude about the complexity of an organism and the number of chromosomes it has? *Hint:* Are there any single-celled organisms in the table?

Lesson 12.2

Data Analysis 17 Base Percentages

Goal

Analyze data and draw conclusions about the relative amounts of nucleotides in DNA.

Skills Focus

Interpret Tables, Graph, Predict

Build Connections

During the middle part of the twentieth century, the race was on to discover what genes were made of. Both chemists and biologists were working on the problem. One important piece of the puzzle fell into place in 1949. The chemist Erwin Chargaff discovered that there is almost always the same amount of adenine (A) as thymine (T) in a sample of DNA. Also, there is almost always the same amount of guanine (G) as cytosine (C) in a DNA sample.

Chargaff noted the pattern. But he did not understand the significance of this data and what it suggested about the structure of DNA. The table shows a portion of the data that Chargaff collected.

Percentages of Bases in Five Organisms

Source of DNA	A	T	G	C
Streptococcus	29.8	31.6	20.5	18.0
Yeast	31.3	32.9	18.7	17.1
Herring	27.8	27.5	22.2	22.6
Human	30.9	29.4	19.9	19.8
E. coli	24.7	23.6	26.0	25.7

Analyze and Conclude

1. **Interpret Tables** What is being measured in the table?

____

2. **Read Tables** Which organism has the highest percentage of A? Which has the highest percentage of T?

____

3. **Predict** If a species has 35 percent A in its DNA, what would you expect its percentage of T to be?

____

4. **Calculate** If a species has 35 percent A in its DNA, what would its percentage of G and C *combined* be? What would its percentage of G be? What would its percentage of C be?

____

5. **Infer** What does the fact that A and T, and G and C, were found in almost equal amounts suggest? What does the fact that the pattern repeats for different organisms suggest?

____

____

____

Build Science Skills

Sometimes patterns are easier to see if you make a model or some visual representation. Make a bar graph of the data in the table. Include a key to show how you are representing each base. In your opinion, does the graph make the pattern more obvious?

____

____

____

____

Data Analysis 18 The Discovery of RNA Interference

Goal

Analyze data to build an understanding of RNA interference.

Skills Focus

Analyze Data, Form a Hypothesis

Build Connections

One way for an organism to turn off gene expression is to interfere with the activity of RNA. In RNA interference, single-stranded microRNA (miRNA) binds to a group of proteins. The complex that forms can destroy complementary messenger RNA (mRNA) molecules and keep mRNA from passing on its instructions.

In 1998, Andrew Fire and Craig Mello did an experiment that helped explain how RNA interference works. They used a large gene called unc-22, which codes for a protein found in muscle cells. Fire and Mello prepared short mRNA fragments that corresponded to two exon regions of the gene. Fire and Mello injected the mRNA fragments into egg cells of the worm *C. elegans.*

Some of their results are shown in the table below. The "sense" strand is the single-stranded mRNA that codes for the protein. The "antisense" strand is the strand that is complementary to the sense strand. Double-stranded RNA is labeled "Sense + Antisense."

Injections of mRNA Into *C. elegans* Eggs

Portion of Gene Used to Produce mRNA	Strand Injected	Result in Adult Worm
Unc-22 (exon 21–22)	Sense	Normal
	Antisense	Normal
	Sense + Antisense	Twitching
Unc-22 (exon 27)	Sense	Normal
	Antisense	Normal
	Sense + Antisense	Twitching

Analyze and Conclude

1. **Analyze Data** When a single strand of sense mRNA was injected into a cell, what was the effect on the adult worm? What was the effect with a single strand of antisense mRNA?

____

____

____

2. **Analyze Data** How did the worm develop when the double-stranded mRNA was injected into the egg cells?

____

____

3. **Form a Hypothesis** When the contractions of muscle cells are not controlled, the muscles twitch. Recall that the unc-22 gene codes for a protein found in muscle cells. What does this experiment suggest about the function of the unc-22 protein?

____

____

4. **Design an Experiment** How could you test your hypothesis? What will your control be? *Hint:* Think about what should be missing from the muscle cells that are twitching.

____

____

____

5. **Infer** The injected fragments came from two different places in the gene and were only a few hundred bases long. The unc-22 mRNA is thousands of bases long. What does this information suggest about how RNA interference takes place?

____

____

Build Science Skills

Many diseases and conditions are related to genetic defects that prevent the body from functioning normally. Why might medical researchers be interested in RNA interference?

____

____

____

Data Analysis 19 The Geography of Malaria

Goal

Analyze map data to understand the relationship between sickle cell disease and malaria.

Skills Focus

Interpret Visuals, Infer

Build Connections

There is an interesting connection between malaria and sickle cell disease. Malaria is an infectious disease. It is caused by a parasite that infects red blood cells. Malaria is transmitted by mosquitoes and can be fatal, especially for children.

Sickle cell disease is a genetic disorder. A person with an allele for the sickle cell trait produces red blood cells that are sickle shaped. These cells cannot deliver as much oxygen to body tissues as normal red blood cells can. A person who is homozygous for sickle cell disease will suffer from damage to different organs and will require ongoing treatment.

People who carry one copy of the allele for sickle cell disease usually do not show signs of sickle cell disease. They are also highly resistant to malaria. The connection between the two diseases became clear when maps showing the distribution of both were put side by side. The dark regions on Map 1 show places where malaria is common. On Map 2, the dark regions show places where many people have the sickle cell allele.

Map 1

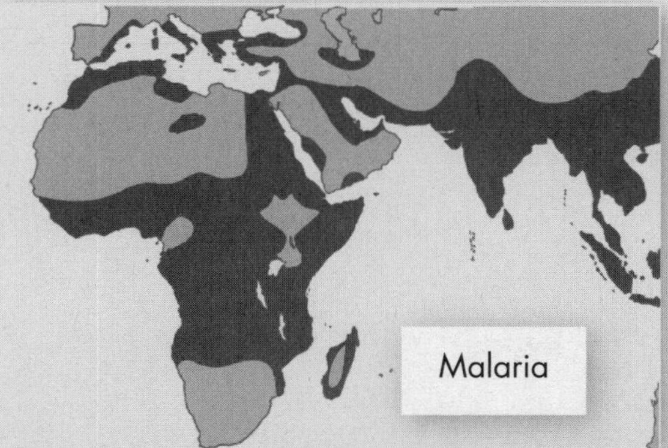

Map 2

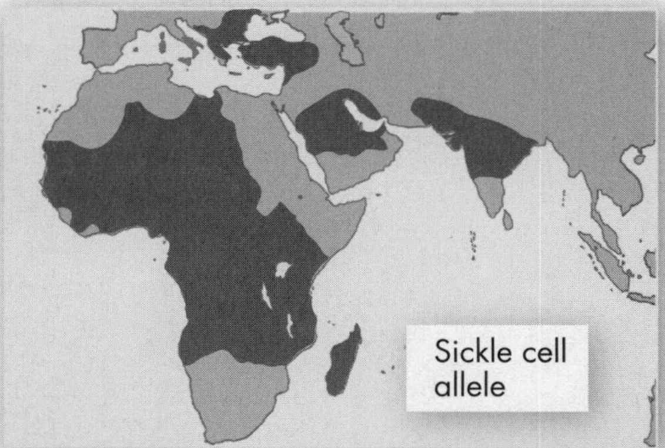

Analyze and Conclude

1. **Interpret Visuals** According to Map 1, where is malaria common? According to Map 2, where is it common for people to have the sickle cell allele?

2. **Analyzing Data** What do you observe about areas where malaria is common and areas where the sickle cell allele is found?

3. **Infer** In 1805, a Scottish explorer named Mungo Park led an expedition of European geographers in Africa. Forty-five Europeans began the journey. While they were in Africa, most of the Europeans died from malaria. Their native African guides survived. Why do you think the guides survived?

4. **Form a Hypothesis** According to Map 2, the sickle cell allele is not common in people native to southern Africa. Form a hypothesis that could explain this fact.

Name ______________________ Class ________ Date ________

Build Science Skills

The sickle cell allele may have become common in African populations as an adaptation to the malaria parasite. After the mutated sickle cell allele appeared in a population, individuals who carried it were more likely to survive malaria. Therefore, they were more likely to reproduce and pass the allele onto their children.

Draw two Punnett squares. In the first, show a cross between a carrier of the sickle cell allele and a person without the allele. In the second, show a cross between two people who are carriers of the allele. Describe the phenotypes that would likely result from each cross. Use *S* to represent the sickle cell allele and *s* to represent the normal allele.

Cross Between Carrier and Person Without Allele

____

____

____

Cross Between Two Carriers

____

____

____

Data Analysis 20 Genetically Modified Crops in the United States

Goal

Analyze data and make inferences about why farmers grow genetically modified crops.

Skills Focus

Interpret Graphs, Infer, Analyze Data

Build Connections

Crops with genetically modified (GM) traits were first introduced in 1996. Some varieties of soybean, cotton, and corn have been modified to survive the use of herbicides. Some varieties of cotton and corn have been modified to be more resistant to insect pests. The graph shows data on the use of different modified crops in the United States between 1996 and 2007. In the legend, "HT" stands for herbicide tolerance, and "Bt" stands for insect resistance.

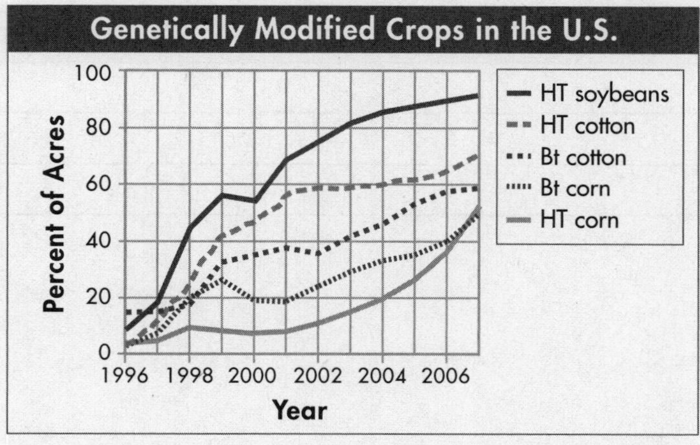

Analyze and Conclude

1. **Analyze Data** Which two GM crops were widely and rapidly adopted by U.S. farmers? Which crop had only a slight increase?

____

2. **Interpret Graphs** Compare the percentage of soybeans that had the HT trait in 1996 to the percentage in 2007.

____

Name ______________________ Class ________ Date ________

3. **Interpret Graphs** Compare the percentage of corn that had the HT trait in 1996 to the percentage in 2007.

4. **Infer** Add up the percentages of acres of GM cotton crops in 2007. Explain your result.

5. **Predict** Do you think that the percentages of HT soybeans and HT corn will continue to rise over the next several years? Use the graph to support your prediction.

Build Science Skills

Why is it important for farmers to have plants that are modified to contain an HT trait, a Bt trait, or both traits? How do these traits help crop yields?

Lesson 16.4

Data Analysis 21 Molecular Homology in *Hoxc8*

Goal

Infer relationships among animals by comparing DNA nucleotides of homologous genes.

Skills Focus

Calculate, Analyze Data, Draw Conclusions

Build Connections

Homologous parts of organisms share certain characteristics that point to their descent from a common ancestor. Forelimbs are a good example. For example, a mouse, a whale, and a chicken appear very different. Yet their forelimbs share similarities in the shape and positions of the bones.

The evidence of homology in evolution is not just limited to parts of the body. Some proteins and genes are also homologous. Like homologous structures, these molecules can be used to infer relationships among species. The diagram shows a small portion of the DNA for the gene, *Hoxc8,* for three animals—a mouse, a baleen whale, and a chicken.

Sequence of Bases in Section of *Hoxc8*																																								
Mouse	C	A	G	A	A	A	T	G	C	C	A	C	T	T	T	T	A	T	G	G	C	C	C	T	G	T	T	T	G	T	C	T	C	C	C	T	G	C	T	C
Baleen whale	C	C	G	A	A	A	T	G	C	C	T	C	T	T	T	T	A	T	G	G	C	G	C	T	G	T	T	T	G	T	C	T	C	C	C	T	G	C	G	C
Chicken	A	A	A	A	A	A	T	G	C	C	G	C	T	T	T	T	A	C	A	G	C	T	C	T	G	T	T	T	G	T	C	T	C	T	C	T	G	C	T	A

Analyze and Conclude

1. **Calculate** What percentage of the nucleotides in a baleen whale's DNA are different from those of a mouse? First, count the nucleotides in one entire sequence. Then, count the nucleotides in the whale DNA that differ from those in the mouse DNA. Finally, divide the number of nucleotides that are different by the total number of nucleotides, and multiply the result by 100.

____

____

2. **Calculate** What percentage of the nucleotides of a chicken are different from those of a mouse?

3. **Draw Conclusions** Do you think a mouse is more closely related to a baleen whale or to a chicken? Explain.

4. **Evaluate** It is not unusual for a gene to have thousands of bases in its sequence. Would you expect that scientists typically use small sections of DNA, like the one in the table, or larger sections to infer evolutionary relationships? Explain.

5. **Infer** What modern piece of technology plays an important role in the ability of scientists to study genes?

Build Science Skills

Hox genes are a group of genes that control the development of an organism. How might the similarity of Hox genes in a mouse, whale, and chicken be related to their homologous forelimbs?

Data Analysis 22 Allele Frequency

Goal

Predict the frequency of genotypes using the Hardy-Weinberg principle.

Skills Focus

Calculate, Predict

Build Connections

The word *frequency* refers to the number of times something happens. Sometimes frequency is easy to figure out. For example, the frequency of the Summer Olympics is once every four years. With allele frequency, or the frequency of a particular genotype in a population, the task is more complex.

A dominant trait expressed in a population can be the result of either a heterozygous or homozygous genotype. Suppose you are doing research on a rare but serious medical condition. You know that the condition is caused by a single recessive gene. You want to know how many people carry this gene. Is it possible that this condition might eventually disappear from the population?

The Hardy-Weinberg principle can be used to predict the frequencies of certain genotypes if you know the frequency of other genotypes. The medical condition being studied is controlled by two alleles *S* and *s*. Because only one gene is involved, inheritance follows the rule of simple dominance.

- The dominant allele is *S*, and the recessive allele is *s*.
- Only homozygous recessive individuals show symptoms.
- The population you are studying has 10,000 individuals.
- There are 36 individuals affected by the condition.

Based on this information, use the Hardy-Weinberg equations to answer the questions on the next page.

Analyze and Conclude

1. **Review** Write the Hardy-Weinberg equations in symbols and in words. What value represents the entire population?

2. **Infer** In the population you are studying, which allele is represented by *p* in the Hardy-Weinberg equation? Which allele is represented by *q*?

3. **Calculate** What are the frequencies of the dominant *S* and recessive *s* alleles in the population?

4. **Calculate** What are the frequencies of the *SS, Ss,* and *ss* genotypes? Show your calculations.

5. **Calculate** What percentage of individuals in the population are likely to be carrying the *s* allele, whether or not they know it? Show your calculation.

Build Science Skills

You need more resources to study the effects of the medical condition caused by the recessive allele. Before you apply for grant money to continue your work, you need to know whether the recessive allele is likely to disappear from the population. What percentage of the population carries the *s* allele but does not show any symptoms. How many individuals does this number represent? Do you think the *s* allele is likely to disappear from the population?

Data Analysis 23 Comparing the Domains

Goal

Interpret data to draw conclusions about the classification of organisms.

Skills Focus

Interpret Tables, Compare and Contrast

Build Connections

Until the twentieth century, classifying life forms was relatively simple. Most biologists classified living things as either plant or animal. Then, in the 1950s, the picture became more complicated as scientists looked more closely. By the 1970s, there were five kingdoms. Four were characterized by eukaryotic cells: plants, animals, fungi, and protists. The bacteria were the one group distinguished by prokaryotic cells. Looking even more closely, scientists realized that a certain group of bacteria had cells that didn't really fit with bacteria or with the eukaryotes. The five kingdoms were replaced by six kingdoms and three domains.

This table compares the three domains and six kingdoms. Use the information in the table to answer the Analyze and Conclude questions on the next page.

Classification of Living Things

Domain	**Bacteria**	**Archaea**	**Eukarya**			
Kingdom	Eubacteria	Archaebacteria	"Protista"	Fungi	Plantae	Animalia
Cell type	Prokaryote	Prokaryote	Eukaryote	Eukaryote	Eukaryote	Eukaryote
Cell structures	Cell walls with peptidoglycan	Cell walls without peptidoglycan	Some cellulose cell walls; chloroplasts in some	Cell walls of chitin	Cell walls of cellulose, chloroplasts	No cell walls, no chloroplasts
Number of cells	Unicellular	Unicellular	Most unicellular; some multicellular; some colonial	Most multicellular; some unicellular	Multicellular	Multicellular
Mode of nutrition	Autotroph or heterotroph	Autotroph or heterotroph	Autotroph or heterotroph	Heterotroph	Autotroph	Heterotroph
Examples	*Streptococcus, Escherichia coli*	*Methanogens, halophiles*	*Paramecium,* amoeba, giant kelp, slime molds	Mushrooms, yeasts	Mosses, ferns, flowering plants	Sponges, worms, insects, fishes, mammals

Name ______________________ Class __________ Date __________

Analyze and Conclude

1. **Interpret Tables** Which domain includes four kingdoms? What are those kingdoms?

2. **Interpret Tables** Which kingdom has cells that lack cell walls?

3. **Interpret Tables** Which domain includes multicellular organisms?

4. **Compare and Contrast** How do all members of domain Eukarya differ from all members of domains Archaea and Bacteria?

5. **Compare and Contrast** On the basis of the information in the table, how are the members of domain Archaea similar to those of domain Bacteria?

Build Science Skills

If you were to observe a multicellular organism without cell walls while looking under a microscope, in which domain and kingdom would you classify it? Explain your reasoning.

Data Analysis 24 Extinctions Through Time

Goal

Interpret graphs to draw conclusions about the rates of extinction over time.

Skills Focus

Interpret Graphs, Analyze Data, Draw Conclusions

Build Connections

The graph shows the percentages of genera (singular: genus) that have gone extinct during different geologic periods. The periods are shown along the top of the graph. Genera are groups of related species. For example, cat species belong to the genus *Felis.*

The most important extinction event for you, as a mammal, comes with the mass extinction that occurred at the end of the Cretaceous Period. At that time, the dinosaurs disappeared and mammal species rose in number. Use the graph to answer the Analyze and Conclude questions on the next page.

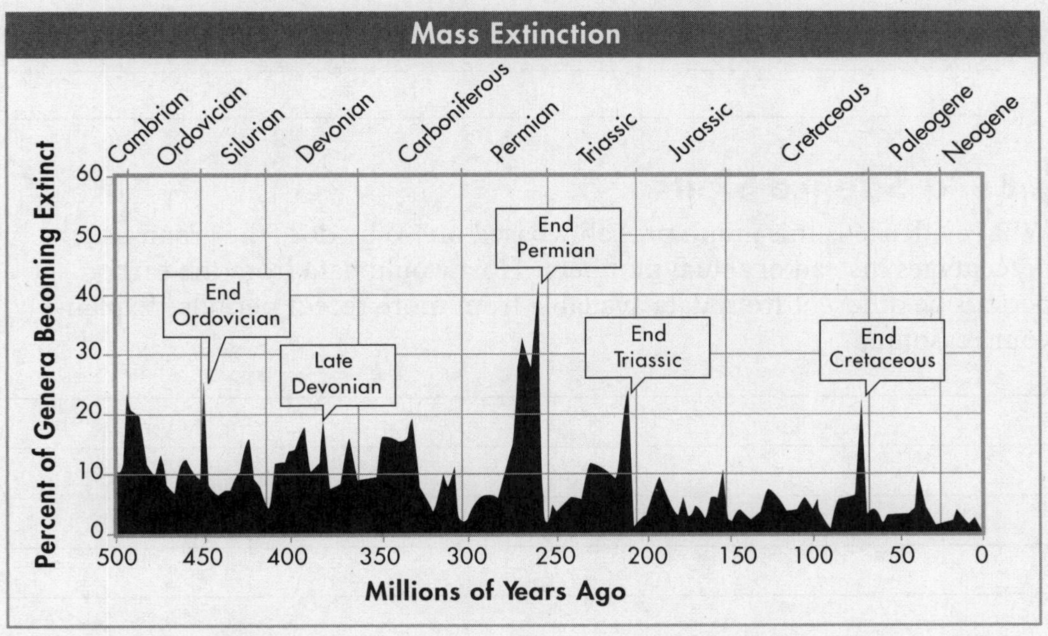

Analyze and Conclude

1. **Interpret Graphs** What is plotted on the *y*-axis?

2. **Interpret Graphs** What do the text balloons in the graph point to?

3. **Analyze Data** Which mass extinction killed off the highest percentage of genera?

4. **Draw Conclusions** Describe the overall pattern of extinction shown on the graph.

5. **Evaluate** Can you conclude from the graph alone the percentage of species that became extinct during different periods? Why or why not?

Build Science Skills

What evidence is this graph probably based on? Why does the graph use percentages instead of actual numbers? How would data from the earlier periods be different from data available from more recent periods? Explain your reasoning.

Data Analysis 25 Comparing Atmospheres

Goal

Interpret and evaluate circle graphs.

Skills Focus

Interpret Graphs, Analyze Data

Build Connections

Many scientists think that Earth's early atmosphere may have been made up of gases similar to those released by a volcano. The circle graphs show the gases in the atmosphere today and the gases released by a volcano.

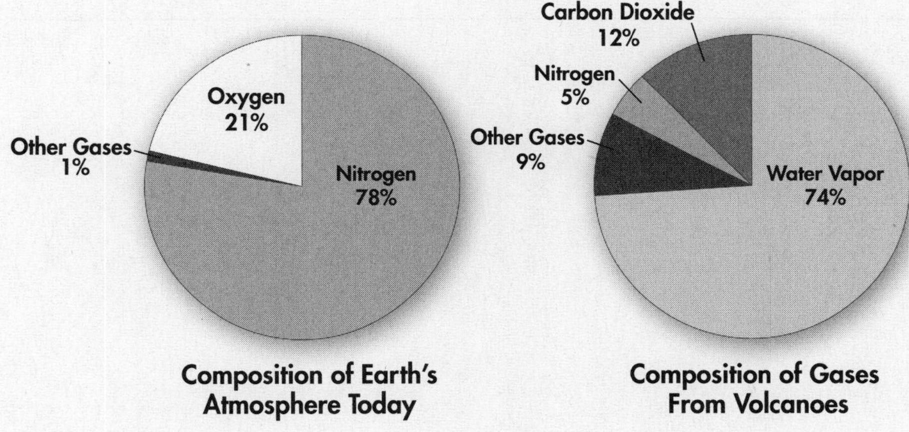

Composition of Earth's Atmosphere Today

Composition of Gases From Volcanoes

Analyze and Conclude

1. **Infer** Compare the two circle graphs. In which graph is the composition of gases most like Earth's early atmosphere?

   ____

2. **Interpret Graphs** Which gas is most abundant in Earth's atmosphere today? What percentage of that gas may have been present in Earth's early atmosphere?

   ____

3. **Analyze Data** Which gas was probably most abundant in the early atmosphere?

   ____

4. Infer Where did the water in today's oceans probably come from? Explain your thinking.

Build Science Skills

Green algae and plants existed on Earth before animals. How did their appearance help to alter the composition of the air and set the stage for the evolution of animals? *Hint:* What ability do algae and plants have that animals do not?

Data Analysis 26 MRSA on the Rise

Goal

Draw a line graph based on a data table.

Skills Focus

Analyze Data, Calculate, Draw Conclusions, Graph

Build Connections

Staphylococcus aureus bacteria are often called "Staph." Most staph bacteria are harmless. One out of three people have staph bacteria living on their skin but show no signs of infection. Antibiotics can cure most staph infections. The problem is when the infection is caused by MRSA (MURS uh), which stands for "methicillin-resistant *Staphylococcus aureus*." This strain of staph is resistant to the antibiotic methicillin and most other antibiotics.

Because it is resistant to so many antibiotics, MRSA is very difficult to control. MRSA infections can spread rapidly in hospitals, where patients have weakened immune systems. It also can spread through nursing homes, gyms, and other crowded places. MRSA passes from person to person by skin contact or by contact with equipment used by a person with MRSA.

Incidence of MRSA in U.S. Hospitals

Year	Hospital Cases Reported
1993	1900
1995	38,100
1997	69,800
1999	108,600
2001	175,000
2003	248,300
2005	368,600

Analyze and Conclude

1. **Calculate** By what percentage did MRSA infections increase between 1995 and 2005? Show your work.

____

2. **Analyze Data** What do all the individuals in the population that was studied have in common? Can the trend in this data be applied to the U.S. population as a whole? Explain your thinking.

____

____

____

3. **Infer** How do you think the perception of MRSA infection levels might have changed between the years 1993 and 1995? Explain your thinking.

____

____

____

4. **Draw Conclusions** A 2007 study reported that the average hospital stay in the United States lasted 4.6 days. For the average MRSA-infected patient, the hospital stay was 10.0 days. Suppose the trend shown by the data in the table continues. What effect will MRSA infections have on future hospital costs? Explain.

____

____

Build Science Skills

Use the grid to draw a line graph showing the number of MRSA infections in U.S. hospitals over time. Describe the trend shown. Does the graph show exponential growth? What shape is associated with exponential growth?

____

____

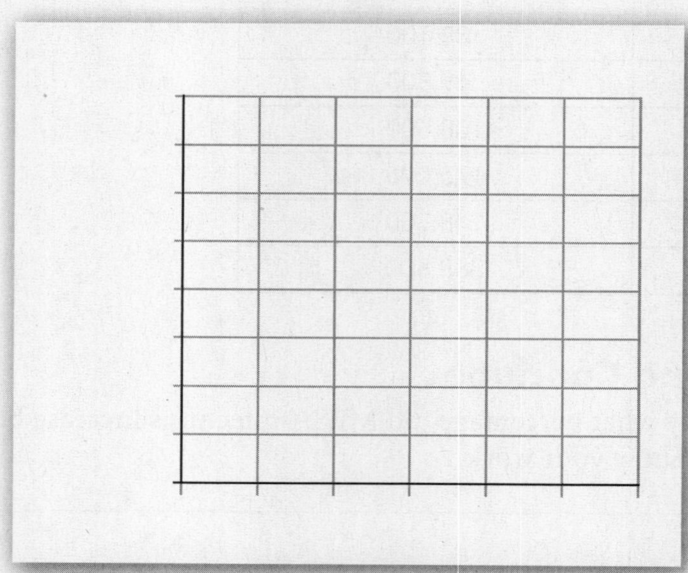

Data Analysis 27 Mycorrhizae and Tree Height

Goal

Draw conclusions about the relationship between mycorrhizae and certain plants.

Skills Focus

Analyze Data, Draw Conclusions, Form a Hypothesis

Build Connections

Mycorrhizae (my koh RY zee) refers to a symbiotic relationship that occurs between fungi and plant roots. Research has shown that 80 to 90 percent of all plant species form mycorrhizae with fungi. The graph compares the height of three tree species. One tree of each species grew with mycorrhizae, and one grew without mycorrhizae.

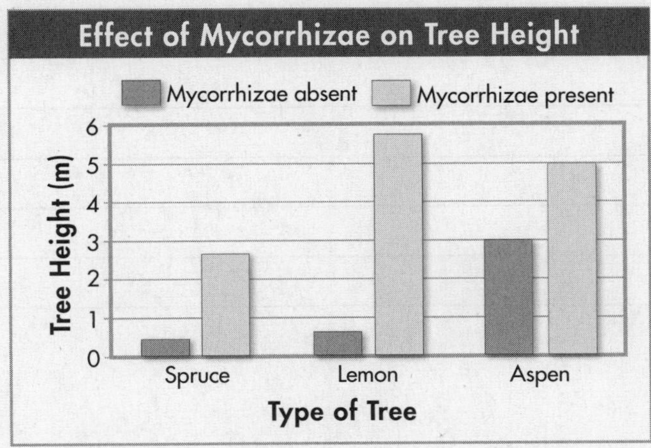

Analyze and Conclude

1. **Read Graphs** What are the three species of trees shown on the graph?

____

2. **Analyze Data** What do the two different shades of bars represent?

____

____

____

Name ______________________ Class __________ Date __________

3. **Calculate** Which lemon tree is taller? What is the difference in height between the taller tree and the shorter tree? What is the percent difference in height? Show your work.

____

____

____

4. **Draw Conclusions** Make a generalization about plants that grow with mycorrhizae.

____

____

Build Science Skills

You work for a nursery that grows lemon trees in large pots. Recently, the nursery started using sterilized soil for repotting the trees. The sterilization process is used to kill organisms that can cause diseases in lemon trees. You observe that many of the repotted trees are not growing as well as the trees that were not repotted. Form a hypothesis that explains your observations. How would you test your hypothesis?

____

____

____

____

____

____

____

Lesson 22.2

Data Analysis 28 Keeping Ferns in Check

Goal

Analyze data to better understand dispersal of fern spores.

Skills Focus

Interpret Tables, Analyze Data, Relate Cause and Effect

Build Connections

Hay-scented fern, *Dennstaedtia punctilobula,* is very common in the eastern United States. It grows in large colonies on forest floors and around wooded areas. It has lacy, light-green fronds. These ferns can form such a thick covering that they block out the sun. Small seedlings of plants and trees cannot grow in the thick shade beneath these ferns. An abundance of ferns makes it difficult for trees to grow again after a forest has been logged.

To understand the hay-scented fern better, scientists measured the number of viable fern spores per square centimeter of soil. They made measurements at different distances from a plot of ferns. The scientists counted spores in July, when the ferns begin to grow, and in November, after the ferns release their spores.

Number of Spores in Soil (per cm^2)

Distance From Plot of Ferns (meters)	Before Dispersal (July)	After Dispersal (November)
0	14	54
2	16	18
4	5	9
10	10	17
50	2	7

Analyze and Conclude

1. **Calculate** What percentage of spores is found 4 meters or less from the fern plot after dispersal? Show your calculations.

____

____

2. **Graph** Make a line graph. Show the number of spores per square centimeter versus distance from the fern plot. Use different colors for the July and November data. Include a title. *Hint:* You may want to use a jagged line at one point along the x-axis.

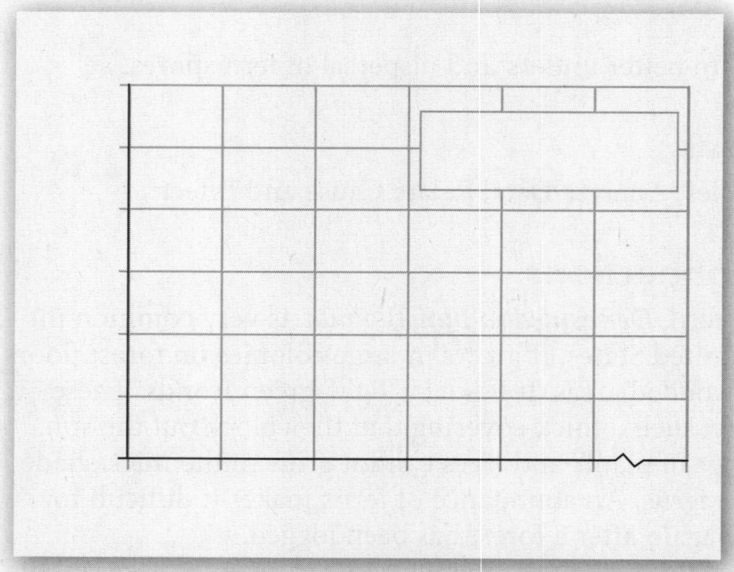

3. **Interpret Graphs** Are spore numbers in the soil higher before dispersal or after dispersal? Explain.

____

____

____

4. **Evaluate** Fertilization for a fern requires a thin film of water. What selective advantage is there for ferns that disperse spores close to the parent plant?

____

____

____

Build Science Skills

You are working on a forest conservation project. Your crew is planting tree seedlings in an area where timber has just been harvested. You notice several clusters of ferns nearby. Should you remove all the ferns to keep them from invading the area around your seedlings? Explain your reasoning.

____

____

____

Lesson 23.3

Data Analysis 29 Reading a Tree's History

Goal

Analyze tree rings to gain knowledge of a tree's growth patterns.

Skills Focus

Analyze Data, Compare and Contrast, Infer

Build Connections

Trees are often used as indicators of weather patterns. By analyzing a tree's rings, you can learn about the conditions in which the tree grew. Each year of growth produces one ring. A thick growth ring indicates that weather conditions that year were good for tree growth. Typically, good conditions include plenty of sun and rain.

In 2005, a large tree in Kensington, Maryland, was uprooted during a storm. The table shows the size of the tree's growth rings. The bold type is used to highlight every fifth year of growth.

Ring Radius (mm)					
Year 1: 10	57	124	212	301	429
13	59	128	216	306	432
15	62	132	220	312	436
17	64	136	224	320	440
19	**69**	**139**	**230**	**325**	**443**
22	71	143	236	332	446
24	74	147	240	337	449
27	78	152	246	342	452
30	79	157	250	350	455
33	**81**	**162**	**255**	**356**	**457**
35	84	165	259	362	459
38	88	170	262	368	462
40	93	174	267	373	465
42	97	178	271	377	468
44	**102**	**182**	**278**	**383**	**470**
46	106	186	282	390	473
48	109	192	286	414	490
51	112	197	289	420	501
53	115	203	293	423	
Year 20: **55**	**119**	**208**	**296**	**427**	

Data from the NASA activity *Sunspots and Tree Rings*

Analyze and Conclude

1. **Interpret Tables** How old was the tree when it came down? About what year was the tree planted?

2. **Analyze Data** What was the diameter of the tree when it came down? Give your answer in both millimeters and meters. *Hint:* How many times would each growth ring be counted if you measured the diameter of the tree?

3. **Calculate** Consider the span of your arms stretched out straight. Assuming you could go back in time, in what year would you have last been able to circle the tree with your arms? Use the formula for circumference: $C = 2\pi r$, where C is the circumference, r is the radius, and $\pi = 3.14$. Remember that $d = 2r$, where d is the diameter. Explain your thinking.

4. **Compare and Contrast** What was the average rate of growth per year for this tree during its lifetime? How does that average compare to its first year of growth? Show your calculations.

5. **Infer** Based on the data, how would you describe the early years of growth compared to later years? What might account for that pattern?

Build Science Skills

Based on the data, were there any unusually good growth years? What would you infer about those years? How could you confirm your inferences?

Lesson 24.2

Data Analysis 30 Temperature and Seed Germination

Goal

Relate seed germination to environmental conditions.

Skills Focus

Interpret Graphs, Analyze Data, Infer, Form a Hypothesis

Build Connections

Arisaema dracontium, also called "green dragon," is a plant that grows in the eastern half of North America. It displays a flame-red cluster of seeds in the fall. The plant's range extends from the southern United States to northern Canada. It is threatened or endangered in Massachusetts, New Hampshire, New York, and Vermont. The graph shows germination rates of green dragon seeds that were (1) collected from two locations and (2) stored at two different temperatures.

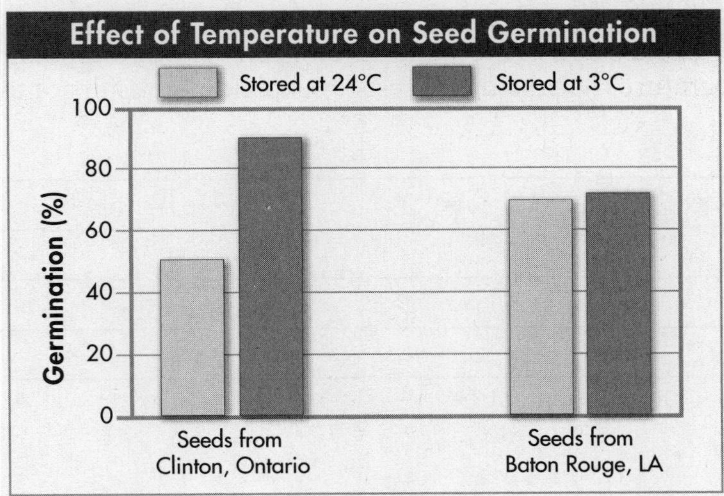

Analyze and Conclude

1. **Interpret Graphs** Where were the seeds collected, and how would the climate of these locations vary?

______

______

______

2. **Interpret Graphs** Why are the bars in the graph two different shades? What does each shade represent?

____

____

____

3. **Analyze Data** At which location did the largest percentage of seeds germinate? At which temperature were those seeds stored? What percentage of seeds stored at that temperature germinated?

____

____

____

4. **Infer** What effect does chilling have on germination of seeds from Ontario? What effect does chilling have on seeds from Louisiana?

____

____

____

____

____

Build Science Skills

The graph shows how seeds from the same species can vary in their response to changes in temperature. Form a hypothesis to explain the results of this experiment.

____

____

____

____

____

Lesson 24.4

Data Analysis 31 Increasing Crop Yields

Goal

Identify factors that affect corn yields.

Skills Focus

Interpret Graphs, Calculate, Infer, Form an Opinion

Build Connections

The amount of a crop that a farmer can harvest per acre is referred to as crop yield. During the 1960s, farmers in the United States saw dramatic increases in the crop yields for corn. The boost in corn yields was due to improved farming methods. For example, most farmers were irrigating crops instead of relying on rain. Most were also using commercial fertilizers instead of animal manure. Recent corn yields tend to range from 125 to 170 bushels per acre. A bushel weighs 60 pounds. There may be between 40 and 60 ears of corn in a bushel, depending on the type of corn. Use the graph to answer the questions on the next page.

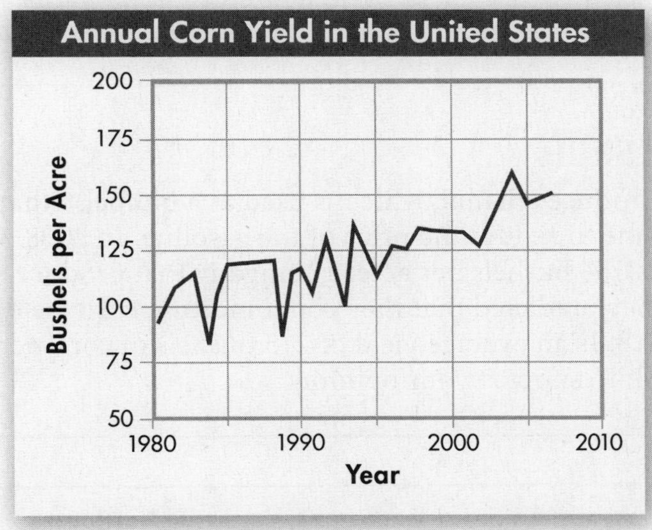

Analyze and Conclude

1. **Read Graphs** What was the corn yield per acre in 1980? What was the corn yield in 2000?

2. **Interpret Graphs** What is the general trend shown in the graph. Draw a line of best fit on the graph to reflect this trend. When drawing a line of best fit, try to position a straight line so that half of the points are above the line and half are below the line.

3. **Calculate** What was the approximate percent change in corn yield from 1980 to 2005? List the data you will use to do the calculation and show your work.

4. **Infer** In 1983 and 1988, major corn-growing regions experienced drought, which means that there was very little rain. Were crop yields affected by the drought? How can you tell?

Build Science Skills

Corn can be used to produce ethanol, which is used as a biofuel. Ethanol can also be added to gasoline to reduce the price of the gasoline. In 2008, when the average corn yield was 154 bushels per acre, a company that produces ethanol made a bold claim. They predicted that they could increase corn yields by at least 40 percent by 2018. Is an average yield of 215 bushels of corn per acre realistic? Use the graph to support your opinion.

Lesson 25.2

Data Analysis 32 Differences in Differentiation

Goal

Graph data to show trends.

Skills Focus

Compare and Contrast, Relate Cause and Effect

Build Connections

The timetable for developmental stages in different species varies greatly. The table shows the length of time it takes four animals to reach important stages in their early development. Use the data to answer the Analyze and Conclude questions.

Time Variations in Developmental Stages of Various Animals

Stage	Chicken	Hamster	Rabbit	Rhesus Monkey
2 cells	3 hours	16 hours	8 hours	24 hours
4 cells	3.25 hours	40 hours	11 hours	36 hours
Three germ layers begin to form	1.5 days	6.5–7 days	6.5 days	19 days
Three germ layers differentiate	3 days	8 days	9 days	25 days
Formation of tail bud	3.25 days	8.5 days	9.5 days	26 days
Birth/Hatching	22 days	16 days	32 days	164 days

Analyze and Conclude

1. **Compare and Contrast** For the four animals, what is the range for the time required for a fertilized egg, or zygote, to divide into two cells? Are these cells haploid or diploid? How do you know?

____

____

2. **Calculate** How much longer does it take a rhesus monkey zygote to reach the 4-cell stage compared to a chicken zygote? Show your work.

____

____

3. **Relate Cause and Effect** Between which stages shown in the table would you place the formation of the blastula? At that point, have the cells differentiated yet?

4. **Compare and Contrast** Which animal takes the most time to reach the differentiation stage? Which takes the least time?

5. **Draw Conclusions** From the limited data in the table, what conclusion can you draw about the time needed for development and the relative size of an organism?

6. **Predict** Use your answer to Question 5 to match the animals with the developmental periods. One match has been done for you.

Cat	600-660 days
Dog	150 days
Pig	336 days
Sheep	65 days
Horse	62 days
Rhinoceros	487 days
Elephant	115 days

Build Science Skills

The three germ layers are called mesoderm, endoderm, and ectoderm. For chordates, such as those in this activity, an internal cavity called a coelom (SEE lum) forms within the body from mouth to anus. Using the prefixes for each of the terms as a guide, indicate the relative position of cells derived from each germ layer, starting with the lining of the coelom. Are the genes in the body cells of each layer the same or different? Are all the genes expressed in every layer?

Lesson 26.2

Data Analysis 33 Feather Evolution

Goal

Analyze data to draw conclusions about evolution.

Skills Focus

Organize Data, Draw Conclusions, Compare and Contrast

Build Connections

One of the most interesting puzzles for biologists is the evolution of birds. Their earliest origins go back to reptiles and the clade that separated and evolved into dinosaurs. None of the dinosaurs shown in the table are direct ancestors of modern birds. Some, however, share a common trait: feathers. The information in the table shows the evolution of feathers in some groups of dinosaurs that preceded modern birds. The groups are listed alphabetically. You will need the information in the table to answer some of the Analyze and Conclude questions.

Group	Feather Status
Allosaurs	No feathers
Archaeopteryx	Flight feathers
Compsognathids	Hairlike feathers
Oviraptors	True feathers
Tyrannosaurs	Branched feathers

Analyze and Conclude

1. **Interpret Diagrams** List the organisms in the cladogram on the next page in order from most ancient to most modern.

____

____

2. **Organize Data** Place the traits from the table as nodes on the cladogram. One node is already placed to get you started. (Recall what you learned about drawing cladograms in Chapter 18.)

3. **Draw Conclusions** Which type of feathers would you expect modern birds to have?

____

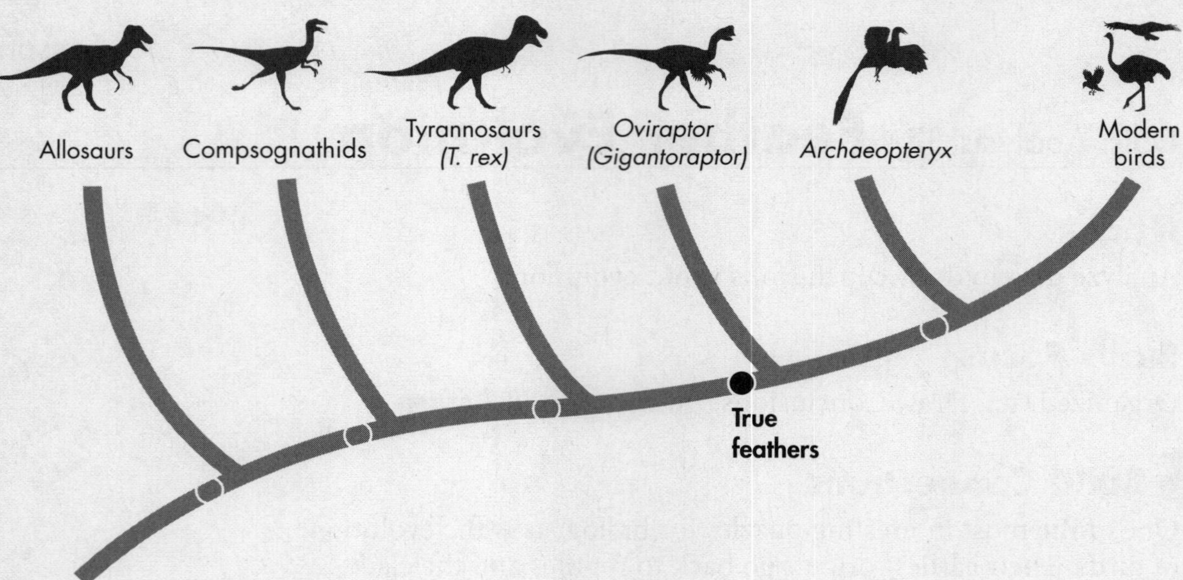

Build Science Skills

The simplified diagram below shows the bones in the wing of a modern bird (a chicken). Compare the wing structure to that of the *Archaeopteryx* fossil shown in Lesson 26.2. Describe the similarities you see. Are these homologous or analogous structures? Explain.

____

____

____

____

Chicken Wing

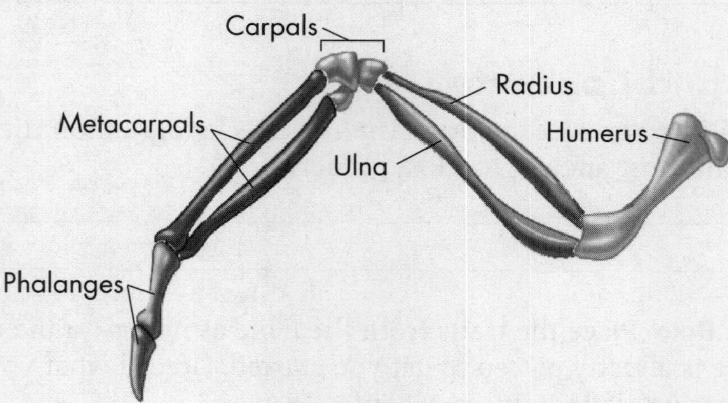

Lesson 27.1

Data Analysis 34 Protein Digestion

Goal

Draw conclusions about the role of pepsin in digestion.

Skills Focus

Interpret Graphs, Infer, Draw Conclusions

Build Connections

An important feature of the digestive system of carnivores is the ability to digest animal protein. A scientist wanted to find out how much time might be needed for a carnivore to digest animal protein. The scientist placed pieces of hard-boiled egg white (an animal protein) in a test tube containing hydrochloric acid, water, and the enzyme pepsin. Pepsin speeds up the rate of protein digestion. The graph shows the rate at which the egg white was broken down, or "digested," over a 24-hour period.

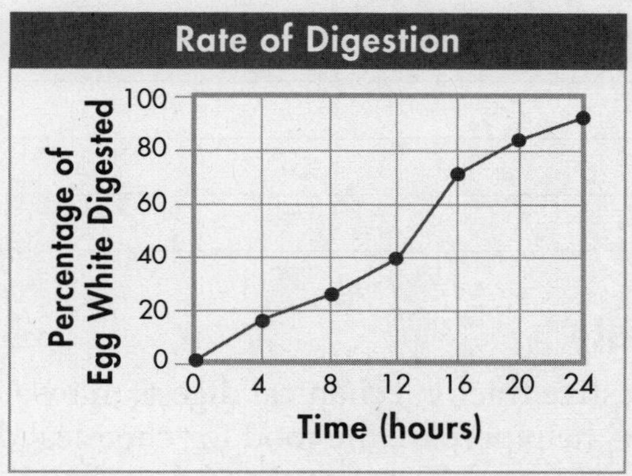

Analyze and Conclude

1. **Interpret Graphs** Identify the dependent and independent variables in the experiment. Which axis is each one plotted on?

____

____

2. **Interpret Graphs** Describe the trends in the rate of protein digestion over the 24-hour period. *Hint:* Look at the slope of the line for the first 12 hours. Then, look at the slope for the next 4 hours, Finally, look at the slope for the last 8 hours.

3. **Analyze Data** About how many hours did it take for half of the protein to be digested?

4. **Infer** While the animal protein is being digested, it is moving through different organs in the digestive system. What has to happen in those organs for digestion to continue?

5. **Draw Conclusions** How would you expect the rate of meat digestion to differ in an animal whose digestive tract releases smaller amounts of pepsin?

Build Science Skills

Before food enters the digestive tract, mechanical digestion by a carnivore's teeth and other mouthparts help prepare the food for chemical digestion. How might the type of mouthparts affect the rate of chemical digestion? *Hint:* Think about the effect of surface area on a chemical reaction.

Lesson 28.4

Data Analysis 35 Soaking Up Sun

Goal

Relate an ectotherm's behavior to its body temperature.

Skills Focus

Interpret Tables, Analyze Data, Predict

Build Connections

Scientists are concerned about how well ectotherms will adjust to the warming trends seen with global climate change. Ectotherms are animals whose body temperature depends on the temperature of their environment. Lizards are ectotherms. Many species of lizard live in very hot climates. How do these lizards maintain homeostasis? A scientist noticed a lizard living outside his desert laboratory. The scientist collected data on the temperature of the lizard and its environment. He also observed the lizard's behavior. Use the data in the table to answer the questions on the next page.

Lizard Activity (12-hour period)

Description of Activity	Time	Temperature (°C)		
		Air	Ground	Body
Leaves burrow	6:00 A.M.	20	28	25.0
Lies flat on rock	7:00	27	29	32.6
Searches for food, water	9:00	31	33	36.6
Enters burrow	Noon	40	54	38.5
Searches for food, water	2:00	39	53	39.5
Climbs cactus, rests	2:30	34	52	38.2
Searches for food, water	3:00	32	50	38.9
Rests, legs extended, tail over head	3:30	29	47	37.1
Enters burrow	6:00	25	26	27.4

Analyze and Conclude

1. **Interpret Tables** Describe the changes in the lizard's body temperature between 6 A.M. and 6 P.M.

2. **Infer** What are three sources of heat that caused the lizard's body temperature to rise during the day?

3. **Interpret Tables** During the hottest part of the day, what were the air and ground temperatures? How did the lizard control its body temperature at this time?

4. **Analyze Data** Identify three behaviors that help the lizard to control its body temperature.

Build Science Skills

With some exceptions, the range of body temperatures for animals falls between 1°C and 45°C. What if temperatures were to rise between 2°C and 5°C in desert areas as a result of climate change? Do you think changes in behavior will be enough for ectotherms to adapt to the changing conditions? Explain your thinking.

Data Analysis 36 Caring for Young

Goal

Interpret a graph to explore how experience affects the breeding success of short-tailed shearwaters.

Skills Focus

Interpret Graphs, Analyze Data, Draw Conclusions

Build Connections

Can experience help animals other than humans care for their young better? Recall that changing behavior in response to experience is a form of learning. The graph is based on data from studies of a seabird, the short-tailed shearwater. A mating pair produces only one egg a year. If the egg breaks or the chick dies, that ends the reproductive cycle for the year. Therefore, a single egg represents the only chance for shearwater reproductive success. By comparison, a loggerhead sea turtle produces about 125 eggs at one time and may nest 4–7 times a year.

The graph shows the percentage of shearwater eggs that develop into independent young. This development is defined as reproductive success. Use the graph to answer the questions on the next page.

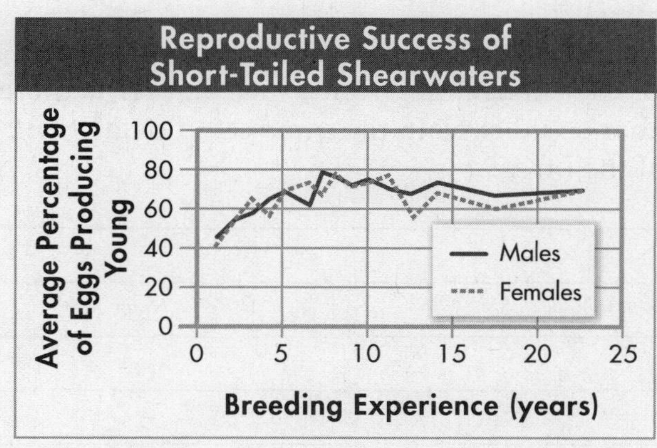

Analyze and Conclude

1. **Interpret Graphs** What was the independent variable in this investigation? What was the dependent variable?

2. **Interpret Graphs** What is the approximate success rate of a female shearwater with five years of breeding experience? Describe that level of success in terms of a hundred shearwater females.

3. **Draw Conclusions** Do older shearwaters have higher reproductive success than younger ones? Use evidence from the graph to support your answer.

4. **Compare and Contrast** Does the graph show differences in reproductive success between male and female shearwaters?

Build Science Skills

Do you think shearwaters learn to raise young more successfully over time? How do you account for the change that occurs later in life? Is there an alternative hypothesis that could explain the same set of data? *Hint:* Think in terms of the life cycle of the birds.

Data Analysis 37 The American Diet

Goal

Analyze data and draw a graph to understand the relationship between nutrition and Calories.

Skills Focus

Calculate, Analyze Data, Evaluate, Graph

Build Connections

Researchers who study eating habits are concerned about the number of fast-food meals Americans eat each week. For example, a researcher in the Midwest studied the eating habits of 2500 teens. She reported that 27 percent of high-school girls and 30 percent of high-school boys eat fast food more than three times a week.

The circle graphs compare a typical American diet to a recommended diet. The graphs show the percent of energy from different classes of nutrients.

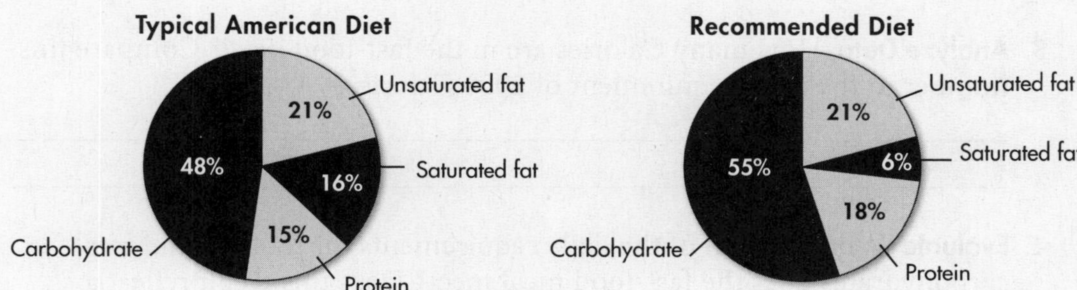

Analyze and Conclude

1. **Calculate** Convert the percentages in the recommended diet into Calories. Assume 2000 Calories are needed per day.

____

____

2. **Calculate** One gram of protein or carbohydrate has about 4 Calories. One gram of fat has about 9 Calories. Calculate the total number of grams of carbohydrate, unsaturated fat, saturated fat, and protein in the fast-food meal.

____

____

The table shows nutritional information from a typical fast-food meal. The fries and the soda are both large. Use the table to answer Questions 3 and 4.

Typical Fast-Food Meal (% daily value based on 2000 C)						
Nutrition Facts	**Burger**	% Daily Value	**Fries**	% Daily Value	**Soda**	% Daily Value
Total Fat	**29.0 g**	**45%**	**25.0 g**	**38%**		
Saturated Fat	10.0 g	50%	3.5 g	18%		
Cholesterol	**75 mg**	**25%**				
Sodium	**1040 mg**	**43%**	**350 mg**	**15%**	**20 mg**	**1%**
Total Carbohydrates	**45.0 g**	**15%**	**63.0 g**	**21%**	**86.0 g**	**29%**
Dietary Fiber	3.0 g	12%	6.0 g	24%		
Sugars	9.0 g				86.0 g	
Protein	**25.0 g**		**6.0 g**			
Vitamin A		6%		0%		
Calcium		25%		2%		
Vitamin C		2%		20%		
Iron		25%		8%		
Calories		**540**		**500**		**310**

3. **Analyze Data** How many Calories are in the fast-food meal? Compare this number to the daily requirement of 2000 Calories.

____

____

4. **Evaluate** What portion of the daily requirements for total fat and total carbohydrates does the fast-food meal meet? Does this result reflect a healthy diet? Explain. *Hint:* Consider other daily requirements and what happens during the rest of the day.

____

____

____

____

Build Science Skills

Make a circle graph in the space below showing the percentage of energy from carbohydrate, unsaturated fat, saturated fat, and protein in the fast-food meal described in the table. You will need to use information from Question 2. *Hint:* The total number of Calories is not 2000. When you are done, compare your graph to the graphs of the typical American diet and recommended diet.

Lesson 31.4

Data Analysis 38 Sound Intensity

Goal

Analyze data to understand the relationship between sound intensity and hearing.

Skills Focus

Compare and Contrast, Relate Cause and Effect

Build Connections

Sound intensity, or loudness, is measured in units called decibels (dB). The threshold of hearing for the human ear—the sound intensity at which people begin to hear—is set at 0 dB. Because the range of intensities the human ear can detect is so large, the scale used to measure sound intensity is based on multiples of 10. For every 10-dB increase, the sound intensity increases ten times. The table lists a typical sound associated with each decibel level. These examples are offered as points of reference.

As the table shows, normal talking has an intensity level of 60 dB. Several hours of listening to sounds above 80 dB and just seconds of listening to sounds at 120 dB can damage hearing. Remember, the closer you are to a sound, the greater its intensity.

Sound (point of reference)	Decibels (dB)	Relative Level of Sound Intensity
Just detectable	0	1
Breathing	10	10
Whisper	20	100
Mosquito	30	
Quiet room	40	10,000
Normal talking (50–60 dB)	50	100,000
Laughter	60	
Hair dryer	70	
Telephone dial tone	80	
Lawn mower	90	
Chain saw	100	10,000,000,000
Rock concert (90–130 dB)	110	
Thunder clap	120	
Jet engine 100 feet away	130	
Air raid siren	140	100,000,000,000,000

Analyze and Conclude

1. **Apply Concepts** For every 10-dB increase, sound intensity increases 10 times. Use this information to complete the third column of the table. How did you know what the missing data should be?

2. **Interpret Tables** What is the sound intensity of a jet plane? How much louder is a jet plane than normal talking? Explain your answer.

3. **Infer** Hearing damage from loud noise usually happens over time. The damage is cumulative, meaning that it increases with repeated exposure. How does this information help explain why older people do not hear as well as younger people?

4. **Relate Cause and Effect** What can you do to prevent hearing loss without giving up listening to music on portable players? *Hint:* Hearing damage is associated with two factors.

Build Science Skills

Doctors report seeing levels of hearing loss in young people similar to those found in much older people. Much of the damage can be traced to the use of portable digital music players. Identify two features of such players that might contribute to hearing loss.

Lesson 32.3

Data Analysis 39 The Rising Rate of Melanoma

Goal

Analyze data to understand the risk of developing melanoma.

Skills Focus

Interpret Graphs, Infer

Build Connections

Melanoma is the most dangerous form of skin cancer, and it is becoming more common. Studies link skin cancer to ultraviolet radiation in sunlight. Yet many people still spend too much time in the sun without adequate protection.

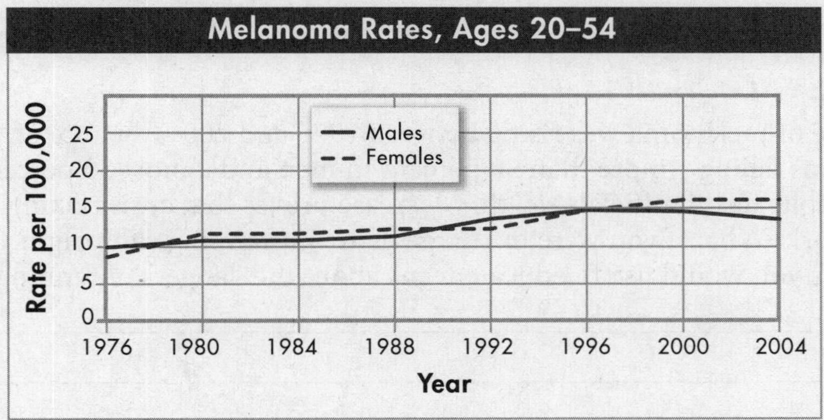

Analyze and Conclude

1. **Interpret Graphs** What does the graph show about the incidence of melanoma in men and women from 1976 to 2004?

____

____

2. **Interpret Graphs** What was the rate of melanoma for men in 2004? If there are 80 million men in the United States, ages 40–54, how many cases of melanoma does that rate represent?

____

____

3. **Calculate** Use the data in the graph to calculate the percentage increase in the rate of melanoma in men and in women from 1976 to 2004.

4. **Infer** Today, despite doctors' warnings, many people still believe that a tan is a sign of good health. What impact do you think that belief has had on the incidence of melanoma in recent years?

5. **Analyze Data** The chance of developing melanoma increases with age. The data in the graph are for people ages 20 to 54. If you looked at similar data for people ages 20 to 75, how do you think the graph would be different? Explain your answer.

Build Science Skills

While the rate of melanoma was rising between 1976 and 2004, the rate of lung cancer was falling—more than 50 percent in men and almost 30 percent in women. Public health officials say this decrease proves that antismoking campaigns work. What if you were in charge of an antitanning campaign? List three methods you would use to educate teens about the dangers of tanning.

Lesson 33.2

Data Analysis 40 Blood Transfusions

Goal

Analyze data to learn how blood type affects the success of transfusions.

Skills Focus

Interpret Tables, Infer, Compare and Contrast

Build Connections

Blood transfusions have been carried out since 1818. Many early recipients, however, had severe reactions, and some died. The problem was blood types. People inherit one of four blood types—A, B, AB, and O. Blood type is determined by the antigens, or lack of antigens, on the surface of blood cells. (Recall that antigens are substances that trigger an immune response.) People with blood type A have A antigens on their blood cells, those with B have B antigens, and those with AB have A and B antigens. Those with O have no antigens.

Transfusions work when the blood types match. They can also work in some cases when the blood types of the donor and the recipient do not match. Use the table to answer the Analyze and Conclude questions on the next page.

Blood Transfusions

	Blood Type of Recipient			
Blood Type of Donor	**A**	**B**	**AB**	**O**
A	✓	×	✓	×
B	×	✓	✓	×
AB	×	×	✓	×
O	✓	✓	✓	✓

× = Unsuccessful transfusion; ✓ = Successful transfusion

Analyze and Conclude

1. **Interpret Tables** One blood type has no antigens. Thus, it is compatible with any blood type and is referred to as the "universal donor." Which blood type is that?

2. **Infer** Which blood type is referred to as the "universal recipient?" Explain this reference in terms of the antigens of the donor and recipient.

3. **Compare and Contrast** In a transfusion involving blood types A and O, does it matter which blood type is the recipient's and which is the donor's? Explain.

Build Science Skills

Use what you know about genotypes and phenotypes to explain why there are four blood types in the ABO blood group. *Hint:* If needed, review the information about alleles in Lesson 14.1.

Data Analysis 41 **Menstrual Cycle**

Goal

Interpret interaction of hormone levels in terms of positive and negative feedback.

Skills Focus

Interpret Graphs, Relate Cause and Effect

Build Connections

The hypothalamus, pituitary, and ovaries make hormones that regulate the menstrual cycle. Changes in the level of hormones form a feedback system that releases an egg and prepares the uterus to accept it. If the egg is not fertilized, menstruation follows and a new cycle begins.

The menstrual cycle is regulated by both positive and negative feedback. Negative feedback, or feedback inhibition, occurs when a stimulus causes a response that has the opposite effect. In a positive feedback system, the stimulus causes a response to intensify. Refer to the diagram as you answer the questions on the next page.

Days	2	4	6	8	10	12	14	16	18	20	22	24	26	28
Phase	Follicular						Ovulation		Luteal					
Hormone Levels in the Blood	FSH		Estrogens				LH				Progesterone			

Analyze and Conclude

1. **Interpret Graphs** A new cycle begins when the hypothalamus detects low levels of estrogens in the blood. It signals the pituitary to produce FSH and LH, which stimulate the development of a new follicle, which releases estrogens. Describe this sequence of events in terms of a feedback system.

2. **Classify** Is the feedback system you described in Question 1 a positive or a negative system? Explain your choice. *Hint:* Is a stimulus being intensified, or is it being inhibited?

3. **Interpret Graphs** As the follicle develops, it releases more and more estrogens. The level of estrogens peaks around Day 12. In response, the hypothalamus signals the pituitary gland. What does the pituitary gland do in response? How can you tell?

4. **Interpret Graphs** After ovulation, the ovary prepares to accept the released egg. Which hormones are needed for this process to occur? How do you know?

5. **Relate Cause and Effect** Why is it important that the levels of FSH and LH drop after ovulation? *Hint:* What is the role of these hormones in the menstrual cycle?

Build Science Skills

If fertilization occurs, the uterus must support the developing fetus. What happens to the levels of progesterone and estrogens? What happens to the levels of FSH and LH? What type of feedback is this? What happens if fertilization does not occur? What type of feedback is this?

Lesson 35.2

Data Analysis 42 Immune System "Memory"

Goal

Analyze data to explore the immune system's first and second response to an antibody.

Skills Focus

Interpret Graphs, Infer, Predict

Build Connections

Your body is able to recognize pathogens as "not self." When cells in your immune system detect antigens on the outer surfaces of pathogens, the cells try to destroy the pathogens. During an initial infection, your body makes memory B cells. These cells allow your body to respond even more quickly if you are infected by the same pathogen again. Memory B cells make new plasma cells very quickly. Plasma cells then make and release antibodies to respond to the antigens on the surface of the pathogen.

The level, or concentration, of antibodies in a person's blood is different for the first and second immune response. Look at the graph. The person was exposed to Antigen A for the first time on Day 1. On Day 28, the person was exposed to Antigen A again and to Antigen B for the first time. One line shows the body's response to Antigen A. The other line shows the response to Antigen B. Use the graph to answer the questions on the next page.

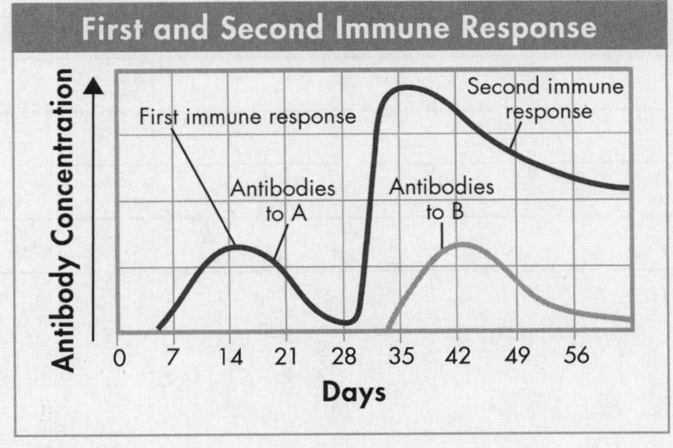

Analyze and Conclude

1. **Interpret Graphs** According to the graph, when did the first immune response reach a level that could be measured?

2. **Infer** What happened on Day 14?

3. **Infer** When did the peak for the second immune response to Antigen A occur?

4. **Compare and Contrast** Did the body respond faster the first or the second time it was exposed to Antigen A? Use the graph to support your answer.

5. **Predict** What do you think will happen when there is a second exposure to Antigen B?

Build Science Skills

In terms of evolution, what selective advantage does having an immune system "memory" give an organism? *Hint:* Think about the body's first reaction to pathogens. Do you think such a "memory" is found in other organisms?

Lesson 35.4

Data Analysis 43 Food Allergies

Goal

Analyze data to make inferences about increasing levels of food allergies among children in the United States.

Skills Focus

Analyze Data, Infer, Calculate

Build Connections

About 4 percent of the children in the United States have food allergies. Eight foods cause 90 percent of all food allergies. These foods are milk, eggs, peanuts, tree nuts, wheat, soy, fish, and shellfish. Food allergies can be very dangerous—they cause about 30,000 emergency room visits and 150–200 deaths each year. Most of the deaths are from peanut allergies. The table shows the percentage of children who were diagnosed with food allergies between 1998 and 2006.

Food Allergies Among Children in the United States

Age	1998–2000	2001–2003	2004–2006
0–4	3.80%	4.20%	4.60%
5–17	3.30%	3.40%	3.90%

Analyze and Conclude

1. **Interpret Tables** In terms of food allergies, what is the general trend for younger children between 1998 and 2006? What is the trend for older children?

____

____

____

2. **Analyze Data** Which age group shows the bigger change between 1998 and 2006?

____

3. Calculate Which age group had the largest percent change from 1998 to 2006? What is the percent change for each group? Show your calculations. *Hint:* More than one mathematical operation is needed to determine the percent change.

4. Calculate In 2006, there were a little more than 20 million children under the age of 5 in the United States. How many children were affected by food allergies? Are food allergies a serious problem among children? Show your calculations.

Build Science Skills

What might be one reason that children 4 years old and younger are more likely to have allergies than older children? *Hint:* Some of the children in one age group enter the next age group during the period of time covered by the table.

Lesson 1.1

Hands-On 1 Asking Questions Scientifically

Goal

Explore what it means to ask questions scientifically by examining a common belief.

Build Connections

There are many common ideas that people accept as true. An idea that is accepted without evidence is called a belief. Here are three common beliefs.

- A piece of buttered bread usually falls buttered-side down.
- When a person's arms are fully extended to the sides, the distance from left fingertip to right fingertip is the same as that person's height.
- It is always darkest just before the dawn.

What makes a scientific idea different from a belief? A scientific idea is based on evidence from the natural world.

Skills Focus

Form a Hypothesis, Design an Experiment

Safety ⚠

Let your teacher know if you plan to use food in your experiment. Do not eat or drink anything while working in the laboratory.

Procedure

In this activity, you will apply scientific process to examine a common belief. You can use one of the beliefs listed above or choose another.

1. Choose a common belief to test scientifically. Write a hypothesis that will allow you to test this belief.

   Hypothesis: ______________________________

   ____

   ____

2. Record your independent and dependent variables.

   Independent Variable: ______________________________

   Dependent Variable: ______________________________

3. Design a controlled experiment based on your hypothesis. Use a separate sheet of paper to record your procedure.
    - Describe how you will measure and organize your data.
    - Decide which variables you will need to control.
    - List the materials you will need to carry out the experiment.
    - List any safety precautions that you will need to take.
4. Give your written procedure to your teacher for approval.
5. Carry out your experiment. Collect and record data.

Analyze and Conclude

1. **Form an Operational Definition** An operational definition is a statement that describes how data collected for an investigation is measured. It provides a way for you to evaluate the results. What operational definition did you use for your investigation?

____

____

____

____

2. **Evaluate** Describe how the hypothesis you wrote helped you test the common belief you chose to investigate.

____

____

____

3. **Draw Conclusions** Is the belief you investigated supported by the evidence you collected? Can you say that the belief is true? Why or why not?

____

____

____

Build Science Skills

Does your experiment qualify as science? Explain your thinking.

____

____

____

____

____

Hands-On 2 Model an Ionic Compound

Goal

Model the formation of an ionic compound.

Build Connections

When sodium metal and chlorine gas react, the product is a white solid known as table salt. The chemical name for this familiar compound is sodium chloride (NaCl). The formula indicates that equal numbers of sodium and chlorine atoms react when sodium chloride is produced.

In this activity, you will work with your classmates to build a model of sodium chloride. Refer to the diagrams below of a sodium chloride crystal as you build your model. The diagram on the left provides a clear view of how the ions are arranged. The diagram on the right provides a more realistic model of how close together the ions are.

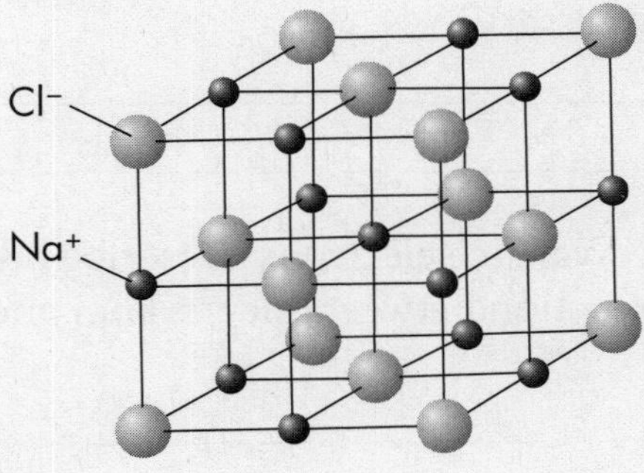

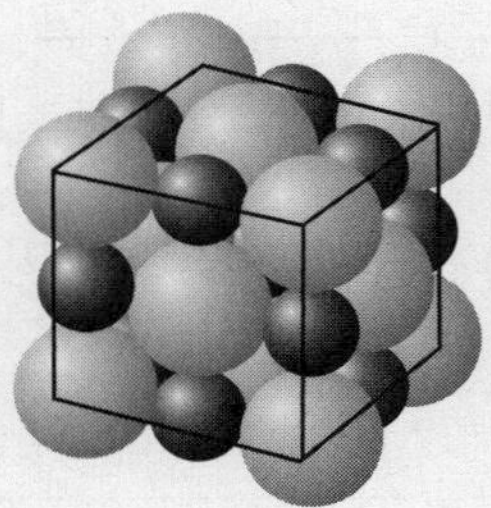

Skills Focus

Use Models, Calculate, Relate Cause and Effect

Materials

- popcorn kernels
- index card
- permanent marker

Safety 

Wash your hands thoroughly with soap and warm water before leaving the lab.

Procedure

In this lab, you will represent the nucleus of an atom. The popcorn kernels will represent your atom's electrons.

1. Your teacher will give you an index card with the symbol Na for sodium or Cl for chlorine.
2. Collect one popcorn kernel for each electron in an atom of your assigned element.
3. Find a partner with whom you can model forming an ionic bond. After you form the bond, use a marker to change the symbol on your card to reflect what happened to your atom as the bond formed.
4. Join with the rest of your classmates to model the arrangement of ions across one plane of a sodium chloride crystal.

Analyze and Conclude

1. **Use Models** How did you model the formation of an ionic bond?

____

____

2. **Relate Cause and Effect** How did you modify the symbol on your index card in Step 3? Why was this change necessary?

____

____

3. **Use Models** Magnesium atoms have two valence electrons. Describe how you would modify Step 3 to show the reaction between magnesium and chlorine.

____

____

4. **Draw Conclusions** What is the main factor that determines the arrangement of ions in an ionic compound? Explain.

____

____

Build Science Skills

Use what you know about ionic bonds to explain why sodium chloride has a melting point of about 800°C.

____

____

____

Hands-On 3 Abiotic Factors: Sand Versus Soil

Goal

Describe how abiotic factors can affect growth in different species of plants.

Build Connections

You may think of plants and animals first when you think of the characteristics of an ecosystem. However, the physical or abiotic factors of an ecosystem determine which plants and animals can live there. Air and water are critical to life. But soil provides the foundation for an ecosystem. Its qualities help to determine what types of plants can be supported. In turn, the types of plants determine which types of animals the ecosystem can support.

Skills Focus

Observe, Infer, Draw Conclusions

Materials

- 4 small paper cups
- tray
- sand
- potting soil
- rye and rice seeds, 10 each
- water

Safety

Wash your hands thoroughly with soap and warm water after handling plants and soil.

Procedure

In this activity, you will plant two different types of seeds in two different types of soil. Once you have planted your seeds, you will make observations over a two-week period.

1. Take four paper cups. Use a pencil to punch three holes in the bottom of each cup. Place the cups on a tray.
2. Fill two of the cups half full of sand. Fill the other two cups half full of potting soil. Label each cup with the type of soil.
3. Use the tip of a pencil to make five shallow holes in the surface of the soil in each cup.

4. Plant five rice seeds in the sand in one cup and five rice seeds in the sand in the second cup. Cover the seeds with a thin layer of sand. Label each cup with the type of seed.
5. Repeat Step 4, using the cups with potting soil.
6. Place all the cups in a warm, sunny location.
7. Each day for two weeks, water the cups equally to moisten the soil. Record your observations.

Analyze and Conclude

1. **Analyze Data** In which type of soil did the rice grow better—sand or potting soil? Which was the better soil for growing rye?

2. **Infer** Potting soil holds more water than sand does. Based on your observations, which kind of environment favors the growth of rice? Which kind of environment favors the growth of rye?

3. **Draw Conclusions** Based on your observations, would rice or rye compete more successfully in a dry environment? Which would be more successful in a moist environment?

Build Science Skills

(1) What were the dependent and independent variables in this experiment? *Hint:* There were two dependent variables. (2) Identify two other abiotic factors that might affect plant growth.

Lesson 4.2

Hands-On 4 Modeling Predator-Prey Interactions

Goal

Model the effects of predation on populations of prey and predators.

Build Connections

One type of interaction between organisms in an ecosystem is predation. A predator is an animal that captures and feeds on another animal, its prey. Predation affects the size of a prey population, and the size of a prey population affects the size of the predator population. In this activity, snakes will be the predators and mice will be the prey. You will record and interpret changes in the populations of both the predators and prey.

Skills Focus

Use Models, Relate Cause and Effect, Draw Conclusions

Materials

- 200 1-inch red squares
- 50 3-inch blue squares

Procedure

In this activity, your desk represents an ecosystem. Use the red squares to represent mice. Use the blue squares to represent snakes—predators that feed on mice. You will work with a partner. Decide which one of you will be the predator and which one will be the prey. As you do the activity, record your results in the data table on the next page.

1. Toss three red squares on your desk. In the data table, write 3 in the column labeled Number of Prey for Generation 1.
2. Toss one blue square on your desk. Write 1 in the column labeled Number of Predators for Generation 1.
3. If the blue square is *touching* one or more red squares, the snake has eaten one or more mice. Remove any red squares that the blue square is touching. Write the correct number of red squares remaining in the column labeled Prey Remaining and 1 in the column labeled Predators Remaining.

4. If the blue square is *not touching* a red square, the snake did not eat. A predator that does not eat will die. Remove the blue square. Write 3 under Prey Remaining and 0 under Predators Remaining.
5. The number of prey doubles in each generation. Multiply the Prey Remaining at the end of Generation 1 by 2. Enter that number under Number of Prey for Generation 2. Add enough red squares to your desk to equal that number. **NOTE:** When you add squares, toss them on the desk to keep the results random.
6. In this activity, if a predator dies, a new predator takes its place. *If your predator died,* add a blue square to your desk. Write 1 under Number of Predators for Generation 2.
7. The number of surviving predators doubles each generation. *If your predator survived,* add another blue square to your desk. Write 2 under Number of Predators for Generation 2.
8. Repeat Steps 3 through 7 for a total of ten generations. **NOTE:** In this activity, if two predators capture the same prey, only one predator can survive.

Data Table: Results of Activity

Generation	Number of Prey	Number of Predators	Prey Remaining	Predators Remaining
1				
2				
3				
4				
5				
6				
7				
8				
9				
10				

Analyze and Conclude

1. **Infer** Why does it make sense to start the activity with a ratio of 3 prey to 1 predator? *Hint:* Think in terms of a food pyramid.

2. **Analyze Data** At what point in the activity did the ratio of predators to prey change? What happens at that point?

3. **Relate Cause and Effect** In well-established communities, the populations of a predator and its primary prey usually increase and decrease in predictable cycles. Why is that the case?

4. **Draw Conclusions** Does the predator-prey relationship provide an advantage for the predator population, the prey population, or both populations? Explain your thinking.

5. **Predict** What would happen to a snake population if all of the mice died of disease?

Build Science Skills

Owls are predators of mice and snakes. How would you expect populations of mice and snakes to change when owls join a community?

Lesson 5.2

Hands-On 5 How Competition Affects Growth

Goal

Explore crowding as a limiting factor in plant growth.

Build Connections

You may think the term *competition* refers only to interactions that occur between species. However, members of the same species also compete for resources in the environment. This competition is a density-dependent factor. It depends on how many members of a species occupy the same area. Too high a density will limit growth of a population. The limit depends on the species.

Skills Focus

Observe, Compare and Contrast, Form a Hypothesis

Materials

- 2 small paper cups
- tray
- potting soil
- 18 bean seeds
- water

Safety

Wash your hands thoroughly with soap and warm water after handling plants and soil.

Procedure

1. Label two paper cups 3 and 15. Use a pencil to punch several small holes in the bottom of each cup. Place the cups on a tray.
2. Fill each cup two-thirds full with potting soil.
3. Plant 3 bean seeds in cup 3 and 15 bean seeds in cup 15. Push the seeds into the soil until they are just covered by the soil.
4. Slowly add water to both cups until the soil is moist but not wet. Try to add about the same amount of water to each cup.
5. Put the tray in a location that receives bright indirect light. Each day for two weeks, add an equal amount of water to the cups to keep the soil moist.

6. Count and record the number of seedlings in each cup every other day. Describe any differences you see in the seedlings.

Data Table			
Day	Number of Seedlings		Observations
	Cup 3	Cup 15	
2			
4			
6			
8			
10			
12			
14			

Analyze and Conclude

1. **Compare and Contrast** What was the difference in the number of seedlings growing in each cup after two weeks?

2. **Compare and Contrast** What differences other than number did you observe about the seedlings growing in the two cups?

3. **Infer** What resources are the seedlings competing for?

Build Science Skills

Write a hypothesis that describes what happened in your experiment. Include details about the design of the experiment in your hypothesis. *Hint:* Use the words *if* and *then* in your hypothesis.

Hands-On 6 Overpackaging

Goal

Examine packaging of a product to compare its cost per unit with the potential cost of the solid waste it produces.

Build Connections

Americans enjoy many food products that are packaged and preserved for convenience. These products typically come in disposable, or throwaway, packaging. But such packaging might end up in a landfill, which is a cost to the environment and society.

Skills Focus

Calculate, Compare and Contrast

Materials

- candy-coated chocolate, single-serving bag
- candy-coated chocolate, large bag
- scissors
- large bowl
- small bowl
- metric ruler
- calculator

Safety  

Do not eat or drink anything while working in a laboratory. Wash your hands thoroughly before and after handling food.

Procedure

1. Record the cost of each bag in the data table on the next page.
2. Cut open both bags. Pour the contents of the large bag into the large bowl. Pour the contents of the small bag into the small bowl. **CAUTION:** Do not eat any of the chocolates.
3. Count and record the number of chocolates in each bag.
4. Flatten each bag. Measure the length and width of each package. Record your data.
5. Calculate the total area of each bag. Multiply length × width to find the area of one side. Multiply this area by 2.
6. Calculate the number of chocolates per square centimeter of packaging. Divide the total area by the number of chocolates.

Data Table		
Property	**Large Bag**	**Single Serving**
Cost		
Number of chocolates		
Dimensions of bag (cm x cm)		
Total area of packaging (cm^2)		
Number of chocolates per cm^2		

Analyze and Conclude

1. **Calculate** Determine the cost per chocolate for each bag. How does the cost of a large-bag chocolate compare to the cost of a small-bag chocolate?

2. **Calculate** Find the cost per square meter of packaging for each bag.

3. **Compare and Contrast** Describe any relationship you see between the cost per chocolate and the cost per square centimeter of packaging.

4. **Infer** What other packaging would be associated with the bags of chocolates when they are shipped from the factory?

Build Science Skills

What does this activity suggest about how food choices can affect your ecological footprint? What can you do to lessen the impact?

Hands-On 7 Making a Model of a Cell

Goal

Build a model to better understand cell structure.

 Build Connections

Each part of a plant cell has a specific function, which is often reflected in the size, shape, and location of the part. For example, the nucleus, which controls what happens in a cell, is located in the center of the cell. In this activity, you will work with your classmates to make a model of a plant cell.

Skills Focus

Use Models, Calculate, Compare and Contrast, Infer

Materials

- craft materials
- index card
- scissors
- tape or glue

Safety

Do not direct the points of the scissors toward yourself or others. Use the scissors only as instructed.

Procedure

Your classroom will represent a plant cell. You will make a model of an organelle or other cell part to place in your classroom "cell."

1. Use the table on page 175 of your textbook to select a part to model. The drawing on page 174 will give you an idea of the relative sizes of cell parts and their positions in the cell.
2. Use the materials provided to build a three-dimensional model of your chosen cell part. Refer to other drawings in Lesson 7.2 to make your model as complete and accurate as possible.
3. Label an index card with the name of your cell part, and list its main features and functions. Attach the card to your model.
4. Place your model at an appropriate location in your classroom.
5. As a class, review the completed model. If necessary, relocate some of the cell parts to reflect the spatial and functional relationships between parts of the cell.

Name ______________________ Class ________ Date ________

Analyze and Conclude

1. **Calculate** A typical plant cell has a width of 50 micrometers (μm), or 5×10^{-5} m. Calculate the scale of your classroom cell model. *Hint:* Divide the width of your classroom by the width of a typical plant cell. Use the same unit for both measurements.

2. **Compare and Contrast** How is your model of a cell part similar to the actual cell part? How is it different?

3. **Infer** How is the structure of your cell part adapted to its function?

Build Science Skills

If you were starting over, what would you do to improve your model?

Hands-On 8 CO_2 and You

Goal

Investigate carbon dioxide as a waste product of physical activity.

Build Connections

Each time you take a breath, an exchange of gases occurs between you and the atmosphere. You take in oxygen-rich air and push out carbon dioxide gas. Oxygen molecules are used to break down food and provide energy for everything you do. One of the products of this process is carbon dioxide. In this activity, you will explore how physical activity affects carbon dioxide production.

Skills Focus

Analyze Data, Infer, Draw Conclusions

Materials

- 4 medium test tubes
- test-tube rack
- 10-mL graduated cylinder
- bromthymol blue solution
- 4 straws
- timer or clock with second hand

Safety

Use a stream of water to rinse bromthymol blue solution from your eyes, skin, or clothing. Try not to inhale the vapors. Tell your teacher if you break a glass object. Wash your hands thoroughly with soap and warm water before leaving the lab.

Procedure

You will use bromthymol blue (BTB) to test for the presence of CO_2. The color of BTB will change when CO_2 is added to water.

1. Put on your safety goggles, plastic gloves, and apron.
2. Label two test tubes with the letters A and B. Put 10 mL of water and a few drops of BTB solution in each test tube.
3. First determine the CO_2 released while at rest. Your partner will time you during this step. When your partner says "go," slowly blow air through a straw into the bottom of test tube A. **CAUTION:** Do not inhale through the straw.

4. When the solution changes color, your partner should say "stop" and then record how long the color change took.
5. Jog in place for 2 minutes. **CAUTION:** Do not do this activity if you have a medical condition that interferes with exercise. If you feel faint or dizzy, stop immediately and sit down.
6. Blow air through a straw into the solution in test tube B. Your partner will watch for the color change and record the time.
7. Trade roles with your partner. Repeat steps 2–6.

Data Table

	Time at Rest	Time After Exercise
You		
Partner		

Analyze and Conclude

1. **Observe** What color was the starting solution of water and BTB? What color was the solution after you exhaled into it?

____

____

2. **Analyze Data** How did exercise affect the time it took the solution to change color? How did your results compare to your partner's?

____

____

3. **Infer** How does exercise affect cellular respiration? How do you know?

____

____

Build Science Skills

BTB is an acid-base indicator. It is blue in solutions that are basic or neutral, such as pure water. Adding CO_2 to water will cause the solution to become acidic. The solution will turn green and then yellow as the acidity increases. Suppose you took a sprig of *Elodea,* which is a water plant, and placed it in the acidic solution in one test tube. Predict what would happen if you were to place the test tube in direct sunlight. Explain your thinking.

____

____

____

____

Lesson 10.1

Hands-On 9 Comparing Surface Area and Volume

Goal

Use models to explore how does cell size affects a cell's ability to function.

Build Connections

In this activity, you will construct a set of paper cubes. The cubes will represent cells at different stages of growth. After you construct your cubes, you will calculate the volume, surface area, and ratio of surface area to volume of each cube.

Skills Focus

Use Models, Calculate, Design an Experiment

Materials

- patterns for 6-cm, 5-cm, 4-cm, and 3-cm cubes
- scissors
- tape or glue

Safety 

Do not direct the points of the scissors toward yourself or others. Use the scissors only as instructed.

Procedure

1. Cut out the patterns on pages 343, 345, and 347 and fold them along the dashed lines. Use the tabs to tape or glue the sides together. Do not tape down the top side.
2. Calculate the surface area of each cube. Find the area of one side of the cube and multiply that area by the number of sides. Record your results in the data table on the next page.
3. Calculate the volume of each cube. Multiply width times length times height. Record the results in the data table on the next page.

4. Divide the surface area by the volume to find the ratio of surface area to volume. Record your results in the data table.

Data Table			
Width of Side	Surface Area (cm^2)	Volume (cm^3)	Ratio of Surface Area to Volume
6 cm			
5 cm			
4 cm			
3 cm			

5. Use your data to calculate the number of 3-cm cubes that would fit in the same volume as the 6-cm cube. Also calculate the total surface area for the smaller cubes.

Number of 3-cm cubes: ______________________

Total surface area of smaller cubes: ______________________

Analyze and Conclude

1. **Review** Describe the function of a cell membrane and its relationship to what happens inside a cell.

____

____

2. **Draw Conclusions** How did the ratio of surface area to volume change as the size of the cubes decreased?

____

3. **Relate Cause and Effect** As a cell grows, what happens to the amount of activity in the cell and the need for materials to be exchanged across the cell membrane?

____

____

Build Science Skills

How could the growth of a cell affect its ability to survive?

____

____

____

____

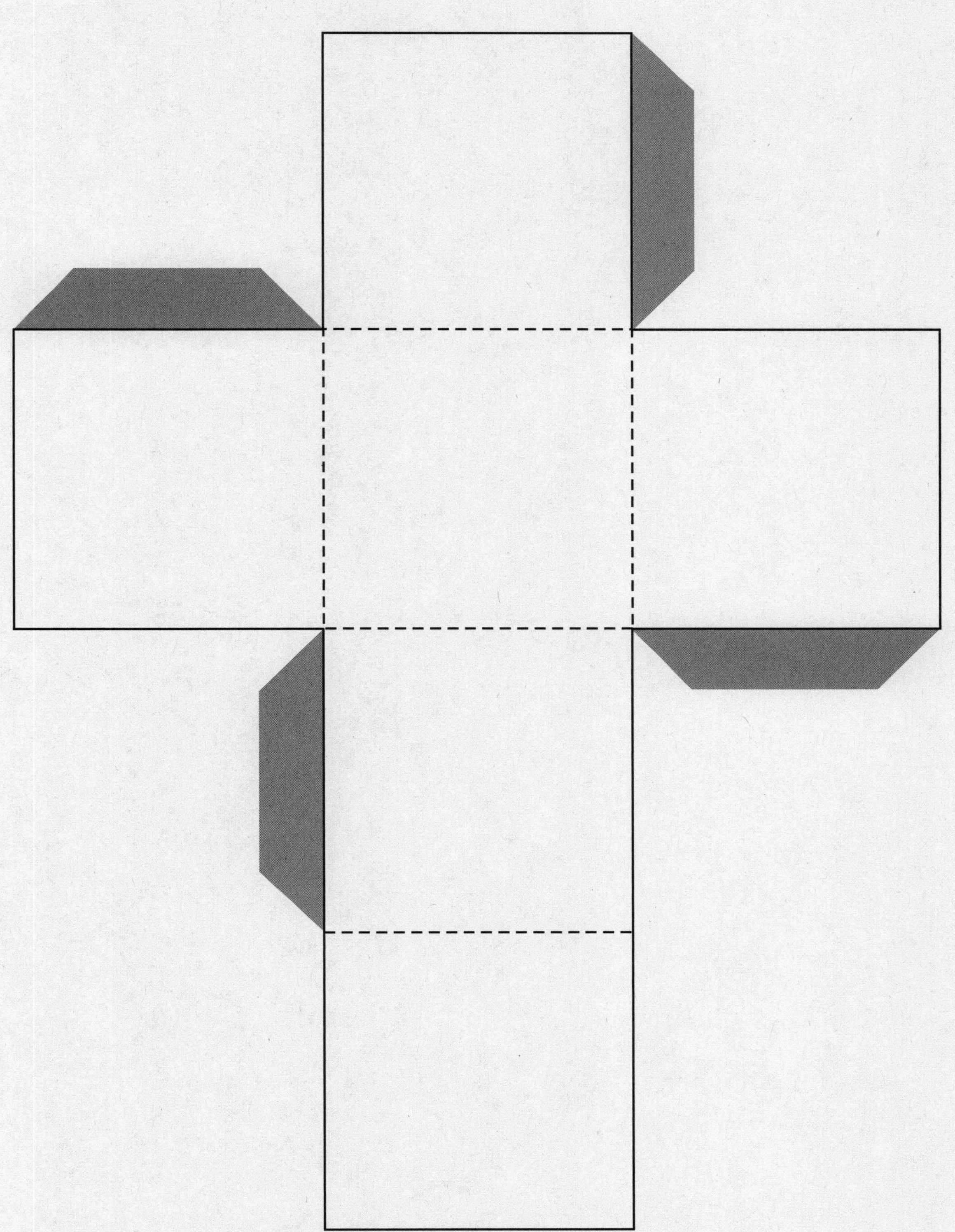

Lesson 11.2

Hands-On 10 How Are Dimples Inherited?

Goal

Predict the outcome of a genetic cross.

Build Connections

Alleles that you inherited from your parents determine whether or not you have dimples. In thisactivity, you will model the inheritance of dimples.

Skills Focus

Use Models, Analyze Data

Procedure

1. Write down the last four digits of a telephone number. You will use these digits to represent the alleles in a gene. Odd digits will represent the allele for dimples, a dominant trait. Even digits will represent the allele for the recessive trait of no dimples. Count 0 as an even digit.
2. Use the first two digits in your number to represent a father's genotype. Use the symbols *D* and *d* to write his genotype. Refer to the example in Figure 1.

   Father's genotype: ______________________

3. Use the last two digits to represent a mother's genotype.

   Mother's genotype: ______________________

Figure 1 Sample of genotype based on four random digits

Father's genotype is *dd* (2 even digits).

Mother's genotype is *Dd* (1 odd digit and 1 even digit).

46 | 38

4. Record the alleles that could be found in all the possible gametes that each parent could produce.

   Father's alleles: ______________________

   Mother's alleles: ______________________

5. Use the Punnett square to predict the genotype combinations for a cross between the father and mother. First, enter the data from Step 4. Place the father's possible alleles in the top row and the mother's possible alleles in the left column. Complete the square by combining the genotypes of the gametes.

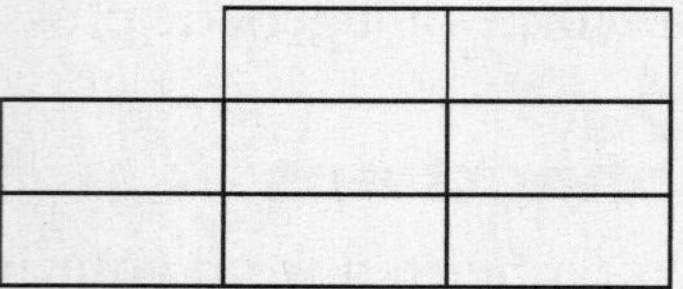

6. Determine the percentage of students in your class who inherited alleles for dimples.

____

Analyze and Conclude

1. **Relate Cause and Effect** What are the possible genotypes for a person with dimples? For a person with no dimples?

____

____

2. **Analyze Data** What is the probability that a child will have dimples when both parents are heterozygous for the gene that determines dimples?

____

3. **Analyze Data** What is the probability that a child will have dimples when one parent is homozygous for the dimple allele and the other is heterozygous for the gene that determines dimples?

____

4. **Analyze Data** What is the probability that a child will have dimples when both parents are homozygous for the no-dimple allele?

____

Build Science Skills

Which type of cross could have produced the percentage of dimples among students in your class?

____

____

Lesson 12.3

Hands-On 11 Modeling DNA Replication

Goal

Use a model to investigate how one strand of DNA acts as a template for the other.

 Build Connections

Body cells in humans have 46 chromosomes. During mitosis, the chromosomes are duplicated, and each daughter cell gets a copy. How is it that the body can continue to copy DNA again and again with such accuracy? The answer lies in the way the copies are made. Each strand of DNA acts as a template. A template is a model or pattern used to make multiple copies of an object.

Skills Focus

Use Models

Materials

- colored paper
- metric ruler
- scissors
- tape

Do not direct the points of the scissors toward yourself or others. Use the scissors only as instructed.

Procedure

Using the pattern shown below, you will construct paper models of the four nucleotides that make up a strand of DNA. The pattern is a simplified version of the nucleotide diagram in Lesson 12.3. You will make a single strand of ten nucleotides to use as a template.

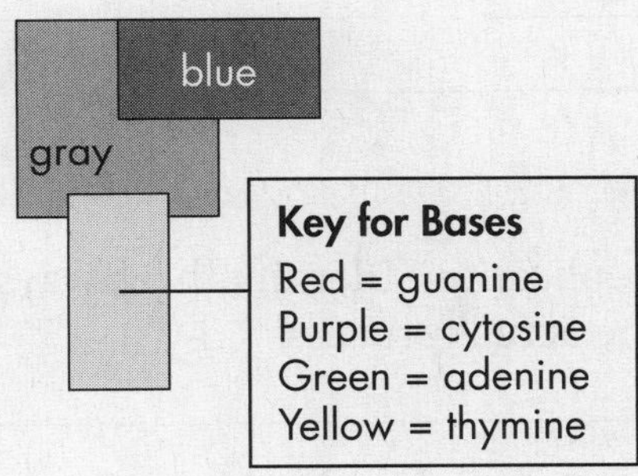

Key for Bases
Red = guanine
Purple = cytosine
Green = adenine
Yellow = thymine

1. Cut out rectangles of colored paper to represent each component of the nucleotides as indicated in the table.

Component	Color	Number of Pieces	Dimensions
Sugar	gray	36	2 cm × 2 cm
Phosphate group	blue	36	1 cm × 2 cm
Guanine (G)	red	12	1 cm × 2 cm
Cytosine (C)	purple	12	1 cm × 2 cm
Adenine (A)	green	6	1 cm × 2 cm
Thymine (T)	yellow	6	1 cm × 2 cm

2. Using the pattern as a guide, tape together 36 nucleotides.
3. To model a single strand of DNA, tape the sugar (gray square) of each nucleotide to the phosphate group (blue strip) of the next nucleotide in the following order: G T T A C A A T C. The bases should all point in the same direction. The sugars and phosphate groups form the "backbone" of the strand.
4. Using your strand as a template, construct a second strand of DNA that is complementary to the first strand.
5. Place the two strands so that they face each other, with the complementary bases opposite each other. Write "original" on each strand.
6. Separate the strands. You and your partner should each take a strand and construct a new complementary strand for each original strand. Write "duplicate" on each new strand.

Analyze and Conclude

1. **Compare and Contrast** Compare the duplicate strands with the strands in the original DNA molecule. Are their nucleotide sequences identical?

____

2. **Use Models** When a cell divides, each daughter cell receives one copy of the original cell's DNA. According to your model, how are the duplicate and original strands divided between the two new daughter cells?

____

____

Build Science Skills

Evaluate your model of DNA replication. Identify three ways in which the model simulates, or imitates, the actual process.

____

____

Hands-On 12 Modeling Restriction Enzymes

Goal

Use a model to investigate how different restriction enzymes cut apart a DNA strand.

Build Connections

Restriction enzymes are used to break DNA molecules into smaller strands. Restriction enzymes are produced in bacteria and archaea. The enzymes offer these single-celled organisms a defense against viruses. When viruses invade a cell, they use the materials in the cell to reproduce themselves. The enzymes limit, or "restrict," the viral DNA by cutting it apart. Restriction enzymes are named after the organisms they are found in. For example, the enzyme *Eco*RI comes from *E. coli* bacteria.

Skills Focus

Use Models

Materials

- colored pencils
- scissors
- tape

Safety

Do not direct the points of the scissors toward yourself or others. Use the scissors only as instructed.

Procedure

The diagram shows three restriction enzymes. You will compare the effect of these enzymes on strands of DNA with 50 base pairs.

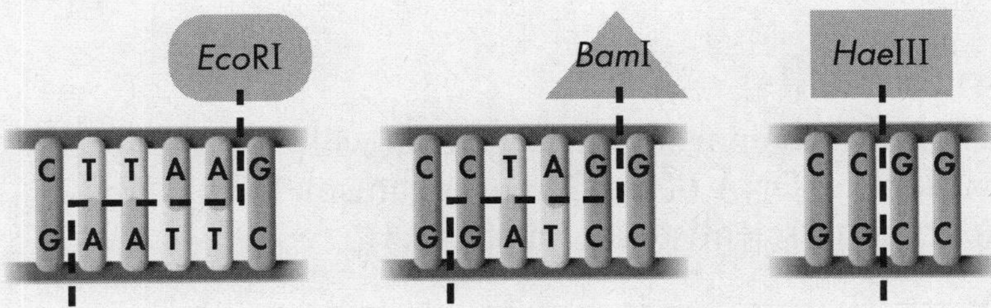

 •

1. Use a different colored pencil to *lightly* color in each DNA sequence on page 355. Then cut out the sequences.
2. Pick one sequence and mark the points on the sequence where it would be cut apart by the *Eco*RI restriction enzyme. Use the marks to cut the sequence apart. Record the color of the strip, the enzyme, and the number of fragments.

   ____

3. Repeat Step 2 with a second sequence and *Bam*I.

   ____

4. Repeat Step 2 with the third sequence and *Hae*III.

   ____

5. To model the building of recombinant DNA, choose one of your DNA fragments. Take your fragment over to another group. Use it to piece together a new strand of DNA by taping your fragment to one or two of their fragments.

Analyze and Conclude

1. **Observe** Which restriction enzyme produced the most pieces? Which produced the fewest pieces?

   ____

   ____

2. **Relate Cause and Effect** Use the structure of the enzymes to explain the result you reported in Question 1.

   ____

   ____

   ____

3. **Evaluate** How well did your model represent the actual process of using restriction enzymes to cut DNA? *Hint:* Contrast the length of your model DNA sequence to the actual length of a DNA molecule.

   ____

   ____

   ____

Build Science Skills

Most restriction enzymes taken from one organism will recognize their restriction sequence in the DNA of a different organism. Why is this characteristic important to scientists studying DNA?

____

____

T A T T C G A A C T T A A G C C G G G C C T A G G C A C C G G T A C T T A A G C C C C G G A T A G A

A T A A G C T T G A A T T C G G C C C G G A T C C G T G G C C A T G A A T T C G G G G C C T A T C T

Sequence 1

A A C T T C C G G A T T T C C G G C T G A G C C G G C C T A G G C T T A A G C G G A C C G G C A T G

T T G A A G G C C T A A A G G C C G A C T C G G C C G G A T C C G A A T T C G C C T G G C C G T A C

Sequence 2

T T C C C T A G G C C T A T A G C C G G C T T A A G T A T T C G A A C C T A G G T T C C G G T C G G

A A G G G A T C C G G A T A T C G G C C G A A T T C A T A A G C T T G G A T C C A A G G C C A G C C

Sequence 3

Cut out these strips to help you identify the restriction sites.

C C G G	C T T A A G	C C T A G G
*Hae*III	*Eco*RI	*Bam*I

Name ______________________ Class __________ Date __________

Hands-On 13 Comparing Bones

Goal

Identify homologous bones in vertebrate forelimbs.

 Build Connections

The term *forelimb* refers to the front leg or arm of a vertebrate. The bones in the forelimbs of modern vertebrates are homologous. These forelimbs evolved from the forelimbs of an extinct lobe-finned fish that lived more than 380 million years ago. If modern vertebrates all had different origins, it would be unlikely for them to have such similar structures.

In this activity, you will compare the bones in the forelimb of a human, cat, and lizard.

Skills Focus

Use Models, Compare and Contrast

Materials

- scissors
- tape

Safety

Do not direct the points of the scissors toward yourself or others. Use the scissors only as instructed.

Procedure

Look at the diagram of the human arm. Note how the upper arm (humerus), lower arm (ulna and radius), and hand bones fit together. Use the diagram as a model to help you piece together the forelimbs of a cat and lizard.

Human Arm

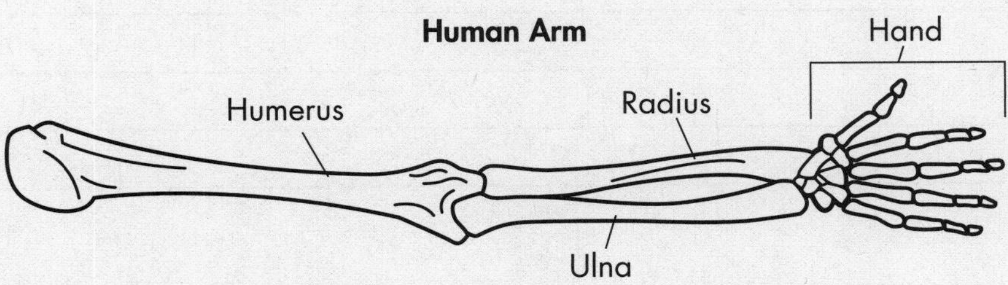

1. Cut out the drawings of bones on page 359.
2. Move the parts around to form a cat forelimb and a lizard forelimb. **NOTE:** The drawings are not drawn at actual size.
3. After you have pieced together both forelimbs, tape the limbs onto a sheet of notebook paper. Label the parts of each forelimb and add a label for the animal name.

Analyze and Conclude

1. **Interpret Visuals** How did the drawing of the human arm help you assemble the cat and lizard forelimbs?

____

____

2. **Classify** Describe how you decided which bones belonged to which animal.

____

____

____

3. **Compare and Contrast** Describe the similarities among the three forelimbs. How would these compare in actual size?

____

____

____

4. **Compare and Contrast** Use your structures and your experience to compare the ways that the three species use their forelimbs.

____

____

____

____

Build Science Skills

How do these homologous structures provide evidence to support the theory that vertebrates evolved from a common ancestor?

____

____

____

____

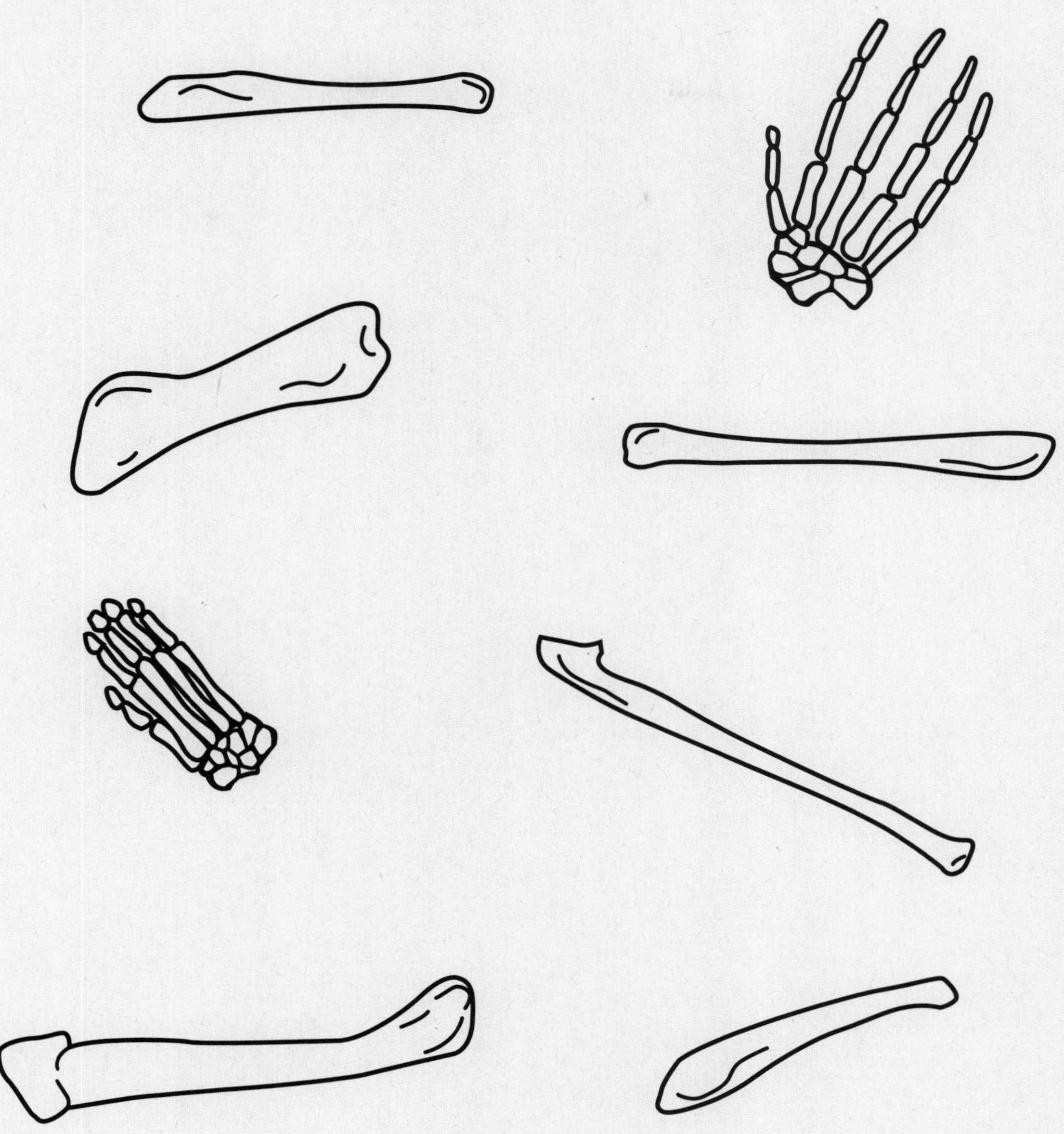

Lesson 17.2

Hands-On 14 Modeling Natural Selection

Goal

Model natural selection pressure on organisms with mutations.

Build Connections

A mutation may offer an organism an advantage for a given environment. For a mutation to be considered an adaptation, it must increase an organism's fitness. Fitness refers to the ability of an organism to survive and reproduce. An organism with increased fitness has a good chance of passing on the trait. Over time, the trait becomes more common in a population.

Skills Focus

Use Models, Organize Data, Graph

Materials

- 75 blue plastic chips
- 75 red plastic chips

Procedure

In this activity, your desktop will represent an environment that goes through a change in climate. The blue chips represent a species that can only reproduce in temperatures between 10°C and 20°C. These are normal breeding temperatures. The red chips represent members of the same species with a mutation. The mutation allows them to reproduce in temperatures above 20°C as well as in the normal temperature range. These organisms are especially tolerant of heat.

As you do the activity, use the data table to record the number of red chips, blue chips, and total chips for each year.

1. Scatter ten red chips and ten blue chips on your desk.
2. In Year 1, the temperatures during the breeding season stay between 10°C and 20°C. Add a red chip or a blue chip for each pair of chips of the same color that are able to breed at these temperatures. Remove one red chip and one blue chip to allow for a death within each of the populations. Record the number of red chips, blue chips, and the total chips for Year 1.
3. During Years 2–4, the climate changes. During the breeding season, the temperatures stay above 20°C. Use this information and the rules described in Step 2 to fill in the table for Years 2–4.
4. During Year 5, the temperatures return to between 10°C and 20°C during the breeding season. Following the rules of reproduction in Step 2, record the population data for Year 5.

	Start	Year 1	Year 2	Year 3	Year 4	Year 5
Red	10					
Blue	10					
Total	20					

Analyze and Conclude

1. **Graph** Make a line graph to compare the growth of the red and blue populations. Remember to title your graph and label both *x*- and *y*-axes. Either label the lines or include a key.

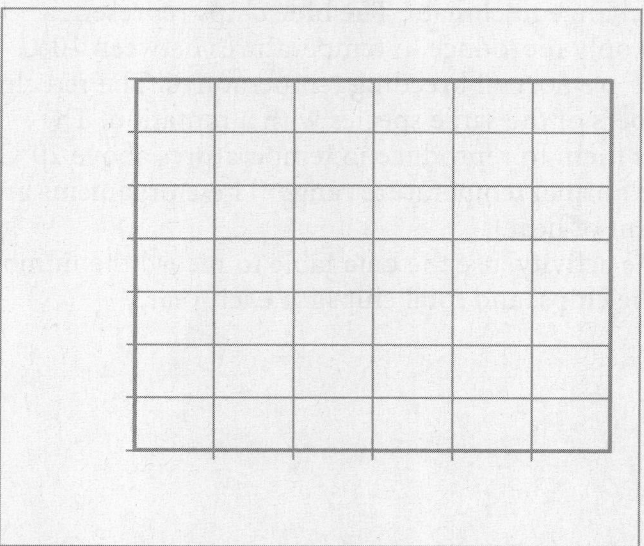

2. **Interpret Graphs** Describe the general trend in temperature over the five-year period. How did this trend affect the size of each population?

3. **Infer** How many offspring can one breeding pair produce in a year? How do you know?

4. **Calculate** How does the percentage of organisms with the mutation change from Year 1 to Year 5? Show your work.

5. **Predict** Assume that the temperatures stay within the normal range over the next five years. What would the populations look like at the end of ten years? Explain your thinking.

Build Science Skills

The model of population growth used in this activity is a very simple one. Identify two ways that the model oversimplifies the interactions of members of this species.

Hands-On 15 Classifying Cerealites

Goal

Create a classification system for a group of unfamiliar organisms.

Build Connections

When you sort a set of objects into groups, you first have to decide which characteristics of the objects to use. You also have to decide the order in which you will apply the characteristics to the group. The order you choose often will affect the final classification.

Skills Focus

Use Models, Classify, Compare and Contrast

Materials

- set of Cerealites
- poster board
- glue
- colored pencils or markers

Safety

Do not eat any of the materials used in this activity. Let your teacher know if you have any food allergies.

Procedure

Pretend you are a space explorer and scientist who has recently arrived on the planet Cereal. The organisms on this planet are called Cerealites. Your assignment is to develop a classification system for Cerealites.

1. Examine your package of Cerealites. Look for similarities and differences. Start thinking about how you can use these characteristics to develop a classification system.
2. Pick at least two characteristics of Cerealites that will be the most important in your classification system. Use these characteristics to classify your organisms into at least three levels.
3. Make a poster that shows and explains your classification. You will probably want to outline your system on a separate sheet of paper before you begin work on your poster.

Analyze and Conclude

1. **Classify** What characteristics did you use to classify the Cerealites? Why did you choose these characteristics?

2. **Interpret Visuals** Look at the posters of other groups. Is there more than one correct way to classify Cerealites? Explain.

3. **Form a Hypothesis** Like the animals of Earth, Cerealites have undergone millions of years of evolution. Which of the Cerealites you observed would you expect to be most closely related? Explain.

Build Science Skills

DNA evidence caused scientists to reexamine the relationship of species that seemed closely related because of structural similarities. Despite the structural similarities, DNA showed that the species were not so closely related. Think of an analogy that might similarly cause you to rethink your classification of Cerealites. *Hint:* Think of an "internal" characteristic.

Hands-On 16 How Do Viruses Differ?

Goal

Use models to help you compare the structure of viruses.

Build Connections

Viruses share a few characteristics with living organisms. Viruses have a genetic code and can evolve. But viruses cannot do many of the things that living organisms do. For example, viruses must invade the cells of living organisms in order to reproduce. Viruses can be classified by the type of organism they infect, such as plants, animals, or bacteria.

In this activity, you will make models of viruses. You will use the models to look for similarities and differences among viruses.

Skills Focus

Use Models, Measure, Calculate, Compare and Contrast

Materials

- craft materials
- scissors
- tape or glue
- metric ruler

Safety

Do not direct the points of the scissors toward yourself or others. Use the scissors only as instructed.

Procedure

Refer to the Viral Structure drawing on page 480 of your textbook as you make your models. Record your measurements and the results of your calculations in the data table on the next page.

1. Use the materials provided to make models of the viruses shown in the drawing.
2. Use the labels in the drawing to label the parts of your models.
3. Measure the length of each model in centimeters. For the influenza virus, use its diameter as its length.
4. Convert the length of each model into nanometers by using the formula 1 cm = 10 million nm.

5. Measure the length of each magnified image in the drawing in centimeters. For the tobacco mosaic virus, measure the vertical rod in the center of the field of view.
6. Divide the length of each magnified image by the magnification to determine the actual length of each virus.
7. Convert the lengths from Step 6 into nanometers.
8. Divide the length of each model by the length of the actual virus to determine how much larger your models are than the viruses they represent.

Data Table			
	T4 Bacteriophage	Tobacco Mosaic Virus	Influenza Virus
Length of model (cm)			
Length of model (nm)			
Length of virus image (cm)			
Actual length of virus (cm)			
Actual length of virus (nm)			
Scale of model to actual virus			

Analyze and Conclude

1. **Compare and Contrast** What do all viruses have in common?

____

____

2. **Compare and Contrast** What structures are found in only some viruses?

____

____

Build Science Skills

Explain why it can be useful to make a large-scale model of a tiny object.

____

____

____

Lesson 22.1

Hands-On 17 Are All Plants the Same?

Goal

Observe and identify different plant structures and functions.

Build Connections

Compared to the other planets in the solar system, Earth is unique for having life. Viewed from space, what you see is a planet dominated by blue water and green plants. Some of the biggest organisms on Earth are plants and so are some of the tiniest. Because plants have adapted to different climates, they have many different forms of roots, stems, and leaves. Yet they share the same basic structure. Plants, as a group, offer a good opportunity to explore one of the most important ideas in biology—the unity and diversity of life.

Skills Focus

Observe, Measure, Compare and Contrast, Classify

Materials

- three different plants
- small paper cup with water
- paper towel
- metric ruler
- hand lens

Safety

Wash your hands thoroughly with soap and warm water after handling plants and soil. Let your teacher know if you have any allergies to plants.

Procedure

In this activity, you will compare the structures of three different plants and use your observations to classify the plants.

1. Collect three plants for your group.
2. Gently remove each plant from its pot and dip it in the water to clean off the soil. Place the plants on a paper towel.
3. Use a hand lens to examine each plant.

4. Measure the height, leaf dimensions, stem length, and root length of each plant. **NOTE:** For the leaves, measure both the length and the width. Use the table to record your data.

Data Table			
	Plant 1	**Plant 2**	**Plant 3**
Height			
Leaf Dimensions			
Stem Length			
Root Length			
Classification			

Analyze and Conclude

1. **Compare and Contrast** How are the three plants alike?

2. **Compare and Contrast** How are the plants different?

3. **Infer** What do the shapes and location of plant structures suggest about their functions?

Build Science Skills

Use your observations to classify the three plants into two groups based only on outward appearance. Explain your reasons for classifying the plants this way.

Hands-On 18 A-Mazing Plants

Goal

Observe the effects of phototropism on plants.

Build Connections

Most plants depend on sunlight to provide energy through photosynthesis. Many plants have adaptations that help them maximize, or take full advantage of, their exposure to the sun. Perhaps you have noticed a plant at home that seems to reach toward the light. If you moved that plant to a new location, you may have seen it grow in a different direction to capture more light in the new spot. This process is called phototropism.

Skills Focus

Observe, Infer

Materials

- paper cup
- potting soil
- 4 bean seeds
- scissors
- cardboard shoe box
- 2 cardboard dividers
- masking tape

Safety  

Do not direct the points of the scissors toward yourself or others. Use the scissors only as intended. Wash your hands thoroughly with soap and warm water after handling plants and soil.

Procedure

In this lab, you will build a maze with a plant on one end and a light source at the other. You will observe the plant over time to see how it responds. To make sure that the plants grow, you will first place the planted seeds in full sun.

1. Add potting soil to the cup until it is about three-quarters full. Use the tip of a pencil to make four holes about 1 cm deep in the soil. Plant the seeds and cover them with a thin layer of soil.
2. Water the soil until it is moist. Set the cup near the window.

3. Cut a hole about 5 cm in diameter at one end of the shoe box. Tape two cardboard dividers inside the box as shown in the diagram. Put the cover on the box and store it in a safe place.

4. Observe the cup each day. Once the seedlings have broken the surface of the soil, place the cup in the box. Place it at the beginning of the maze, away from the hole. Put the lid on the box. Put the box near the window, with the hole facing the sun.
5. Over the next 2 weeks, open the box every 2 to 3 days to water and observe the seedlings. **CAUTION:** Do not remove the cup to water the plants. Record what you observe.

   Observations: ____

   ____

   ____

Analyze and Conclude

1. **Observe** Summarize what happened to the seedlings.

   ____

2. **Infer** What stimulus did the seedlings respond to? What was happening within the cells of the plant to cause this response?

Build Science Skills

What adaptive advantage does the growth pattern you observed give a plant? What situation in a natural setting does this activity model?

____

____

____

Lesson 27.1

Hands-On 19 How a Bird "Chews"

Goal

Use a model to explain how a bird's gizzard works.

Build Connections

Breaking down food into smaller pieces is an important part of digestion for most animals. Humans use their teeth to grind up food. This mechanical digestion produces pieces that can be more easily digested by enzymes and other chemicals.

Birds also use both mechanical and chemical processes to break down food. One interesting aspect of a bird's digestive system is that birds do their "chewing" at the end of the process, not the beginning. This "chewing" takes place in the gizzard—an organ located below the bird's stomach. How do birds chew without teeth? You may have seen a bird swallowing small pieces of stone and gravel. These pieces of stone end up in the gizzard, where the food is ground up before it enters the bird's small intestine.

In this activity, you will make a model of a bird's gizzard and use it to imitate mechanical digestion.

Skills Focus

Observe, Compare and Contrast

Materials

- plastic jar with lid
- soda cracker
- several small pebbles

Safety

Do not eat or drink anything while working in a laboratory. Alert your teacher if you have any food allergies.

Procedure

1. Place the cracker, along with several small pebbles, in the plastic jar. Put the lid on the jar.
2. Shake the jar for 30 seconds. **CAUTION:** Make sure the lid is secured tightly on the jar before you shake the jar.
3. Open the jar and observe the cracker.

Analyze and Conclude

1. **Observe** What happened to the cracker? Describe the relative size of the pieces.

2. **Compare and Contrast** How is the model like a bird's gizzard? How is it different? *Hint:* Think about the nature of an organ.

Build Science Skills

Scientists view it as an important development when humans first picked up rocks and sharpened them to make arrow heads and other tools. Through toolmaking, humans could change their environment in a way that helped them. Is it an accident that a bird will pick up tiny bits of sand and gravel? Does the bird mistake them for food? Explain how natural selection might favor birds with this behavior.

Hands-On 20 Binocular Vision

Goal

Observe the usefulness of binocular vision for humans.

Build Connections

Eyes almost always exist in pairs. When scientists think about how eyes function, one thing they think about is the field of view. Animals that have eyes placed on each side of their head typically have a wide field of view. Animals with eyes close together often have a much smaller field of view.

When the area that is seen by one eye overlaps the area seen by the other, this type of vision is called binocular vision. You have binocular vision. It allows you to determine how far away you are from an object. When you hit a baseball, swat a mosquito, or drive a car, you rely on binocular vision. In fact, you use it all the time, as you move from place to place and interact with your environment.

Skills Focus

Graph, Infer, Compare and Contrast

Materials

- sheet of paper crumpled into a ball
- graph paper

Safety ⚠

Do not aim the ball at your partner's face.

Procedure

In this activity, you will try to catch a paper ball with one hand, first with both eyes open and then with only one eye open.

1. Stand about 2 meters from your partner. Throw the ball to your partner. Do this five times. Use the table on the next page to record the number of times your partner caught the ball.
2. Now have your partner close one eye. Repeat Step 1.
3. Switch roles and repeat Steps 1 and 2 with your partner throwing the ball to you.
4. Collect the class data on the board.

Number of Catches		
	Both Eyes Open	One Eye Shut
You		
Your partner		

Analyze and Conclude

1. **Interpreting Graphs** On a separate sheet of paper, make a bar graph comparing the results with both eyes open and the results with one eye shut. What trend does the graph show?

2. **Infer** Judging from your experience, what ability did you lose when you attempted to catch the paper ball with one eye shut?

3. **Compare and Contrast** Look toward one area of the classroom. Shut one eye and notice how much of a wall you can see. Keeping your head in the same position, do the same with the other eye. How much area for each eye overlaps the other? Describe what one eye sees that the other does not.

Build Science Skills

Most prey animals, such as rabbits and antelopes, have eyes on the sides of their heads. In comparison, many predators have binocular vision. Think in terms of predator-prey interactions and natural selection. What is the adaptive advantage for each type of vision?

Name ______________________ Class ________ Date ________

Hands-On 21 Maintaining Temperature

Goal
Model maintaining a stable body temperature.

 Build Connections
Have you ever been outside on a day when you feel hot in the sun but cold in the shade? On a day like that, you can adjust to the changes in temperature by dressing in layers. You can put on a sweater or jacket to keep warm in the shade. You can take a layer off when you are standing in the sun. You make those choices consciously, responding to the conditions of your environment. Inside your body, adjustments to body temperatures are made constantly, without your realizing it. In fact, your body maintains a fairly constant temperature of about 37.0°C (98.6°F).

Skills Focus
Use Models, Design an Experiment

Materials
- three 250-mL beakers
- water
- thermometer

Safety

Wear protective gear and use heat-resistant gloves to handle beakers of hot water. Tell your teacher if you break a glass object.

Procedure
In this activity, you will design a way to maintain the temperature of a beaker of water.

1. Your teacher will provide you with a thermometer and three beakers of water at the following temperatures: 25°C, 35°C, and 40°C.
2. The beaker of 35°C water represents your body temperature. Develop a method to keep the temperature of the water in this beaker within one degree for a period of 15 minutes.

Analyze and Conclude

1. **Use Visuals** Draw a feedback loop similar to those in Lesson 30.1 to show what actions you took to maintain a constant temperature.

2. **Compare and Contrast** How is what you did to maintain a constant temperature similar to what happens in your own body during temperature regulation? How is it different?

Build Science Skills

Identify two responses your body uses to help it adjust to low and high temperatures.

Lesson 33.3

Hands-On 22 Modeling Breathing

Goal

Use a model to explore how air moves into and out of the lungs.

Build Connections

There are times when you might notice your breathing; for example, when running to catch a bus or climbing a steep hill. But most of the time, you probably are not aware of your breathing. While you focus on other things, your nervous system controls the movement of air into and out of your lungs.

When the level of carbon dioxide in your blood rises, sensory neurons send impulses to a breathing center in your brain. The breathing center responds by sending impulses that cause your diaphragm and muscles between your ribs to contract. Your rib cage rises and air rushes into your lungs. When your diaphragm relaxes and your rib cage lowers, air is exhaled from your lungs.

How does the movement of the diaphragm and rib cage cause air to be inhaled or exhaled? In this activity, you will make a working model of human lungs that will help you answer this question.

Skills Focus

Use Models, Relate Cause and Effect

Materials

- small, clear plastic bottle
- scissors
- small round balloon
- one-hole rubber stopper
- large round balloon

Safety

Use the scissors only as instructed. Do not direct the points of the scissors toward yourself or others. Tell your teacher if you have an allergy to latex.

Procedure

Use Figure 1 to guide you as you construct your model.

1. Place a clear plastic bottle on its side. Press one point of the scissors through the side of the bottle about 1 cm from the bottom. **CAUTION:** The tough plastic may cause the scissors to slip when you try to puncture the bottle.
2. Using the scissors, cut off the bottom of the bottle. Trim any rough spots from the edge.
3. Stretch the small balloon. Then blow into the balloon until it expands. Release the air. Repeat this action two more times.
4. Pull the opening of the small balloon over the bottom of a one-hole rubber stopper.

Figure 1 Completed Model

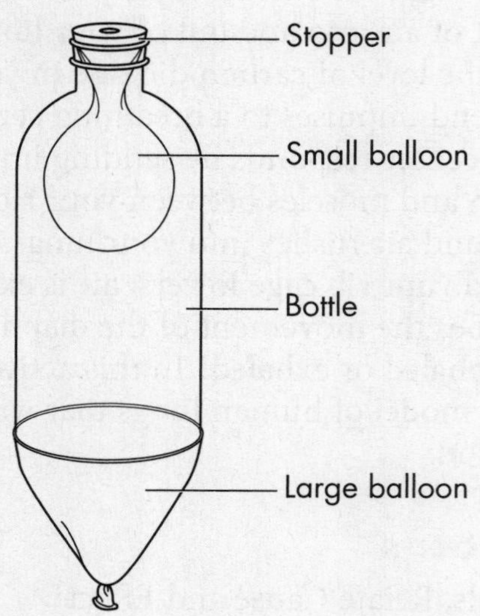

5. Insert the balloon through the mouth of the bottle. Press the stopper tightly into the bottle so that it holds the lip of the balloon in place.
6. Stretch the large balloon. Then blow into the balloon until it expands. Release the air. Repeat this action two more times.
7. Make a cut across the rounded, closed end of the large balloon about 1 cm from the end. Tie the other end closed.
8. Stretch the large balloon far enough over the cut end of the bottle to keep it from slipping off the bottle.
9. Watch the small balloon as you pull down on the knot of the large balloon. Continue watching the small balloon as you push up on the large balloon. Record your observations.

   Observations: ____

   ____

   ____

Name ______________ Class ________ Date ________

Analyze and Conclude

1. **Use Models** In your model, which balloon represents the lungs and which represents the diaphragm?

____

____

2. **Use Models** In your model, what does the bottle represent? What does the hole in the rubber stopper represent?

____

____

3. **Observe** What happened to the volume of air in the bottle when you pulled down on the large balloon? What happened to the volume when you pushed up on the large balloon?

____

____

____

4. **Infer** How did the changes in volume affect the air pressure in the bottle? *Hint:* The relationship between the pressure and volume of a gas is an inverse relationship, which means as one increases the other decreases.

____

____

____

5. **Relate Cause and Effect** Explain how the changes in air pressure in the bottle caused the movement of air into and out of the small balloon.

____

____

____

____

6. **Use Models** What part of the breathing process were you modeling when you pulled down on the large balloon? What part of the process were you modeling when you pushed up on the large balloon?

____

____

____

Build Science Skills

Suppose the skin and muscles of the chest were punctured by a sharp object. Air would be able to enter the chest cavity through the wound. How would such an injury affect a person's ability to breathe? How could you change your model to represent the situation described? How could you use the modified model to test your prediction about the effect of a puncture wound?

Lesson 34.4

Hands-On 23 **Growing Up**

Goal

Identify some changes in body proportions that occur as the body develops.

 Build Connections

It is natural for humans to vary in size, shape, and appearance. Yet the human body tends to follow certain patterns when it comes to proportion. For example, a person's face is about the same length as the person's hand. The proportions, or relative sizes, of some parts of the body change during the course of development.

Skills Focus

Calculate, Analyze Data, Organize Data

Procedure

The diagram shows figures for different development stages drawn against a graph showing percentages. You will use the diagram to compare the lengths of two major body parts to each figure's height. Record your results in the table on the next page.

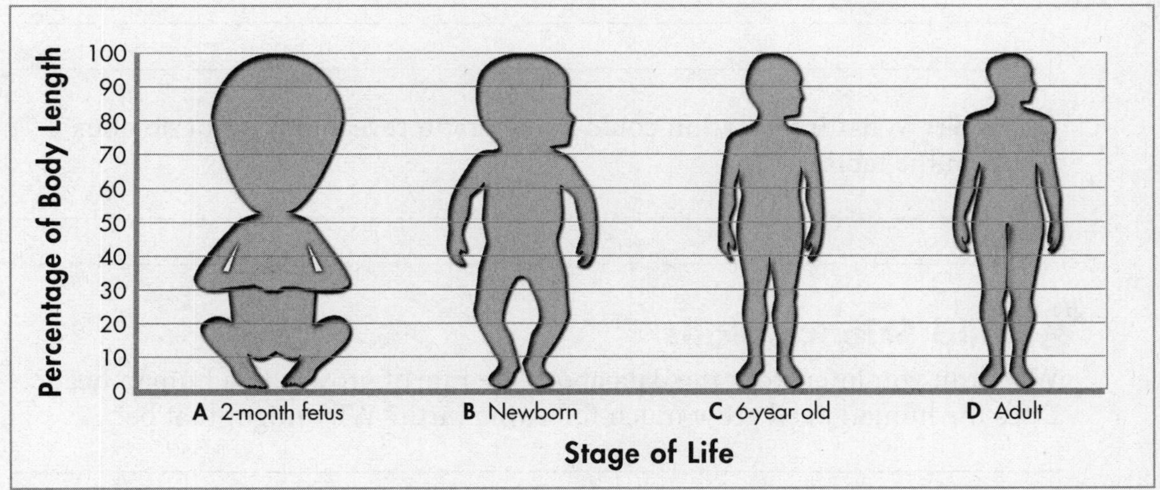

1. Look at Figure D. The head is about 15 percent of the adult's full height (100% – 85%). Use this same approach to figure out the percentage of total height that the head makes up in Figures A through C.

2. Now compare the length of the legs to the total body height for Figures B through D. Do not include the hips. Record your results. **NOTE:** An estimate is given for Figure A because the legs are shown folded.

Data Table		
Stage	Head Size (% of body length)	Leg Length (% of body length)
Fetus at 2 months		25
Newborn		
6 years old		
Adult	15	

Analyze and Conclude

1. **Analyze Data** How do the percentages for head size and leg length change from infancy to adulthood?

2. **Organize Data** If you were to make a line graph using the data, which variable would you place on the horizontal axis? Which would you place on the vertical axis? How many lines would your graph have?

3. **Predict** What information could a line graph reveal that is not obvious from the table?

Build Science Skills

What can you infer from the data about the rate of growth of a human head? Does the human head grow much following birth? Why might that be?

Name ______________________________ Class __________ Date __________

Lesson 35.3

Hands-On 24 How Do Diseases Spread?

Goal

Model the way an infectious disease can spread.

Build Connections

It may seem obvious now. But until the late 1800s, scientists were not able to recognize the connections among germs, hygiene, and infectious diseases. With better microscopes, scientists could see the bacteria and viruses that cause many infections. Once the cause was known, it was easier to see how an infection could spread. One way that infections are spread is through physical contact with objects touched by others who are infected.

Skills Focus

Infer, Draw Conclusions

Materials

- fluorescent material
- ultraviolet lamp

Safety 

Do not look directly at the fluorescent light. Wash your hands thoroughly with soap and warm water after the lab.

Procedure

In this lab, you will model the way an infectious disease can spread through touch. Your teacher has placed a fluorescent material in the classroom to represent a virus.

1. Walk around the classroom, touching only those objects your teacher has said you can touch.
2. Shake hands with a few of the other students. Keep track of the objects and the people you have touched.

   Contacts: ____

   ____

   ____

   ____

3. Use an ultraviolet (UV) lamp to check for the "virus" on your hands and objects you have touched since entering the classroom. Circle any contacts on your list that tested positive. **CAUTION:** Do not look directly at the UV light.
4. Once you have checked your hands, wash them thoroughly with soap and warm water.
5. Compare results with your classmates to determine how the "virus" spread through the classroom.

Analyze and Conclude

1. **Infer** What can you infer about how the "virus" spread through the classroom?

______

______

2. **Draw Conclusions** How does thorough hand washing help prevent the spread of diseases?

______

______

______

Build Science Skills

Viruses and bacteria reproduce within a human body. When you cough or sneeze, the viruses are released into the air and land on surfaces that will be touched by other people. Will covering your mouth when you cough or sneeze completely solve the problem?

______

______

______

______

______

Appendix A How to Form a Hypothesis

What is a hypothesis?

A hypothesis is a possible explanation for a set of observations or a possible answer to a scientific question. A hypothesis is designed to be tested in an experiment. Thus, hypotheses are a central part of scientific methodology. Knowing how to form a hypothesis is an important skill.

Many scientific investigations begin with observations. For instance, you may notice that one pond has more algae growing in it than another, or that a bumblebee in a field visits one type of flower more than others. Observations like these often lead to questions such as, "Why does one pond have more algae than another pond? Why do bumblebees seem to prefer one type of flower more than others?" To answer questions like these, you must first make a hypothesis.

Why should you make a hypothesis?

The main purpose of a hypothesis is to set up a statement that can be supported or disproved by evidence. Once you've made a hypothesis, you can design an experiment to help you determine whether it is right or wrong.

Sometimes what you observe and the data you collect will not support your hypothesis. In science, the important thing is not whether a hypothesis is right or wrong. The important thing is what you learn from an experiment. In fact, for scientists, a hypothesis that is wrong can be just as valuable as a hypothesis that is right.

You will need to design a procedure for some experiments. But often you will be asked to do experiments that have been designed for you. A hypothesis is a useful tool even when you are following a predesigned procedure. Making a hypothesis will ensure that you understand the purpose of a lab and why you will be asked to make certain types of observations.

This appendix describes the "full version" of a hypothesis, which tends to be long and full of details. Such detailed statements are essential for a scientist who is doing research. But for most of the labs in this manual, it will be acceptable for you to write shorter hypotheses with fewer details.

How is a hypothesis related to experimental design?

Most experiments test the relationship between two factors. You change the independent variable. Then you observe whether the dependent variable changes in response. A useful hypothesis should state how you think the variables are related. In the full version, you must also state how the relationship will affect the results of the experiment.

The following statement is a fully developed hypothesis. *If the presence of fertilizer is related to increased algal growth, then algae that are provided with fertilizer will exhibit greater growth than algae that are not provided with fertilizer.* Is this hypothesis useful? Yes, because it relates the use of fertilizer to the growth of algae. It also describes what results to expect if the hypothesis is correct.

Practice Identify the variables in this hypothesis. *If the heart rate of* Daphnia *is related to the concentration of salt in their water, then changing the salt concentration of a* Daphnia's *water will cause its heart rate to change.*

Dependent variable: ______________________

____

Independent variable: ______________________

____

How can you evaluate a hypothesis?

For a hypothesis to be of value during the experimental design process, it must be possible to test the hypothesis. This rule is true whether the hypothesis is fully developed or a shorter version with fewer details.

A statement like "My cat's favorite food is tuna" may or may not be true, but there is no way to test it. However, it would be possible to test the statement "If a cat prefers tuna to dry cat food, then the cat will eat the tuna first when the two foods are placed side by side."

A hypothesis should also contain language that suggests *how* it can be tested. A useful hypothesis often will take the form of an "if, then" statement. In the first part of the statement, you should summarize the relationship you think might be taking place *(If the presence of fertilizer is related to algal growth in ponds...).* In the second part, you should predict how you think this relationship will affect the results of your experiment *(...then algae that are provided with fertilizer in the laboratory will exhibit greater growth than algae that are not provided with fertilizer).*

Comparison of Hypotheses

Poor Hypothesis	Useful Hypothesis
Salt water will decrease plant growth.	*Full version:* If a high concentration of salt in water causes decreased plant growth, then potted plants that are given salt water will grow more slowly than potted plants that are given tap water. *Short version:* Plants that are given salt water will grow more slowly than plants that are given tap water.
The effectiveness of enzymes may be affected by water temperature.	*Full version:* If the effectiveness of enzymes is related to water temperature, then the amount of product from an enzyme-catalyzed reaction will vary at different temperatures. *Shorter version:* The amount of product from an enzyme-catalyzed reaction will vary at different temperatures.
Bumblebees prefer yellow flowers to red flowers.	*Full version:* If bumblebees visit yellow flowers more often than red flowers, then bumblebees that are kept in the laboratory will visit a fake yellow flower more often than a fake red flower. *Shorter version:* When both types of flowers are present, bumblebees will visit fake yellow flowers more often than fake red flowers.

Practice Your Skills

1. Both of these hypotheses are in the form of an "if, then" statement. Which hypothesis is more useful, and why?

   a. If heart rate is related to caffeine intake, then coffee drinkers will have higher heart rates.

   b. If a higher heart rate is related to caffeine intake, then the heart rate of most people will be higher 30 minutes after they drink a cup of coffee.

2. Write the missing "if" statement for this "then" statement: …then ants placed halfway between solutions of sugar and an artificial sweetener will move toward both solutions with equal frequency.

Rewrite the hypotheses in Questions 3–5 so that they are more useful for experimental design.

3. Mouthwash A will kill more bacteria in laboratory cultures than Mouthwash B will.

4. Colonies of *E. coli* bacteria will grow faster in culture dishes kept at 35°C than in dishes kept at 25°C.

5. Bean plants will grow more slowly when exposed to acid rain.

Name ______ Class ______ Date ______

Appendix B Presenting Data

When you do a lab, you may be asked to record your observations in words or drawings. You may have to make and record measurements. How you organize the data you collect can affect your ability to analyze the data, which is an important part of the experimental process. When you present data in a clear and logical way, you also make it easier for others to interpret and evaluate your results.

Using Data Tables

When scientists do experiments, they typically do many trials using the same procedure. Once the scientists analyze the results, they may adjust the procedure and do more trials. This process can continue for months or years, resulting in a vast amount of data. Data tables are an excellent way to organize large amounts of data.

Example A team of researchers collected venom from ten different species of snakes. They tested the venom to determine how toxic each sample was. They also collected data about people who died after being bitten by each type of snake. Compare the following description of the data they collected with the same data presented in a data table. In which format are the results easier to analyze?

For the southern United States copperhead, the death rate was less than 1 percent. For the western diamondback rattlesnake, the rate was 5–15 percent. The rate was 5–20 percent for the eastern coral snake and the king cobra. For the Indian krait, the rate was 77 percent. For the European viper, the rate was 1–5 percent. The rate was 100 percent for the bushmaster and 10–20 percent for the fer-de-lance. For both the black-necked cobra and the puff adder, the death rate was 11–40 percent.

Death Rates After Snake Bites

Type of Snake	Death Rate (%)
Black-necked cobra	11–40
Bushmaster	Typically 100
Copperhead	Less than 1
Eastern coral snake	5–20
European viper	1–5
Fer-de-lance	10–20
Indian krait	77
King cobra	5–20
Puff adder	11–40
Rattlesnake	5–15

Each column in a data table should have a head that describes the data in the column. In the table about snake bites, the column heads are the independent variable (Type of Snake) and the dependent variable (Death Rate). When the variable is a measurement, the unit of measurement, such as (cm) for length or (g) for mass, is often included with the head.

The rows in a table may be arranged by trial (Trial 1, Trial 2, and so on) or by the days on which measurements are made (Day 1, Day 3, Day 5, and so on). But sometimes the choice is less obvious.

Practice How are the rows ordered in the snake-bite table?

______

How might you rearrange the rows to make the data easier to analyze?

______

______

______

Once you have a completed data table, you can apply another important scientific skill—posing questions. For example, scientists looking at the data on snake bites might wonder about the reliability of the data. They might ask questions such as, "What procedure did the researchers use to gather this data?" "How large were the samples that were used to calculate the percentages?"

Practice Some of the ranges in the snake-bite table are very broad—the 11–40 percent death rate for the puff adder, for example. Perhaps data from different sources were combined. If so, think of a follow-up question that a scientist might want to ask.

Follow-up question: ______________________

____

____

Have you ever jotted down notes while working in the lab and been unable to locate the notes later? Have you found the notes but been unable to figure out what you meant? Making a data table in advance helps ensure that the data you collect will not get lost and that all the data will be recorded.

For some labs in this manual, a data table will be provided for you to fill in. For other labs, you will be asked to construct an appropriate data table. You will need to decide how to best arrange the data in the table. Experiments often require a data table with more than two columns.

Example Students who were studying inherited physical traits collected data on hair color from three different classes.

Class 1	**Class 2**	**Class 3**
Black: 2	Black: 0	Black: 4
Blond: 3	Blond: 7	Blond: 12
Brown: 20	Brown: 18	Brown: 15
Red: 0	Red: 1	Red: 0

The hair-color data could be arranged in a table as follows. This arrangement draws attention to differences among the classes.

Distribution of Hair Color by Class

Hair Color	Class 1	Class 2	Class 3
Black	2	0	4
Blond	3	7	12
Brown	20	18	15
Red	0	1	0

Practice The table could be constructed to focus more on hair color and less on the individual classes. The rearranged data has been entered in the table below. Complete the table by filling in the missing heads.

Hair Color of Students

	2	3	20	0
	0	7	18	1
	4	12	15	0
Total	6	22	53	1

Making a table in advance also gives you a chance to evaluate your experimental design before you begin. While constructing a data table for the study on hair color, you might be prompted to think, "How will I decide whether to classify a color as dark brown or as black?" "Will all the hair colors I observe be natural?" "Will I be able to draw any useful conclusions if I survey only three classes?"

Using Graphs

A graph is a pictorial representation of data. Graphs are used to show a relationship between two or more factors. Plotting the data you collect on a graph may reveal a pattern that isn't obvious when data is organized in a table. Before you plot your data, you will need to decide which type of graph to use.

Line Graphs

A line graph has one or more lines connecting a series of data points. A line graph is often the best choice for showing how an independent variable is related to a dependent variable. With a line graph, you are also able to estimate values for points that lie between or beyond the measured data points.

Example This line graph relates the length of a tortoise shell to the age of a tortoise. One line shows data for a tortoise that was raised in a zoo. The second line shows data collected from wild tortoises of the same species. Having the two lines on one graph makes it easier to compare the effect of a third variable—the conditions under which growth occurred.

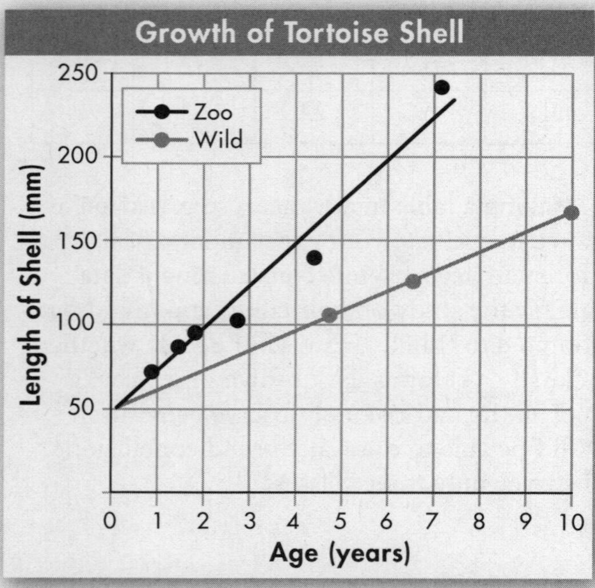

Practice Fish "breathe" by pumping water through their mouths and over their gills, where oxygen is extracted. Use the data in the table to make a graph that relates the temperature of the water to the breathing rate of a fish.

Decide which variable is the independent variable and place it on the horizontal axis, or x-axis. Place the dependent variable on the vertical axis, or y-axis. Label the axes.

Choose a scale for each axis. Consider the range of data and the number of available squares. If your scale unit is too large, your graph will be too small and difficult to read. If your scale unit is too small, some of your data will not fit on the graph. Units that are multiples of 1, 2, 5, and 10 are easiest to work with.

Temperature (°C)	Rate (per minute)
10	15
15	25
18	30
20	38
23	60
25	57
27	25

Bar Graphs

You can also use a bar graph to compare data. Like a line graph, a bar graph has an x-axis and a y-axis. But instead of points, a bar graph uses a series of columns, or bars, to display data. Bar graphs are especially useful when the data is not continuous—when you cannot use the graph to estimate values that were not measured. On many bar graphs, the x-axis lists categories rather than a numerical scale.

Example A driver must be alert and able to react quickly to changing road conditions or to the actions of other drivers. The following bar graph shows how alcohol can affect a driver's ability to react. What is the relationship between the blood alcohol concentration and the reaction time?

____

____

____

____

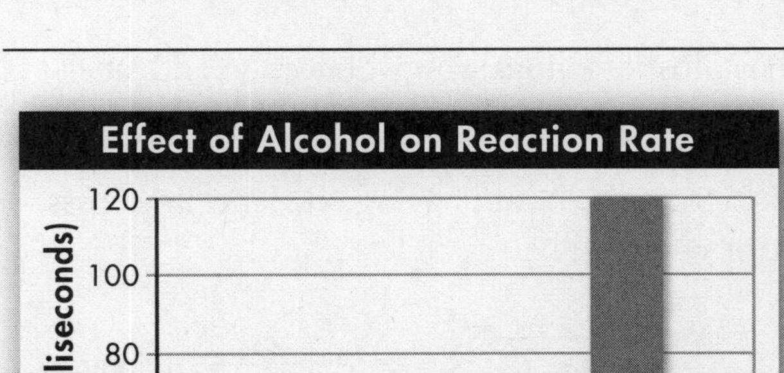
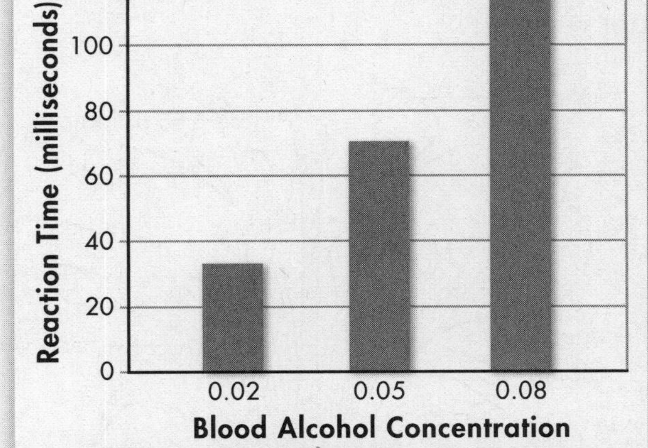

Recall that you can introduce a third variable to a line graph by adding lines. You can do something similar with the bars on a bar graph.

Example The following bar graph compares the fat content of butter, margarine, and olive oil. For each source, the data is divided by type of fat—saturated, unsaturated, and trans fat.

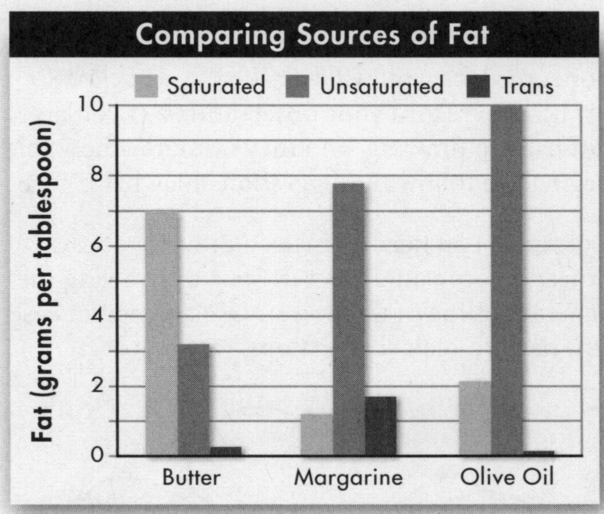

Practice Use the table to make a bar graph showing the percentage of students at each grade who take part in vigorous physical activity. Place the grades on the x-axis and the percentage on the y-axis. Start your y-axis scale just above the jagged line. Use different colored bars for males and females, and add a legend.

Grade	Males	Females
9th	74%	64%
10th	71%	58%
11th	70%	52%
12th	63%	49%

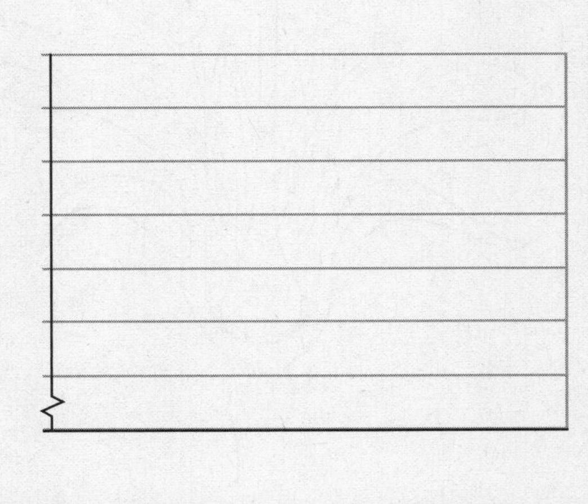

Name ______________________ Class __________ Date __________

Using Drawings

For some labs, you will be asked to make a drawing to record your observations. If you are not used to drawing, you may not know how to begin. The following suggestions may help.

Example You need to make a drawing of a flower before you dissect it. Start by drawing the general outline of the flower. Use a pencil in case you need to make corrections.

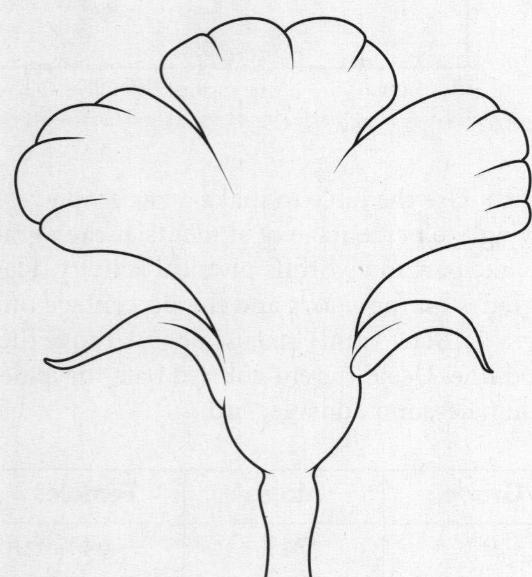

Next, add the different structures. Focus on the general shape and location of each structure.

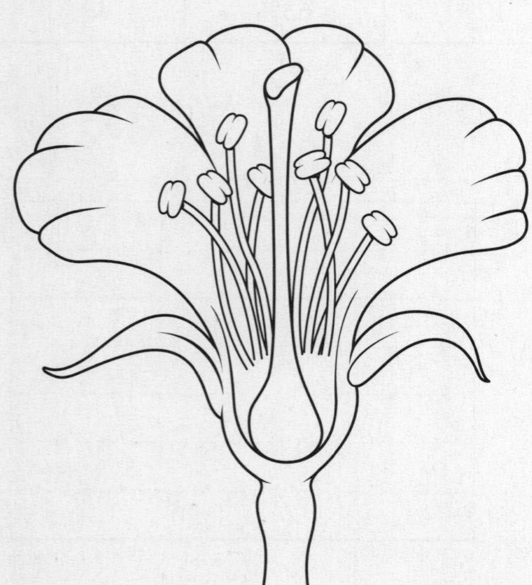

You may choose to use shading to highlight some features of your drawing. The shading in this drawing emphasizes the path that the pollen travels to reach the ovary.

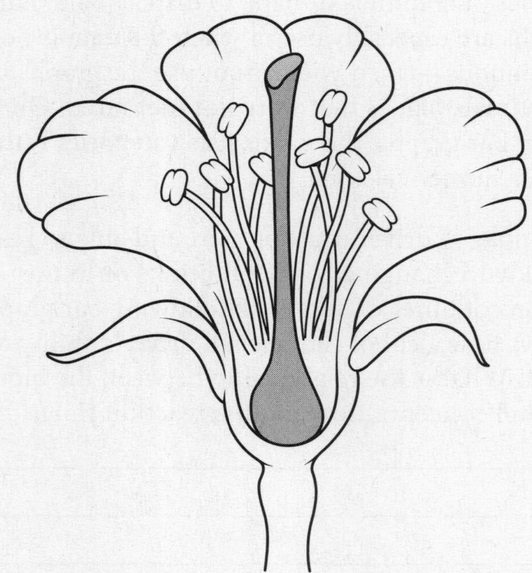

For most drawings, you will need to add labels. Print the labels and position them horizontally. Use a ruler to draw a line between the label and the structure. Avoid having one label line cross over another.

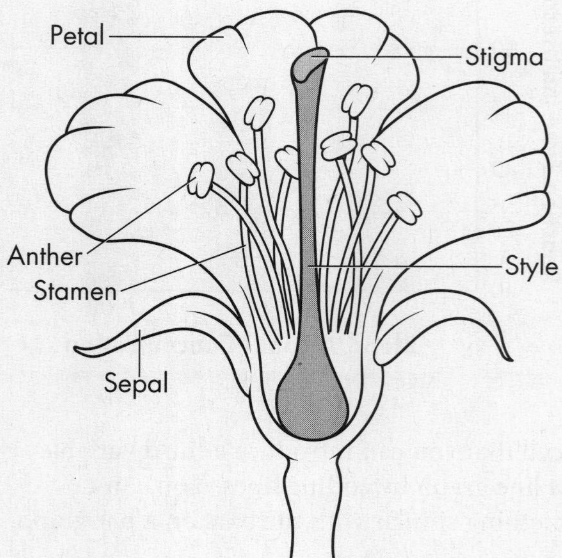

When you draw objects that you view with a microscope, use a circle to represent the field of view. Also include the magnification at which you viewed the object.

Appendix C Measurements and Calculations

The Metric System

The measurement system used by scientists is the International System of Units (SI). Because SI is a metric system, all SI units are related by a power of 10, which makes it easy to convert one SI unit to another. In the lab, you will mainly measure length, mass, volume, and temperature.

Length The SI unit for length is the meter (m). A meter is slightly longer than a yard.

Mass The SI unit for mass is the gram (g). A paper clip has a mass of about one gram.

Volume of a Liquid The SI unit for the volume of a liquid is the liter (L). A liter is slightly more than a quart.

Temperature The SI unit for temperature is degrees Celsius (°C). Water freezes at 0°C and boils at 100°C.

The table lists some SI prefixes. *Larger* and *smaller* refer to what happens when a prefix is placed before a unit. For example, the *c* in the unit cm indicates that a centimeter is 100 times smaller than a meter.

Common SI Prefixes

Prefix	Symbol	Meaning
kilo-	k	1000 times larger
hecto-	h	100 times larger
deka-	da	10 times larger
deci-	d	10 times smaller
centi-	c	100 times smaller
milli-	m	1000 times smaller
micro-	μ	1 million times smaller
nano-	n	1000 million times smaller

Accuracy and Precision

Your measurements need to be both accurate and precise. Accuracy refers to how close a measurement is to the actual value. Precision refers to how close a group of measurements are to each other. The level of precision that is possible depends on the measuring instrument. For example, on one ruler, the smallest unit is a centimeter. On a second ruler, the smallest unit is a millimeter. Measurements made with the second ruler will be more precise than those made with the first ruler.

Significant Figures

The number of significant figures you record for a measurement depends on the precision of the measuring instrument. Significant figures are all of the digits that are known in a measurement, plus one added digit, which is an estimate.

Example Look at the measured lengths of the peanut in the drawing. With Ruler A, the length has two significant figures because the estimated digit is the distance between centimeter marks. With Ruler B, the length has three significant figures because the estimated digit is the distance between millimeter marks.

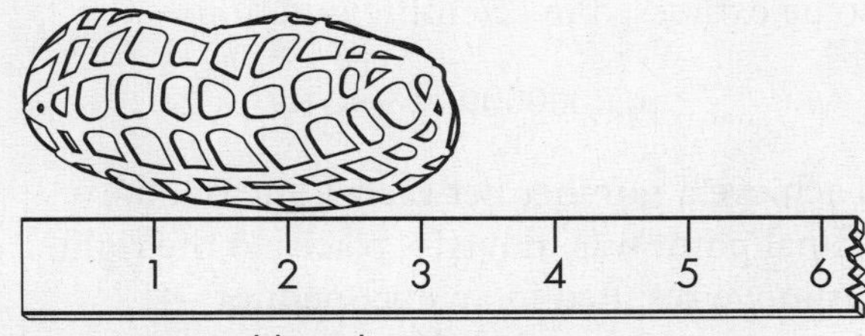

a. Measured length = 3.3 cm

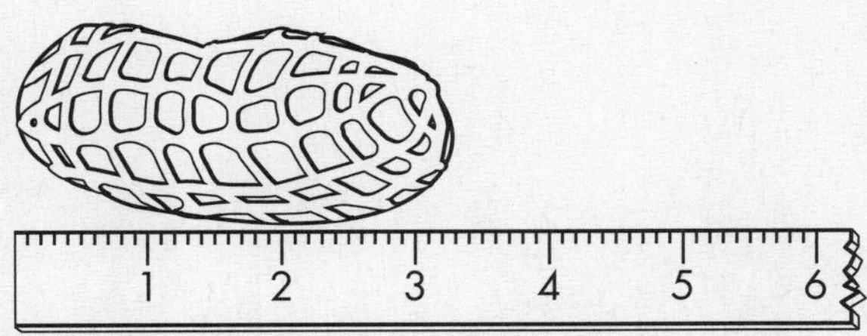

b. Measured length = 3.29 cm

Scientific Notation

Using scientific notation makes it easier to work with numbers that are very large or very small. For example, the diameter of a bacterial cell might be 0.9 micrometers, or 0.0000009 µm. A number with so many zeros is difficult to work with, especially if you need to do a calculation.

Numbers can be expressed as a base and an exponent. The exponent tells you how many times the base is multiplied by itself. The number 15,625, for example, can be expressed as follows:

$$15{,}625 = 25 \times 25 \times 25 = 25^3$$

In this example, the base is 25 and the exponent is 3. In scientific notation, the base is always the number 10. A number written in scientific notation is expressed as the product of two factors, a number between 1 and 10 and the number 10 with an exponent.

Example The number 51,203 can be expressed in scientific notation as follows:

$$51{,}203 = 5.1203 \times 10^4$$

To achieve a number between 1 and 10, the decimal point was moved 4 places to the left. This move resulted in an exponent of 4. Note that the first factor includes all the significant digits in the original number.

Example Numbers that are less than zero can also be expressed in scientific notation.

$$0.0000009 = 9 \times 10^{-7}$$

To achieve a number between 1 and 10, the decimal point was moved 7 places to the right. This move resulted in an exponent of –4.

Calculating Averages

When you do an experiment that includes multiple trials, you will usually be asked to calculate an average. However, an *average* can be calculated in several ways. The method you will use will depend on what you are trying to learn from the data. Scientists often use the term *central tendency* to refer to the "middle," or typical, value in a set of data.

Mean In common usage, the term *average* refers to a numerical average, or *mean*. The mean is the sum of the data divided by the number of items. Consider the following data:

6.2 mL, 8.0 mL, 6.4 mL, 6.2 mL, 6.7 mL

The mean for this data is 6.7 mL. In this case, the mean is probably higher than it should be because of the 8.0 mL data point, which is not typical. The median might be a better choice.

Median The median is the middle number in a set of ordered data. Often the data needs to be ordered before you can determine the mean. For example, 6.2 mL, 8.0 mL, 6.4 mL, 6.2 mL, and 6.7 mL would be reordered as follows:

6.2 mL, 6.2 mL, 6.4 mL, 6.7 mL, 8.0 mL

There are an equal number of data points above the median, which is 6.4 mL. When the number of data points is even, the median is the mean of the two middle points.

Mode The number that appears most often in a set of data is called the mode. In the example above, the mode is 6.2 mL. The mode is useful when you are dealing with categories of data, such as T-shirt sizes. Knowing the mode would help a buyer who is ordering stock for a store.

Name ________________ Class ________ Date ________

Practice Your Skills

1. How much smaller is a milliliter than a liter? How much larger is a centimeter than a millimeter? How many grams are in a kilogram?

2. You are using a 25-mL graduated cylinder to measure the volume of a liquid. The smallest marked unit on the cylinder is a milliliter. The volume is more than 10 mL and less than 15 mL. How many significant figures can you report in your answer. Explain.

3. For adult women, the average number of white blood cells per liter of blood is 5.8 billion. Express this data in scientific notation. *Hint:* You may want to write out the number with all its zeroes first.

4. In a garden, the heights of five sunflowers are 135.0 cm, 162.5 cm, 180.0 cm, 185.0 cm, and 167.5 cm. Calculate the mean and the median for this data.

5. In a second garden, the heights of five sunflowers are 130.0 cm, 162.5 cm, 165.0 cm, 160.0 cm, and 162.5 cm. For this data, would you use the mean or the median, and why?

6. What is the mode for the data in Question 5?

Appendix D Laboratory Techniques

Measuring Volume

The instruments you will use to measure the volume of a liquid are graduated cylinders and pipettes.

Graduated Cylinders

A liquid in a graduated cylinder has a slightly curved surface called a meniscus. To obtain an accurate measurement, read the volume with your eye at the same level as the bottom of the meniscus. To make the meniscus easier to see, place a dark piece of paper behind the cylinder while you make the reading.

Your readings will be more precise if you choose the smallest cylinder that will contain the liquid. Make sure the volume does not exceed the graduated part of the cylinder.

Types of Pipettes

Pipettes are used to transfer a liquid from one container to another or to measure and dispense a specific amount of a liquid. In a few labs, you will use a pipette to move a tiny organism from one container to another. The drawing shows four types of pipettes.

Volumetric Pipettes These pipettes are designed to dispense a specific fixed volume of liquid. They have only one mark. When the pipette is filled to that mark, it will deliver the exact volume etched on the side of the pipette.

Graduated Pipettes These pipettes have a series of marks along the length of the pipette similar to the marks on a graduated cylinder. You take a reading before and after you release liquid from the pipette. The difference between the readings is the volume of the released liquid. A volume measured with a graduated pipette will be less accurate than the same volume measured with a volumetric pipette.

Dropper Pipettes These pipettes have no markings. They are used to transfer liquid from one container to another or to add liquid to a container one drop at a time.

Micropipettes As their name implies, these pipettes are designed to dispense small amounts of a liquid—less than 1 milliliter. Micropipettes are especially useful when a scientist is working with very small samples, such as those used to analyze DNA.

Volumetric Pipette

Graduated Pipette

Dropper Pipette

Micropipette

Using a Volumetric Pipette

Pipettes allow you to draw up and release a liquid in a controlled way. Suction is used to pull the liquid into the pipette. To create the suction with a volumetric pipette, you may use a pipette pump. Or you may use a plain rubber bulb or a bulb with an automatic valve. These instructions are for the bulb without a valve.

CAUTION: Never use your mouth to draw a liquid into a pipette.

1. If you are right-handed, hold the pipette in your right hand and the bulb in your left. Do the opposite if you are left-handed.
2. Place the tip of the pipette into the liquid.
3. Compress the bulb, and press the hole in the bulb against the upper end of the pipette. Insert the end of the pipette a tiny bit into the bulb to create the seal. **CAUTION:** Do not push the pipette too far into the bulb.
4. Slowly release pressure on the bulb so that liquid is drawn into the pipette to a level about 2 cm above the marked line.
5. Remove the bulb and put your index finger over the end of the pipette at the same time.
6. With your index finger pressed firmly against the end of the pipette, remove the pipette from the liquid.
7. Slowly reduce the pressure from your finger to allow some liquid to drain into a waste container. Stop when the bottom of the meniscus is at the marked line.
8. Release the remaining liquid into the receiving container. Wait 20 seconds.
9. Gently touch the pipette tip to the inside of the container. Do not worry about the small amount of liquid that remains in the tip.

Using a Dropper Pipette

The action of a dropper pipette is similar to that of an eye dropper. The bulb is part of the pipette. It is used to draw in and release liquid.

Using a Micropipette

A plunger controls the movement of a liquid into and out of a micropipette.

1. Some micropipettes have a set volume. Others have rings in the center of the pipette to set a volume. Turn the rings clockwise to increase the volume and counterclockwise to decrease the volume. **CAUTION:** Do not set a volume beyond the marked range of the micropipette.
2. Attach a tip to the end of the pipette.
3. When you push down on the plunger, it will stop at a point that is determined by the set volume. When you push harder, the plunger will stop at a second point, beyond which the plunger cannot go.
4. Push down on the plunger to the first point. Place the tip just below the surface of the liquid. When you slowly release the plunger, liquid will be drawn up.
5. Push the plunger to the second point to release the liquid into a container.
6. Use the tip discarder to remove the tip.

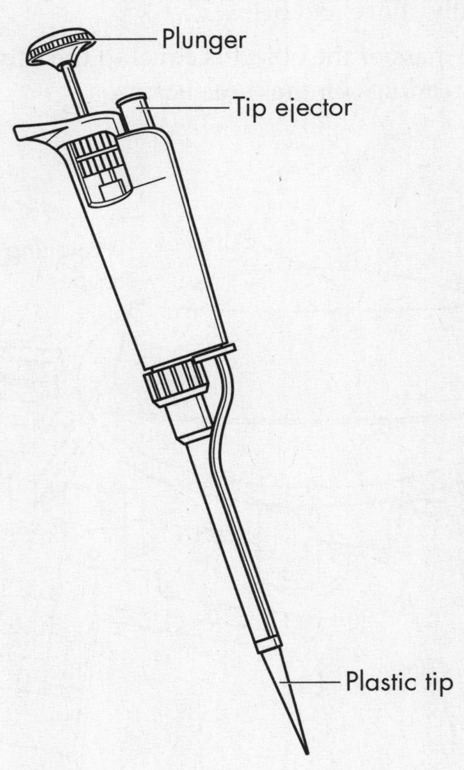

Measuring Mass

When you determine the mass of an object, you are comparing its mass with a known mass. There are many types of laboratory balances, but triple-beam balances are fairly common.

Using a Triple-Beam Balance

Refer to the drawing as you read these steps.

1. Move all the riders to the left side of their beams.
2. Check to see that the scale is balanced. The pointer should move an equal distance above and below the zero line or come to rest at the zero line. If necessary, use the zero adjustment screw.
3. Place your object on the pan. Slide the riders gently along the beams, one at a time, starting with the largest rider. If a beam is notched, be sure that the rider is in a notch.
4. Moving the riders increases the mass of the beams. When the added masses of the moved riders are equal to the mass of the object, the pointer should come to rest at zero or swing evenly above and below zero.
5. The mass of the object is equal to the sum of the readings on the three beams.

Caring for a Triple-Beam Balance

A balance is a precision instrument that must be handled with care. Follow these rules to keep from damaging your balance.

1. Any object placed on the balance must be dry and at room temperature.
2. Do not place chemicals directly on the pan of a balance. Place liquids in containers. Find the mass of the empty, dry container first. Place solids in a container or on weighing paper. If you use weighing paper, zero the balance with the paper on the pan.
3. If you spill a chemical on or near a balance, notify your teacher and clean up the spill immediately.
4. Never try to measure an object with a mass that is likely to exceed the capacity of the balance.
5. When you are done, return all riders to the zero position, remove your sample, and, if necessary, clean off the pan.

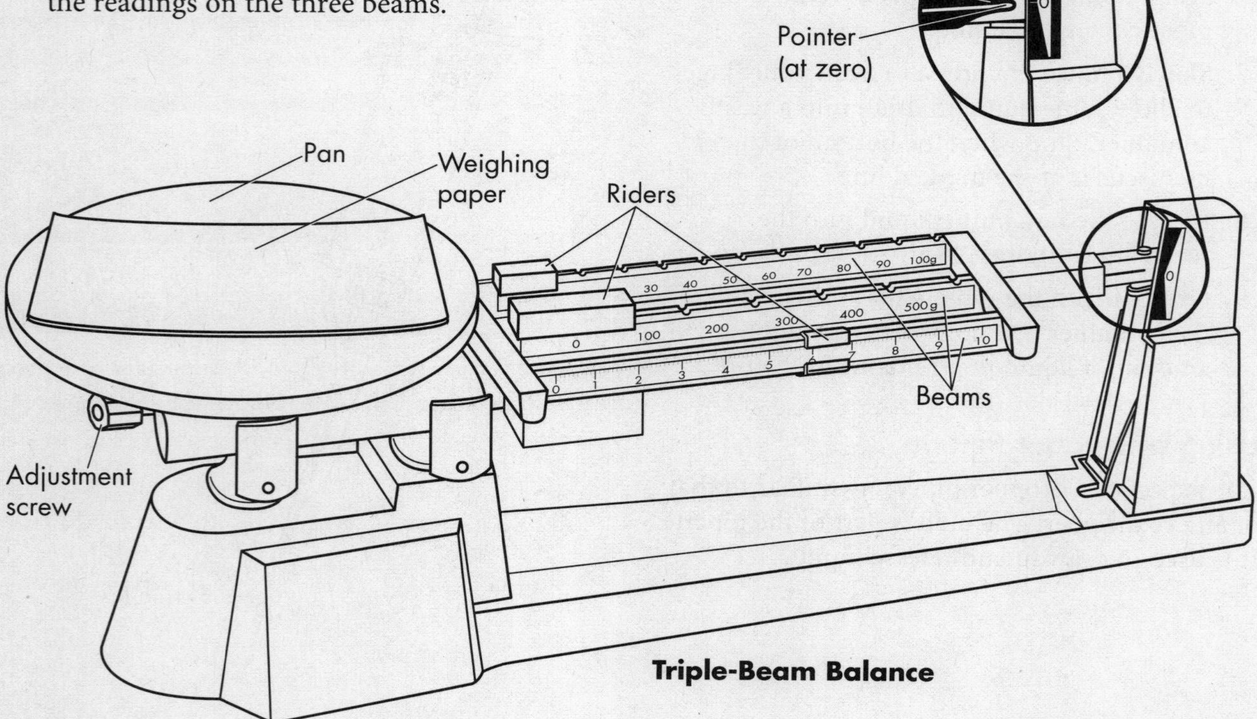

Triple-Beam Balance

Name ______ Class ______ Date ______

Caring for Your Microscope

The microscope used in most biology classes is a compound microscope with a combination of lenses. The eyepiece lens is located in the top part of the microscope. Other lenses, called objective lenses, are at the bottom of the body tube on the revolving nosepiece. By rotating the nosepiece, you can select an appropriate objective with which to view your specimen.

The magnification for each objective is etched on its side. To determine the total magnification, multiply the power of the objective by the power of the eyepiece lens.

Rules for Using a Microscope

A microscope is a precision instrument that requires careful use. To protect the microscope, follow these rules.

1. Always carry a microscope with two hands. Grasp the arm of the microscope with one hand, and place your other hand under the base. Hold the microscope in an upright position so that the eyepiece cannot fall out.
2. Place the microscope on a flat surface with the arm facing you and the base about 10 cm from the edge.
3. Always start with the low-power objective in position. If necessary, rotate the nosepiece to bring the lens into position. A click will indicate that it is in position.
4. Always view the microscope from the side when you rotate the nosepiece to avoid damaging an objective or a slide.
5. Use the coarse adjustment knob to move the low-power objective as close to the stage as possible without touching the stage. Always view the microscope from the side as you move an objective *toward* the stage.
6. As you view a slide through the eyepiece, turn the coarse adjustment knob to move the low-power objective *away* from the stage until the object comes into focus.
7. To avoid eyestrain, keep both eyes open when you look through the eyepiece.
8. When you view an object with the high-power objective, use the fine adjustment knob to obtain a sharper focus. Never use the coarse adjustment.
9. To avoid scratching the lenses, always use lens paper to clean the lenses. Use a new piece of paper for each lens.

1. **Eyepiece:** Contains a magnifying lens
2. **Arm:** Supports the body tube
3. **Low-power objective:** Provides the least magnification and largest field of view
4. **Stage:** Supports the slide being observed
5. **Opening of the stage:** Permits light to pass up to the eyepiece
6. **Fine adjustment knob:** Moves the body tube slightly to adjust the image
7. **Coarse adjustment knob:** Moves the body tube to focus the image
8. **Base:** Supports the microscope
9. **Illuminator:** Produces light or reflects light up toward the eyepiece
10. **Diaphragm:** Regulates the amount of light passing up toward the eyepiece
11. **Stage clips:** Hold the slide in place
12. **High-power objective:** Provides greater magnification and a smaller field of view
13. **Nosepiece:** Holds the objectives and can be rotated to change the magnification
14. **Body tube:** Maintains the proper distance between the eyepiece and the objectives

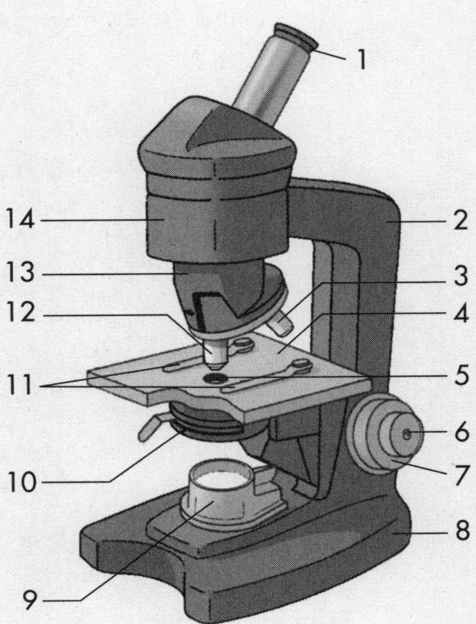

Using a Gas Burner

Many labs use hot plates as a heat source, but some labs still use gas burners. The two most common models are the Bunsen burner and the Tirrell burner. With both models, you can adjust the flame by controlling the amount of air and the amount of gas that mix in the tube.

Both types of burners have a device on the tube (or barrel) to adjust the amount of air. With both types of burners, the amount of gas can be controlled at the main gas valve. With the Tirrell burner, a valve at the base of the burner can also control the flow of gas.

Refer to the drawings of the burners as you read these instructions.

1. Examine your burner to determine which model you have.
2. Connect the burner to the gas outlet with rubber tubing. **CAUTION:** Do not use a gas burner to heat flammable materials.
3. Close the air vents by rotating the sleeve on the Bunsen burner or adjusting the height of the tube on the Tirrell burner.
4. If you have a Tirrell burner, also close the gas control valve at the base of the burner.
5. Hold a lit match about 2 cm above and just to the right of the tube. **CAUTION:** Make sure you use a safety match.
6. If you have a Bunsen burner, slowly open the main gas valve. If you have a Tirrell burner, first open the gas supply fully, and then slowly open the gas valve on the tube. **CAUTION:** If the flame goes out after you light it, reduce the amount of gas.
7. If you have a gas lighter, hold the striker about 2 cm above and just to the right of the tube. With a gas lighter, you must produce the spark as you open the main gas supply on the Bunsen burner or the gas valve on the Tirrell burner.
8. The hottest and most efficient flame is blue and has the distinct regions shown in the drawing. Open the air vents slowly until you have a light-blue, cone-shaped flame.

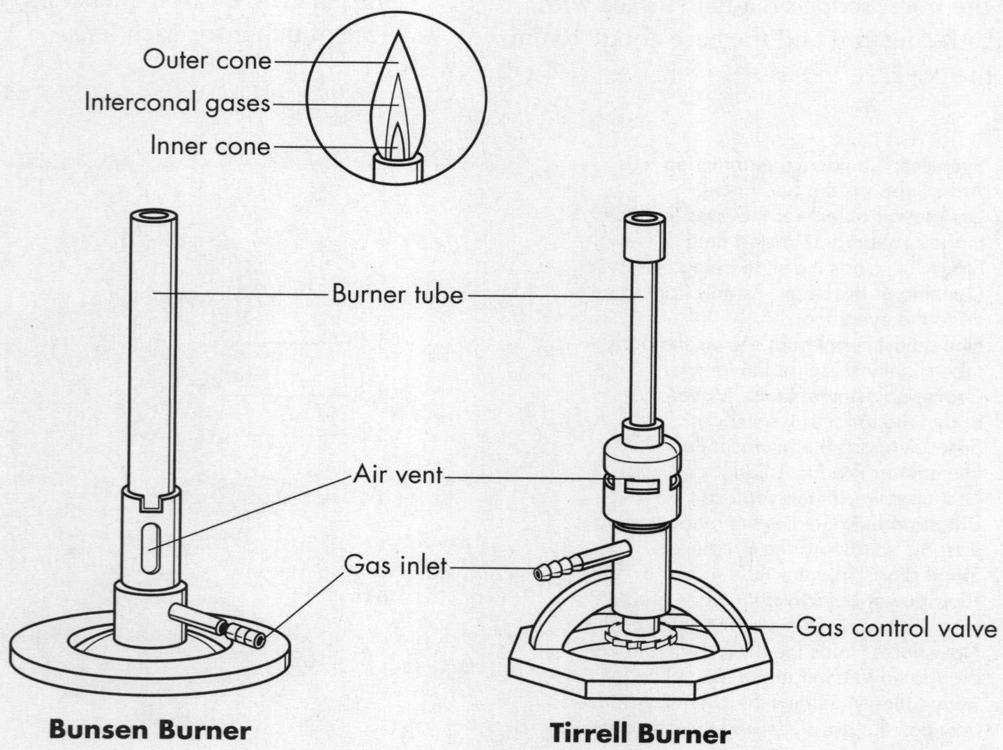

Appendix E Science and Technology

Part 1: Technology

What is technology?

Technology is an application of science to meet specific needs. The need may be global, such as, an application that will protect crops from insects. The need may be practical, such as, an application that cleans clothes or dishes. The need may be personal, such as, an application that makes music portable. All technology involves the handling of materials and an understanding of the processes needed to make the best use of different materials. Technology changes the way people live and how they interact with the world.

A technological application is human-made. It does not occur naturally. For example, until the late nineteenth century, a common way to relieve a toothache was to chew on the bark of a willow tree. The bark contains salicin, a naturally occurring substance that relieves headaches and muscle pain. A derivative of salicin, salicylic acid, is the key ingredient in aspirin, which was first sold in 1899. Both satisfy the same need, but only the aspirin is an application of technology. Chewing willow bark is not.

Different areas of science are used in technology. Consider, for example, *biotechnology,* the combination of biology and technology. Pest-resistant crops, artificial insulin to treat diabetes, and enzymes to clean clothes have all come from biotechnology.

How are science and technology related?

Science is the study of the natural world to understand how it functions. Technology is the use of this understanding to make devices that can change how people interact with the natural world. In the example of the aspirin tablet, basic science provided an understanding of the compound salicin and how to isolate it as crystalline salicylic acid. Technology provided the means of making a tablet that is easy to swallow and can be widely available.

Another example of how an advance in science contributes to advances in technology is the discovery that a changing magnetic field can produce an electric field. This knowledge led to the development of the electric motor. Compared to previous ways of harnessing power, such as windmills to grind flour or horses to haul loads, the electric motor is a significant advance in technology.

Just as advances in science contribute to advances in technology, advances in technology contribute to advances in science.

- The microscope is an example of an advance in technology that contributed to advances in science. Microscopes allow us to see beyond the visual range of humans.
- The application of computers and technological processes for copying and manipulating DNA has resulted in a detailed map of the human genome.

How does technology progress?

Two factors drive technological progress: (1) an increase in people's knowledge or understanding of science and (2) the needs people seek to satisfy. With factor 1, the more you know, the more you get to do. With factor 2, the more you do, the more you may want to do even more.

Think about how technology has affected communication in just the last 50 years. The phone your grandparents used when they were your age was much bigger and heavier than a cellphone, and was permanently attached to a wall. There were no cellphones, no texting, no talking while walking around outdoors.

If you needed to call someone and were not at home, you would have to find a pay phone. Pay phones used to be everywhere. They met a common need and were a profitable business. Today, cellphones have made public pay phones practically *obsolete*—they have been replaced by a better, alternative technology.

What is a technological system?

Applications of technology often involve groups of parts that work together as a system. A technological system has an overall *purpose,* or goal, and four basic parts to meet that goal: the *input,* the *process,* the *output,* and *feedback.*

For example, the *purpose,* or goal, of your school's central heating or cooling system is to heat or cool the classrooms. The *input* is the fuel that makes the system work: electricity, natural gas, geothermal heat, oil, or solar panels. The *process* is the sequence of actions that the system undergoes to reach its goal. Here, the process includes distributing hot or cool water or air to your classroom. The *output* is the hot or cool air. The *feedback* is a device, such as a thermostat, that measures temperature and controls when the system turns off and on.

Feedback is the information that a system uses to monitor the input, processes, and output so that it can adjust itself to meet the goal. Because any technological system can fail, system feedback is a necessary element. Feedback lets you know whether the system is functioning as intended.

What are trade-offs?

When designing a technological system, there may be *trade-offs* to consider. A *trade-off* is an exchange in which one benefit is given up in order to obtain another.

Suppose a family is trying to decide on the heating system for a new house. The *input* is the fuel. What trade-offs are involved in choosing the fuel? The local electric plant is coal-fired. The family is concerned about the effect of fossil fuels on the environment. They might trade off, that is give up, a cheaper mechanical system and choose a more expensive system of solar panels.

Consider trade-offs for designing a *process.* Should the family pipe hot water under the floors or along the baseboards for heat? If they decide to run the pipes under the floor, then they are trading off easy access to the plumbing for a better distribution of heat.

After considering all the options, the family will want to avoid making trade-offs that will compromise the system's goal of providing a reliable source of heat.

What are side effects?

Technological systems usually have *side effects.* Side effects are harmful secondary effects that result from some function of the system. For example, medicines often have side effects. Some side effects, such as sleepiness caused by an allergy medication, are minor. Other side effects, such as internal bleeding caused by a painkiller, can be serious.

What is risk-benefit analysis?

In deciding whether to use a particular technology—or how to use it—you must analyze its possible risks and benefits. For example, the drugs used for cancer treatment often cause nausea, fatigue, and hair loss. In such cases, the benefits of such treatment usually outweigh the risks. Risk-benefit analysis can involve a consideration of human values—principles or goals, such as health or personal freedom, that a person or society thinks are important. For example the use of insecticides to protect crops might be considered too great a risk if it endangers a community's water resources.

How do engineering and technology differ?

Engineering is the use of devices and processes produced by technology to design and manufacture complex systems and structures. Advances in technology lead to advances in engineering. For example, technology helps manufacturers produce a steel I-beam that is strong and carries weight efficiently. Engineering helps designers put together a system of I-beams and other structures to make a bridge or high-rise building. Like technology, engineering involves the application of scientific principles to solve problems. It also relies on math and technical skill.

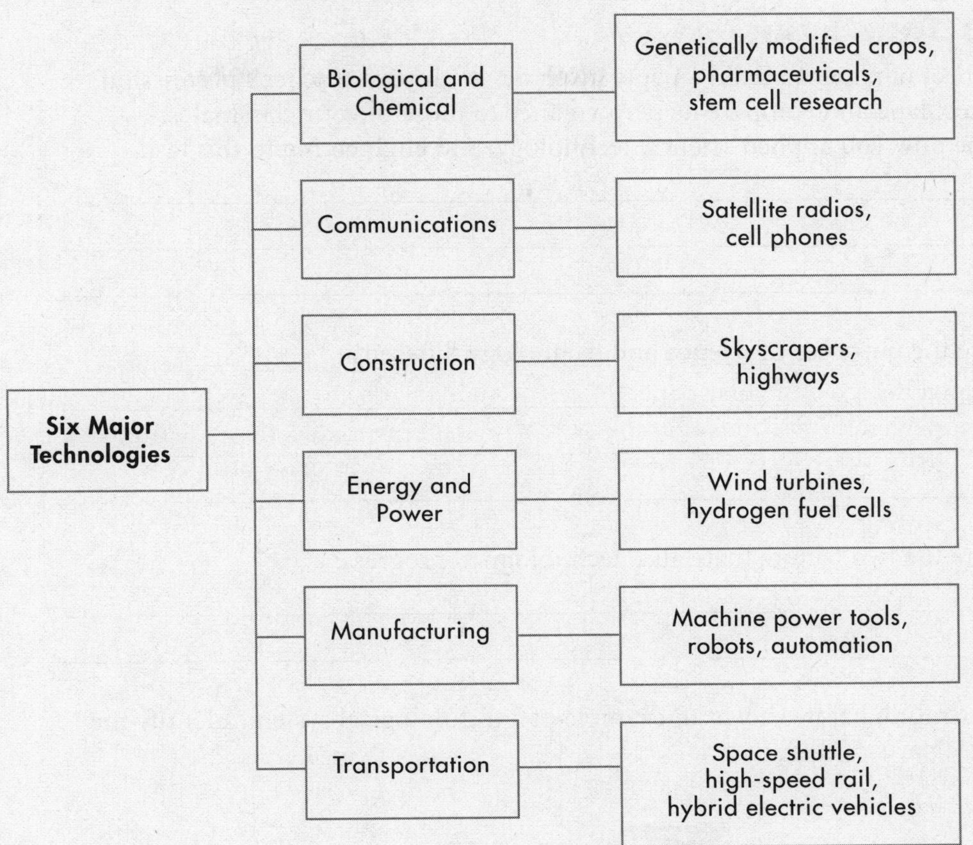

Is technology a product or a process?

Technology is not an object. It's not a DVD player or a satellite or a gaming system. Technology is the *process* through which such objects are made. Innovations in technology have advanced human civilization over thousands of years. Technology has led to ways to harness power and store energy. It has led to more fuel-efficient cars and smaller computers. Technology is neither inherently good nor inherently bad.

What are major areas of technology?

The diagram shows six major technologies and a few examples of each. Notice how different areas of technology overlap. For example, advances in several technologies have led to today's faster and more fuel-efficient cars. Advances in energy and power technology have led to better fuel sources. Manufacturing technology is what allows people to make use of lightweight yet strong materials. Transportation technology has improved car design with more efficient engines and streamlined bodies. Construction technology provides the roads and bridges that allow people to travel great distances over rough terrain, rivers, and other obstacles.

What might the future hold?

As society advances, what works today may be obsolete by the next generation. The changes you can expect to see in your lifetime will depend on both technological advances and society's values.

Transportation is a good example. As we learn more about climate change and habitat loss, changes in thinking may affect the way vehicles are designed and how people think about highway systems. Communities might decide to design transportation systems and ways of living that make commuting by car obsolete. Imagine ribbons of highway turned into green spaces that provide bike trails, skateboarding arenas, and pedestrian walk zones.

Practice Your Skills

1. Use a sheet of paper to build a paper airplane. With your teacher's permission, fly the airplane and compare its performance to those of your classmates. Describe how you applied science, technology, and engineering to this task.

2. How are the purposes of science and technology different?

3. What are the two factors that cause technology to progress?

4. The illustration below shows an example of a technological system. Identify the four basic parts of this system.

5. Name one way that people traveled long distances in the past that is now obsolete. What are two ways that people travel long distances today? How might people travel long distances in the future?

Part 2: Evaluate a Design

The goal of technology is meeting a specific need or solving a problem. The best designs are often collaborations in which people from different backgrounds work together to design the best solution or product. A manufacturing company might have a design team with artists, scientists, mathematicians, and engineers. An *engineer* is a person who is trained to use both technology and scientific knowledge to solve practical problems.

How does the design process work?

Product design teams follow a process that has six basic phases.

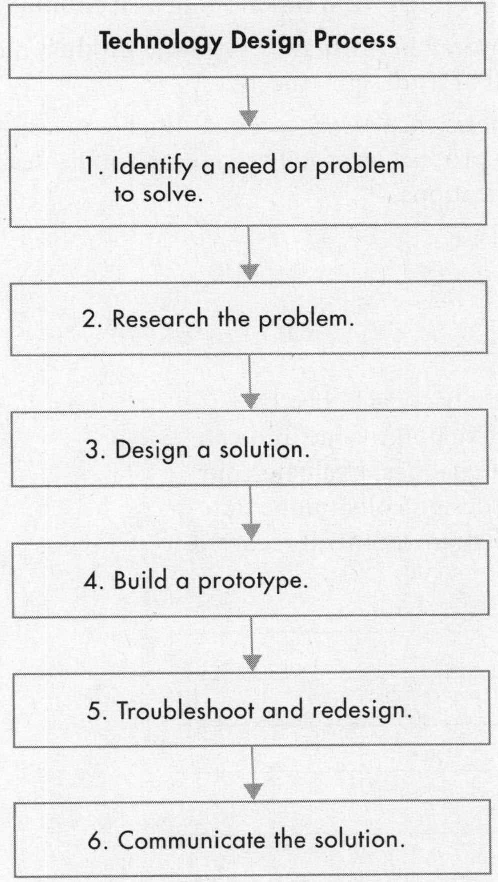

Technology Design Process
1. Identify a need or problem to solve.
2. Research the problem.
3. Design a solution.
4. Build a prototype.
5. Troubleshoot and redesign.
6. Communicate the solution.

An important part of designing a solution through teamwork is *brainstorming.* Brainstorming provides members of the design team the opportunity to freely suggest any creative solution to a problem. The free exchange of ideas can inspire further creativity among the team and lead to the best solution.

How do technology and product design influence one another?

Sometimes product designs push improvements in technology. An inventor may come up with a product idea that requires the development of the manufacturing technology needed to produce the product.

In 1941, George de Mestral, a Swiss engineer, came up with the idea for a product you now know as Velcro. His invention came from a simple observation: While removing the burs attached to his dog's fur, he wondered what it was that made the burs take such a strong hold. He took a closer look at the burs. Under the magnifying glass, he could see that the burs had tiny hooks. From this observation came inspiration.

At the time, the technology needed to manufacture Velcro was not available. It took about 10 years to create a loom that could produce the specialized fabrics with hooks and loops. At first, Velcro was mostly used in highly specialized applications. For example, the aerospace industry of the 1960s used Velcro to enable astronauts to more easily get in and out of their bulky space suits. Today, Velcro is a common substitute for zippers and shoelaces.

Improvements in technology can also push innovation. Lasers are devices that produce beams of light from electromagnetic radiation. The first lasers were of interest mostly to the scientific community, who began studying their properties in the 1960s. Certain types of lasers were used in industrial applications, for example, in welding. Today, a day probably doesn't go by without your using laser technology. Lasers are used to read compact discs and DVDs. They are also used in the optical fibers that supply digital information to your computer.

What are limiting factors in design?

Sometimes, the finished product does not match the original product design. The differences can be due to the *limiting factors* that affect the design. A limiting factor is any characteristic or feature of the finished product that most affects the design. With Velcro, the first limiting factor was technology. There were no technological means available to manufacture the product as designed. Other limiting factors can include cost and materials. In the case of Velcro, the first strips were manufactured using cotton. The cotton was soon replaced by synthetic fibers, which offered greater strength and durability.

Some inventors and design teams conceive of products that cannot be manufactured and sold because the designs are based on an *emerging technology*. Scientists and engineers understand the science, basic principles, and theory behind the product design. However, the design cannot be implemented until the technology is fully developed. One such example is the use of stem cells to reverse paralysis due to spinal cord injuries.

What is a patent?

A *patent* is a legal document issued by the government that gives an inventor legal rights over an invention so that no one can copy it. In the United States, a patent typically lasts for 20 years. George de Mestral was issued a U.S. patent for Velcro in 1955.

How is a product design evaluated?

The evaluation of a design takes into account three basic criteria.

1. Functional requirements: does the product do what it's supposed to do?
2. Constraints: are there any factors that limit the design from functioning as it should?
3. Overall performance: does the product meet all of its design objectives?

A *performance metric* is a quantifiable measure of the product's capacity to meet all of its design specifications.

Practice Your Skills

1. One product that is part of almost every student's life is a backpack. List five qualities you value in a backpack and assign each a relative point value. Indicate if there are any design constraints associated with those qualities. Evaluate your own backpack in terms of functional requirements and design constraints. Rate its overall performance using your scale, indicating how many points it received against the possible total.

2. One recent technological advance in backpack design is the rolling pack. In addition to shoulder straps, a rolling pack has a pair of wheels at its base and a retracting handle so that you can pull the pack. Identify at least two trade-offs with this design.

3. The data table provides dimensions for two models of backpacks. Determine the carrying capacity, or volume, of each (volume = length × width × depth). Both are sold for the same price. What does this information suggest about a design constraint in the manufacturing process?

Comparison of Backpack Types

Type of Pack	Length (cm)	Width (cm)	Depth (cm)	Volume (cm)
Shoulder pack	48	35	25	
Rolling pack	44	24	20	

4. Assume the average textbook is 28.5 cm × 23.0 cm × 4.5 cm. How many textbooks do you typically carry to school each day? Is each pack capable of carrying all your textbooks? Which value determines this?

5. Are you carrying more than the maximum safety load? How do you know?

6. Apply a risk-benefit analysis to the following situation. Dylan plans to purchase a shoulder pack or a rolling pack. The mass of a backpack should be no more than 15 percent of a person's body mass. Dylan weighs 115 pounds and typically carries five textbooks each day. Calculate the total mass of Dylan's textbooks, assuming an average mass of 1.65 kg each. Determine Dylan's maximum safe load in kilograms and make a recommendation. *Hint:* To convert weight in pounds to mass in kilograms, multiply the pounds by 0.45 and round up.

____

____

____

____

____

____

7. If you invented a product, would you obtain a patent? Explain the advantages of a patent.

____

____

____

____

8. Some biotechnology companies have patented certain gene sequences that may have medical applications. From the point of view of societal values, what might be the problem with allowing such patents?

____

____

____

____

____

Part 3: Prototypes and Scale Models

Technology is developed to meet a specific need or solve a particular problem. Once the problem is defined, a team will be chosen to work on the problem. Engineers usually have a central role on the team. Engineers are trained to use both technological and scientific knowledge to solve practical problems.

In the early stages of the design process, the engineers will spend time researching the problem fully. They are likely to spend time reading books and articles to gather background information. They may attend conferences where the latest ideas in their field are discussed. They may also perform experiments related to the technology being designed. The engineers may be working to develop a new product or improve an existing one. Either way, they may want to talk to potential customers to find out what the customers want. This part of the process is called market research.

During the development process, engineers often need to make technical drawings, or blueprints, and build prototypes.

What is a blueprint?

With the results of their research in hand, the design team will identify the materials and processes needed. They will make a sketch of their proposed solution and then make technical drawings. A technical drawing shows the dimensions of the design product and indicates the materials to be used. It contains all the information needed to build the product.

An engineering drawing is often referred to as a *blueprint*. The name comes from a printing process that was once used to produce many copies of a hand-drawn technical drawing. Today, engineers use computers to create technical drawings of their designs. Computers have made the job of creating technical drawings much easier. They enable the design team to view their design in three dimensions and make adjustments.

What is a prototype?

A design team may choose to build a prototype of their product design. A *prototype* is a working model used to test a design. Prototypes are used to test the operation of a product, including how well it works, how long it lasts, and how safe it is to use. Sometimes the prototype is built as a *scale model.* A scale model has the same proportions as the product but is built to a different scale.

Prototype testing allows the design team to identify problems with their design. The process of analyzing a design problem and finding a way to fix it is called *troubleshooting.* Based on the testing, the engineers may need to redesign the product, or some part of it, to address one or more design problems. With the testing done and adjustments made, the design product can then move on to the manufacturing stage.

Practice Your Skills

1. Suppose a wealthy inventor who once went to your school has returned to announce a team competition. She has convinced the principal to make available a little-used alcove outside the main office. The competition is to design an ideal locker, which the inventor will then manufacture. Your team's goal is to design the ideal locker and build a prototype or produce a scale drawing. To begin, you need to do some research, using your own locker. Describe the design features of your locker, including materials.

2. The alcove is located in the main hallway and measures 10 feet high by 6 feet wide by 2 feet deep. There is an electrical outlet located in the floorboards. Consider whether all that space is usable space. Identify one design constraint in making use of that space for student lockers.

3. Work with your team to brainstorm features of your ideal locker. Make a list of your requirements and determine the locker's dimensions. Remember to keep in mind that the locker you design is part of a system of lockers that must fit into the alcove. Consider how many lockers you want to put in that space. Identify the materials you would like to use.

4. Build a scale model of your ideal locker or make a scale drawing. Evaluate your ideal locker design. Does it meet all the specified requirements? How does it compare to your current locker?

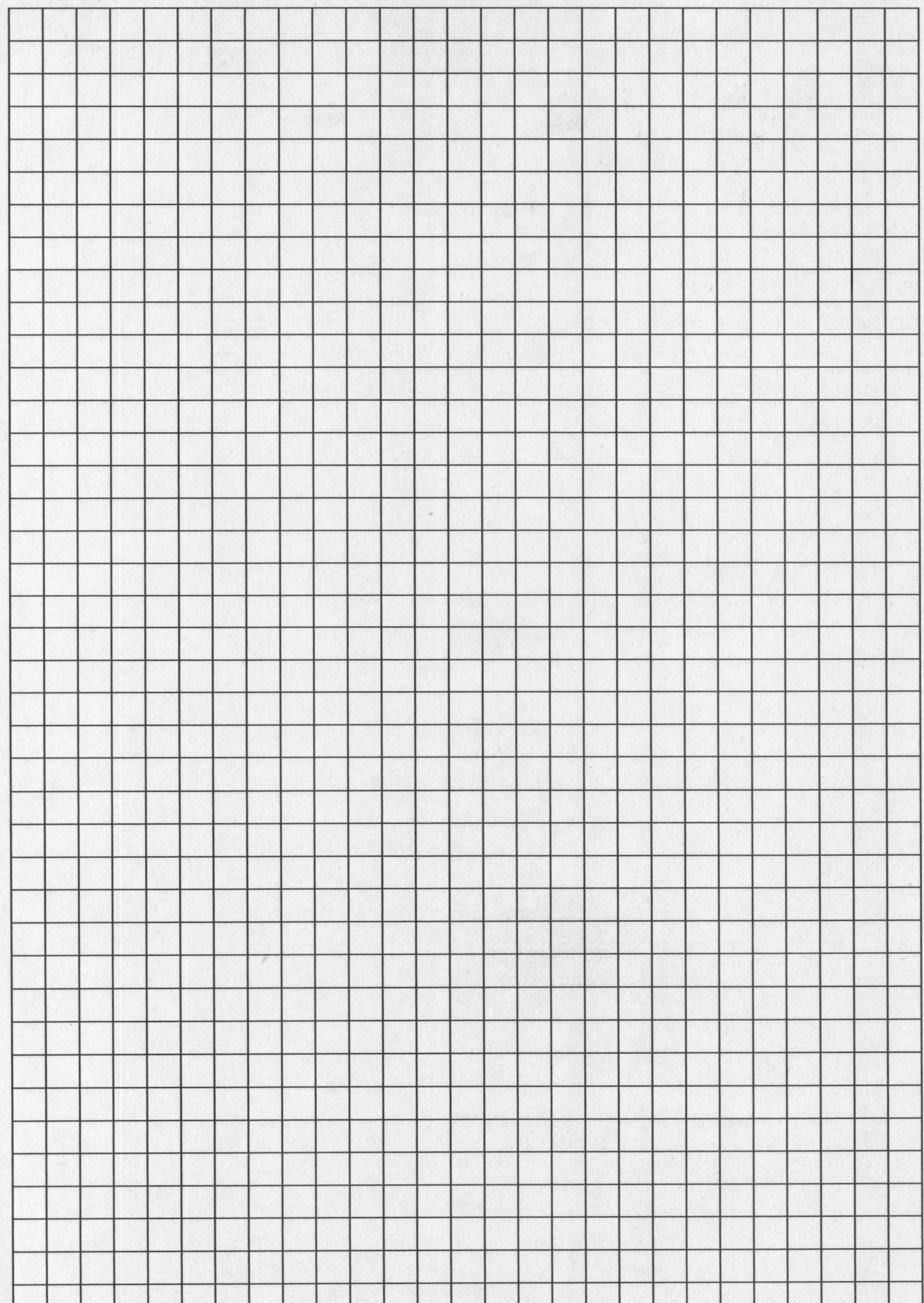

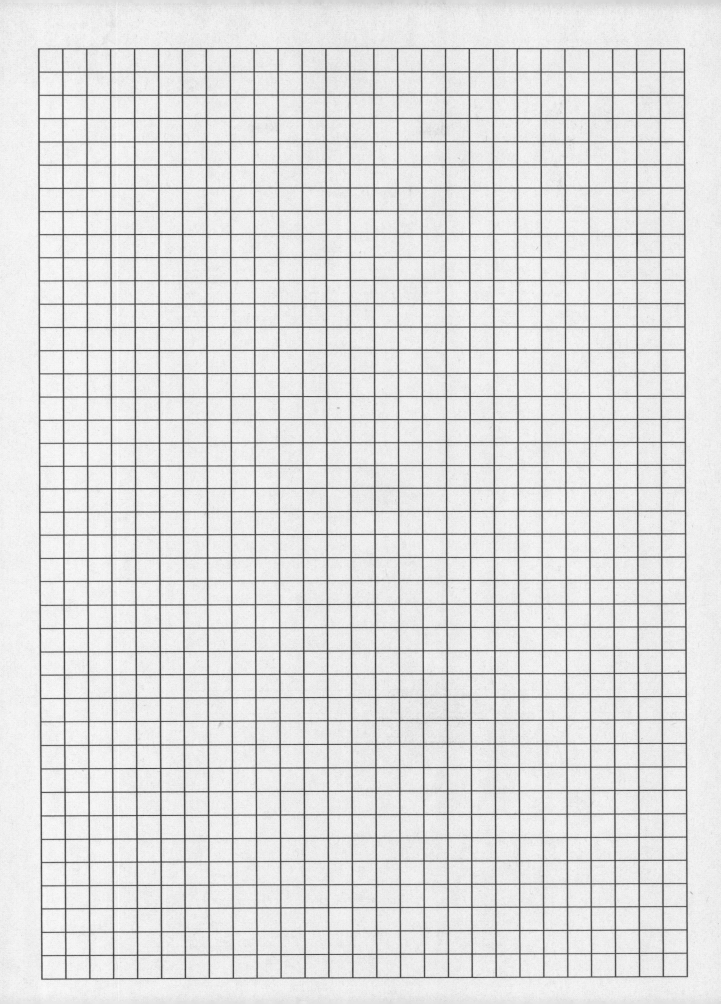

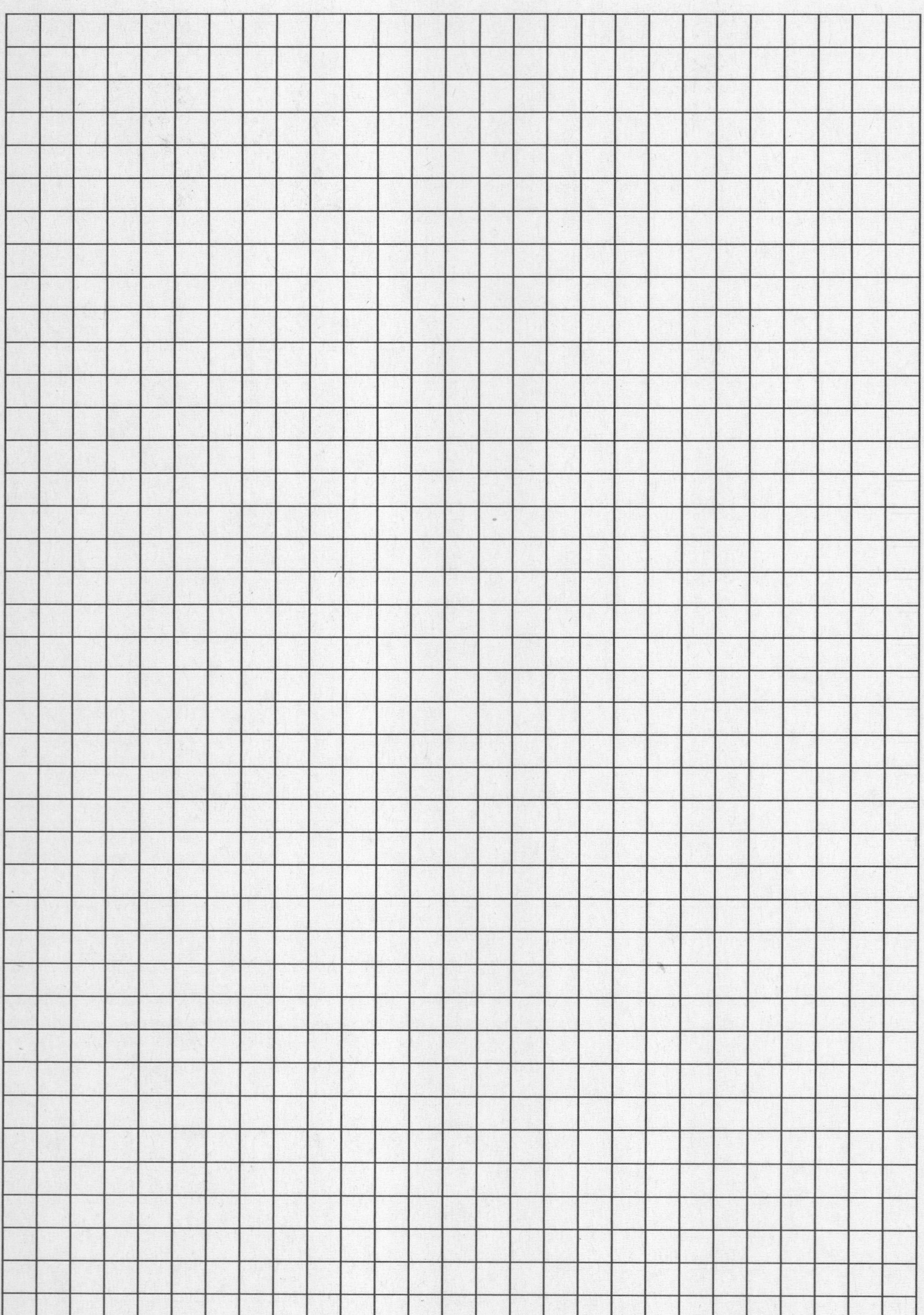

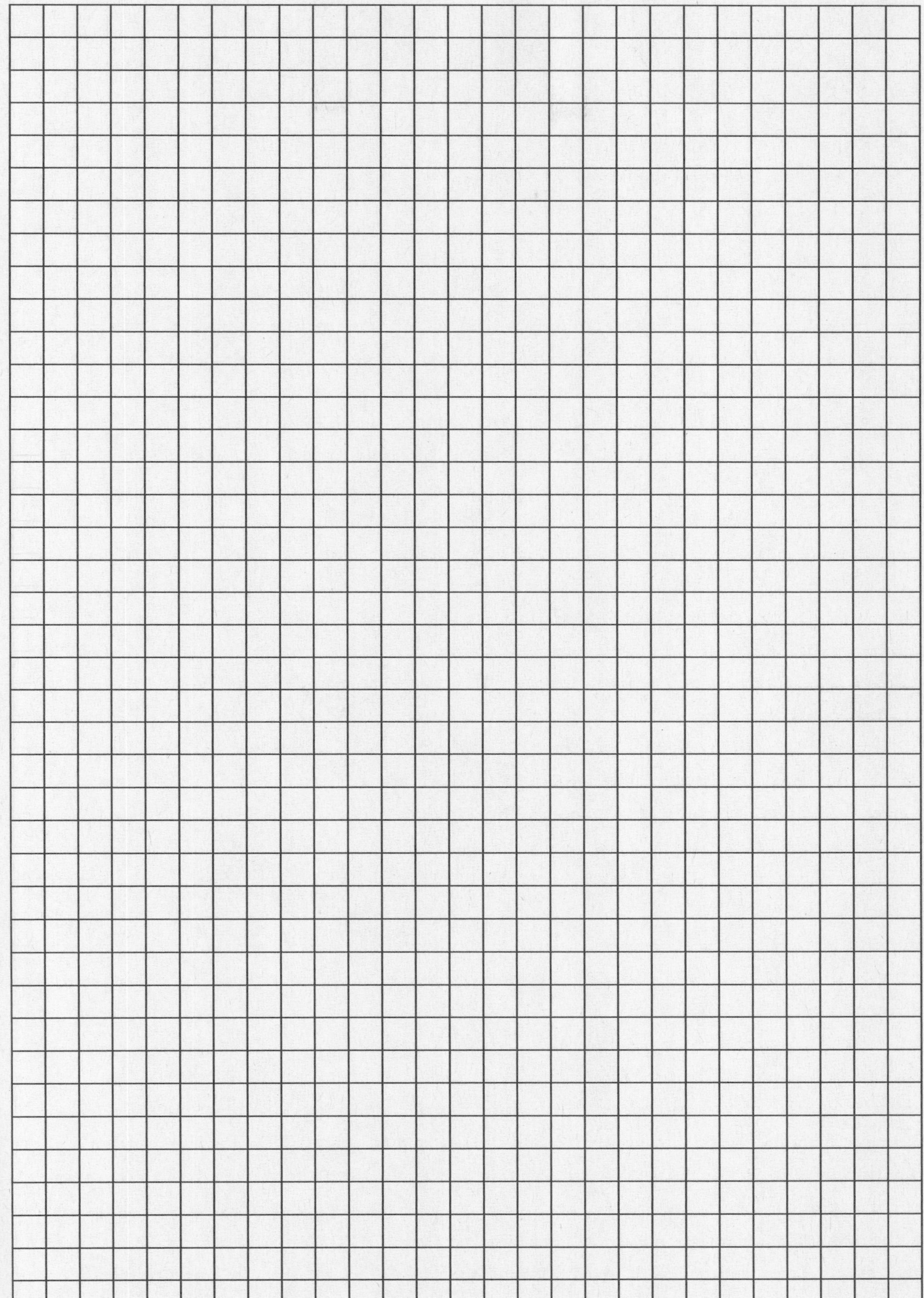

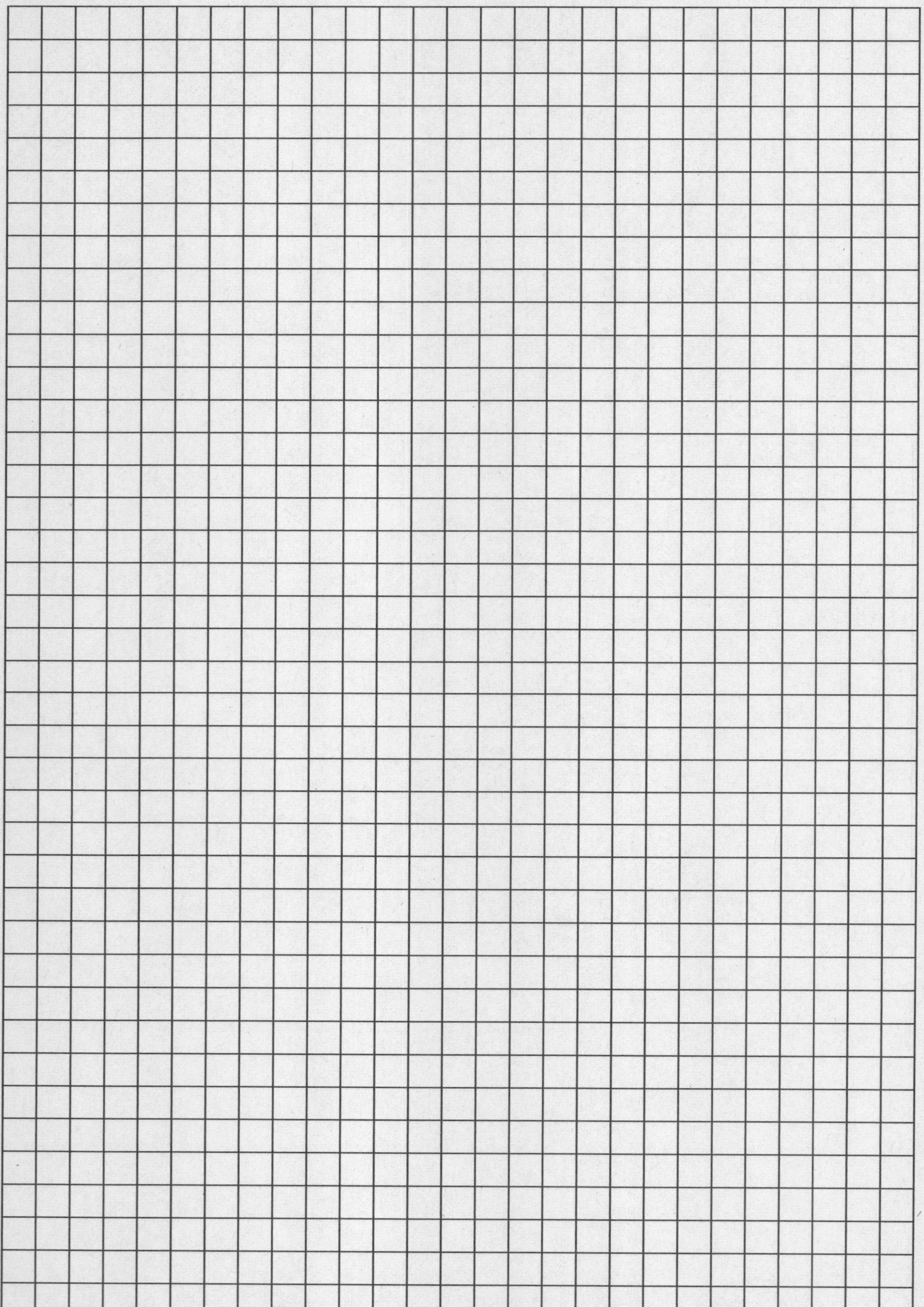

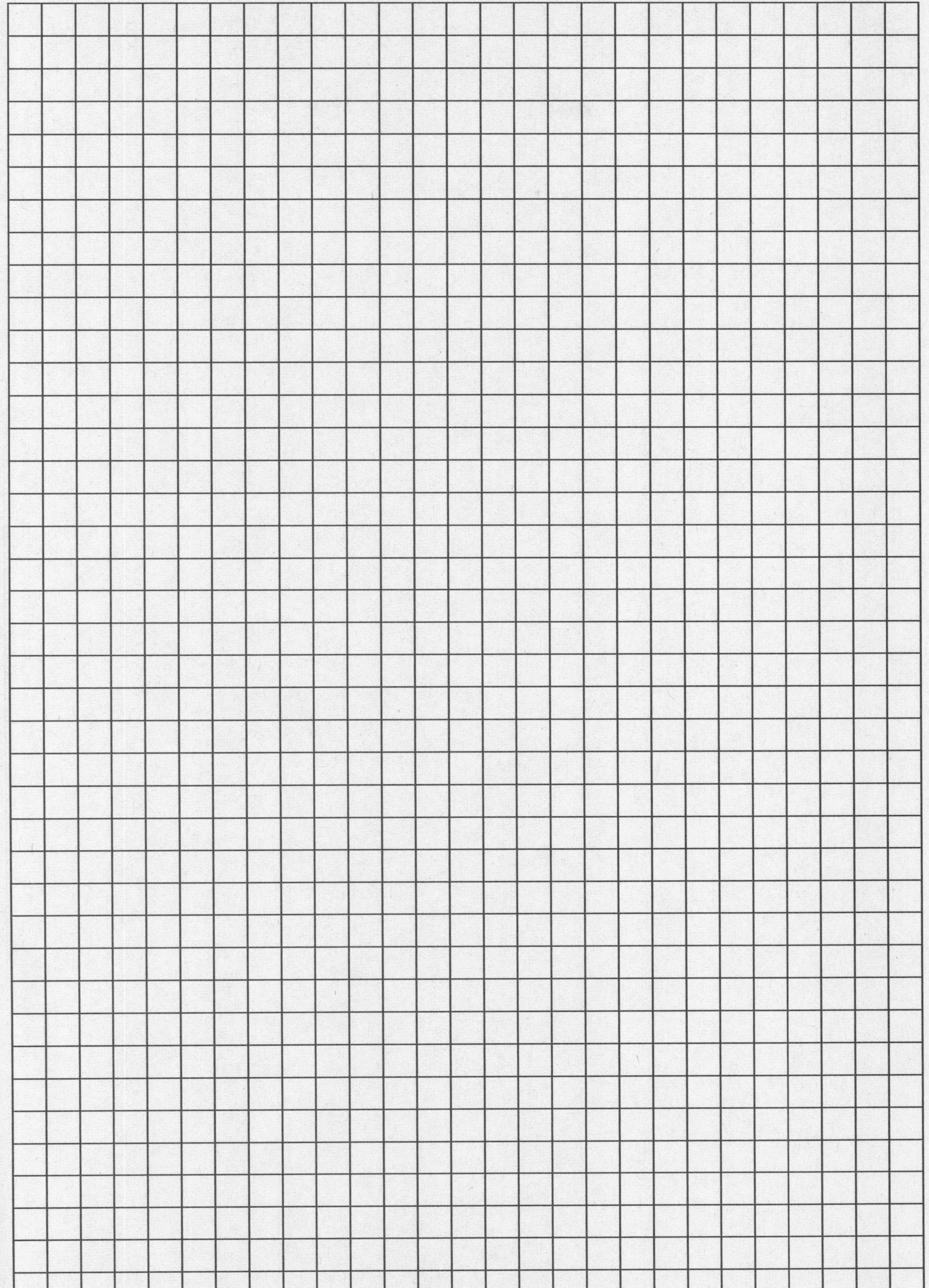

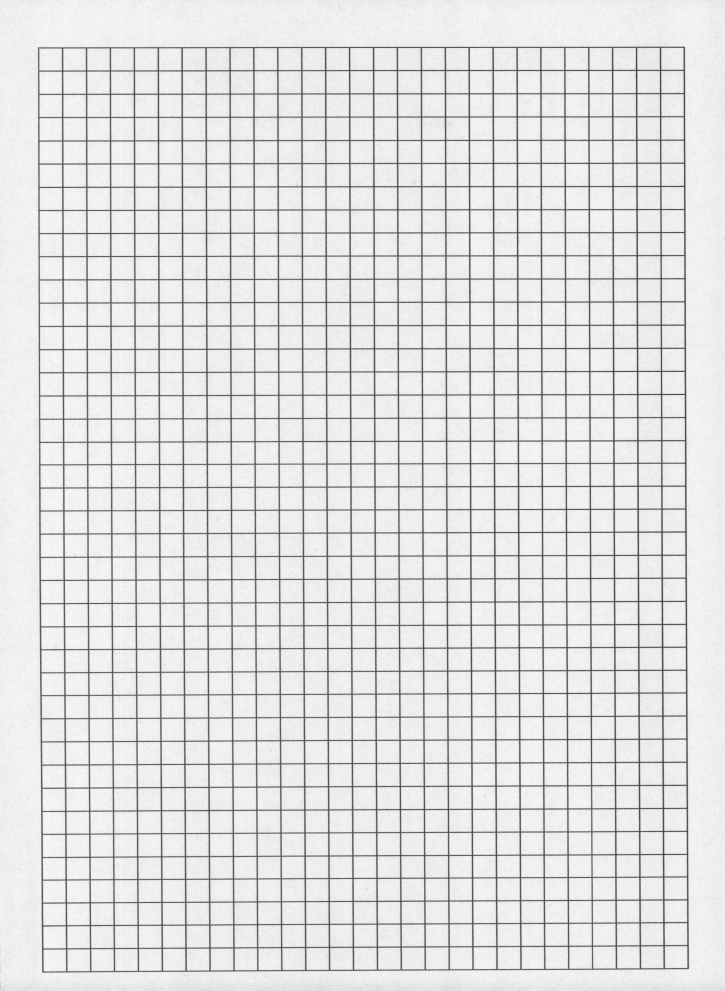

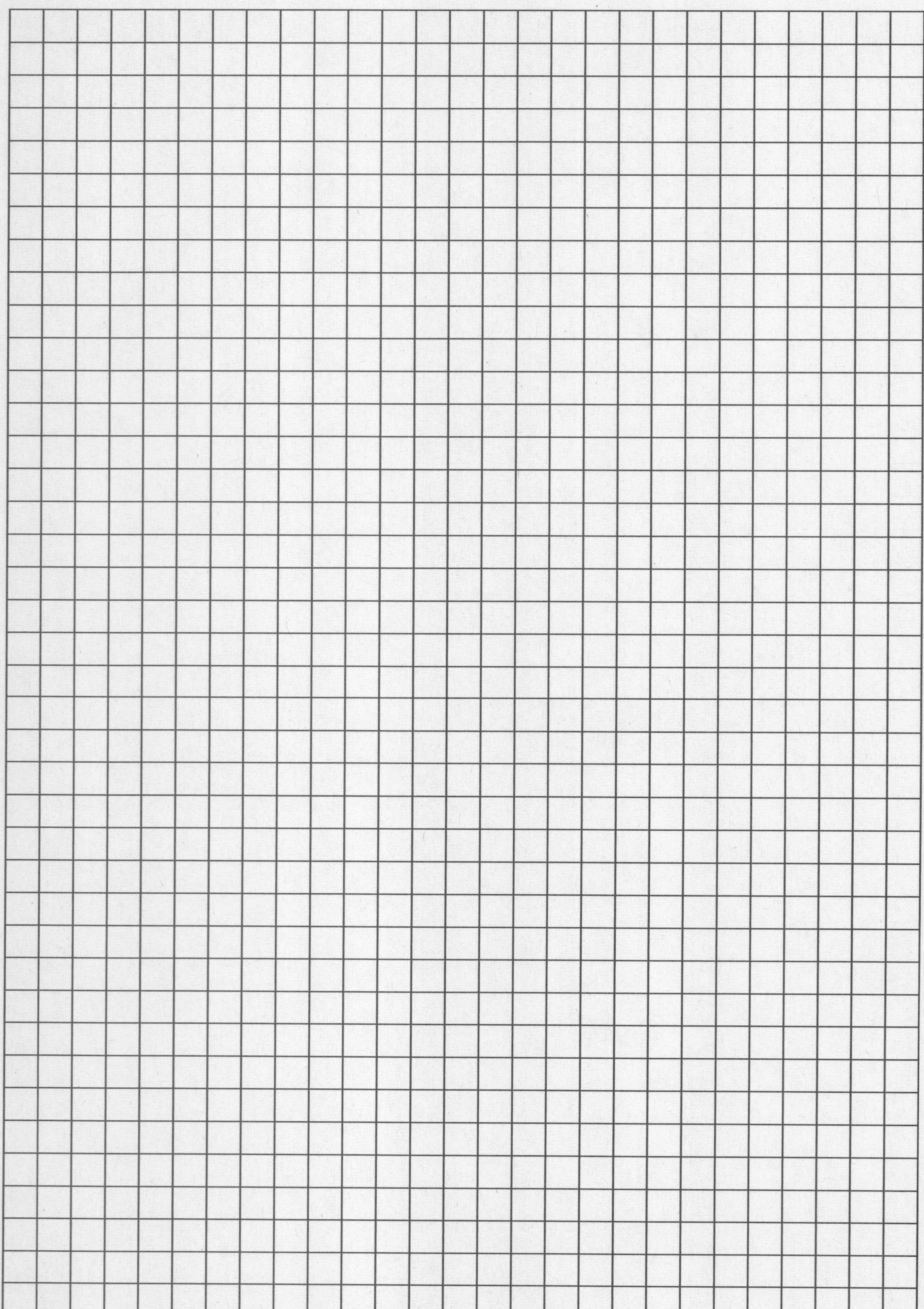

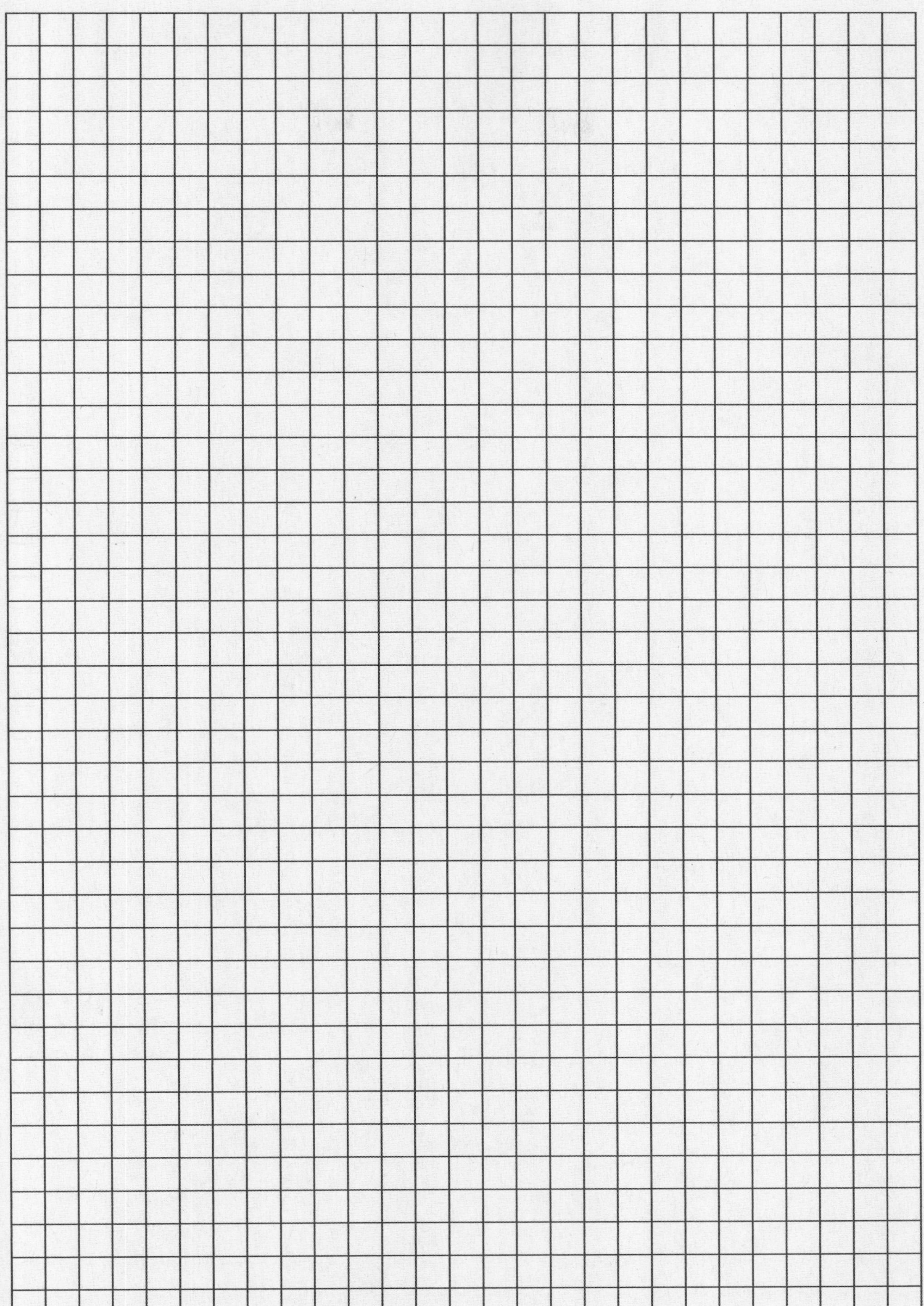

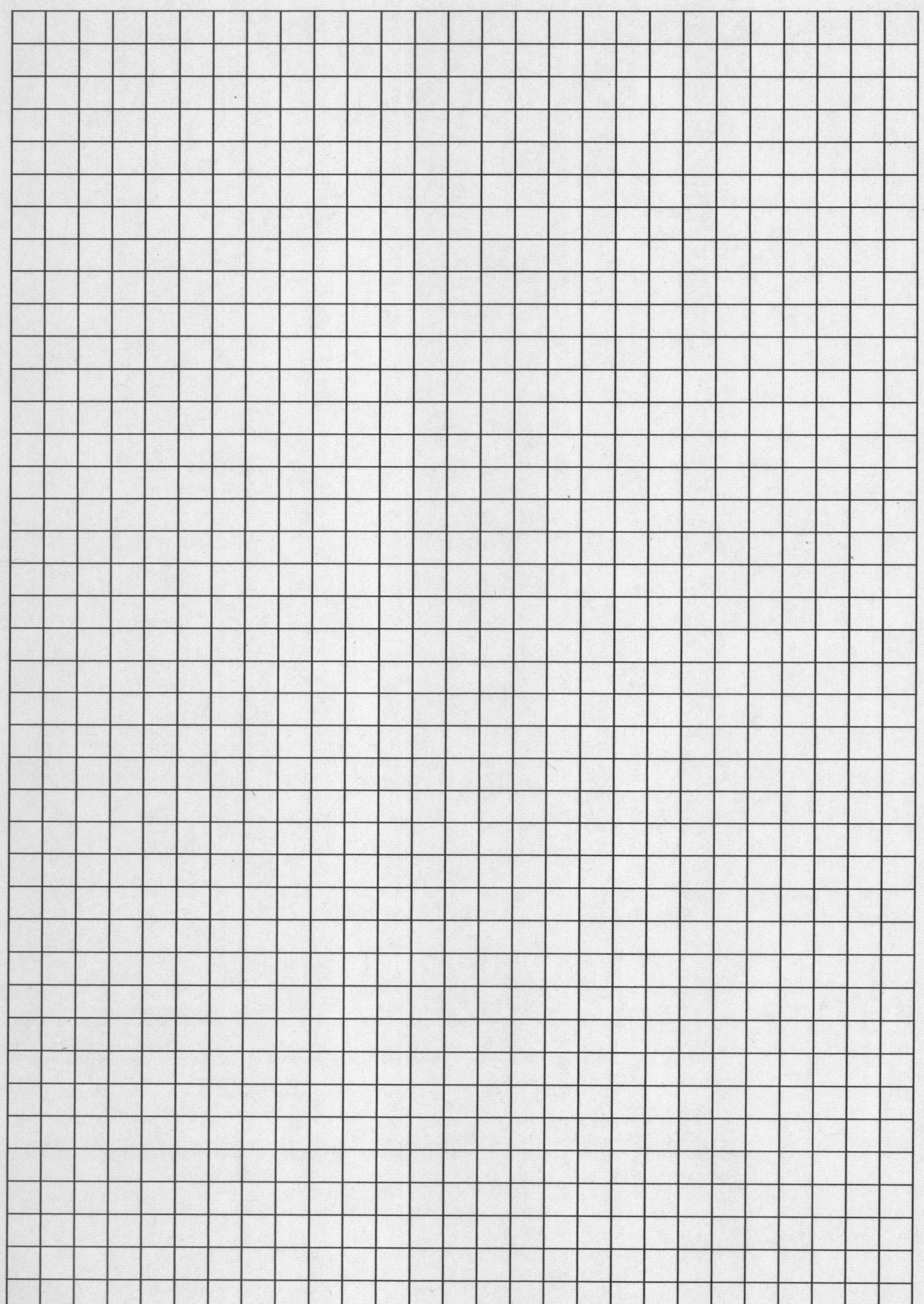

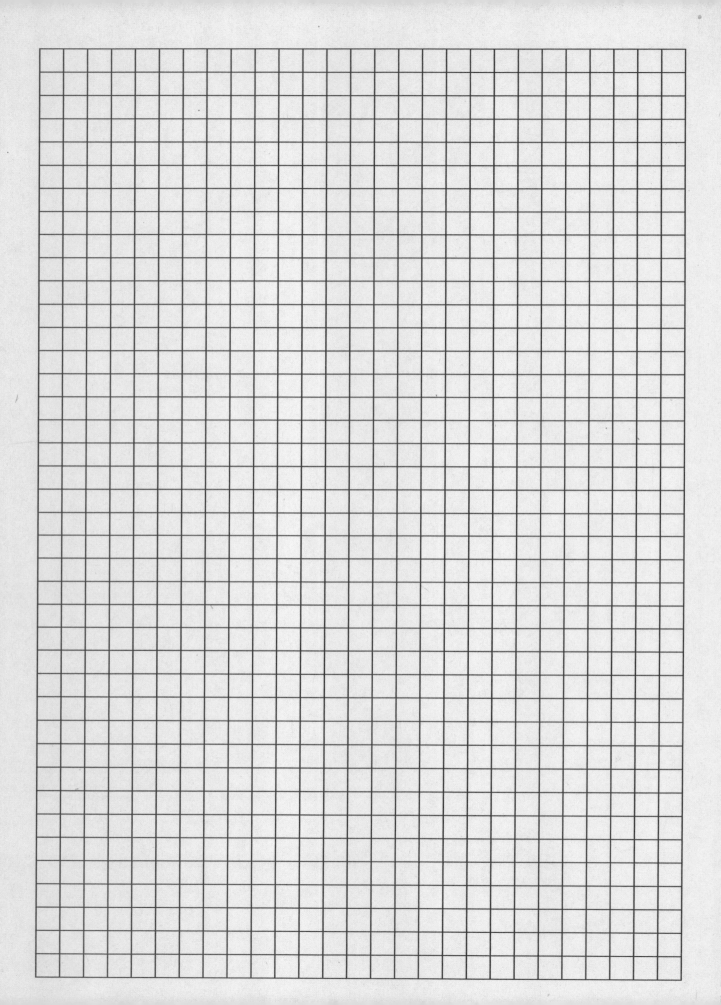